D0758264

Praise for
The Jane Austen Remedy

'While Ruth Wilson would never make such a claim for herself, she emerges from this discreet, wry memoir as quietly defiant as any heroine from the Jane Austen novels she so admires . . . All lovers of literature will relish Wilson's skilful study of how the books we love become woven into the fabric of our lives, evolving with us as we age and helping us to grow up'

Sydney Morning Herald

'*The Jane Austen Remedy* is a memoir, a guide to living a full and intelligent life, a work of thoughtful literary criticism, and also feels like an extended chat with a Jane Austen-reading friend . . . Elegantly and incisively written, full of insight and wisdom, moving and inspiring, this is a book you want to start reading again, as soon as you have finished'

**Susannah Fullerton, OAM, FRSN,
President of the Jane Austen Society of Australia**

'Ruth Wilson's *The Jane Austen Remedy* isn't just a beautiful and brilliant homage to the great novelist. It's a tour de force memoir on the power of reading to light up a life at any age'

Devoney Looser, author of *The Making of Jane Austen*

'This thoughtful, provocative book offers a window into a reading life and the ideas that have shaped a curious mind over more than eighty years. Books can make us better, Wilson urges, in this prescription for attentive, empathetic reading. *The Jane Austen Remedy* may just be the cure for what ails us'

Olivia Murphy, author of *Jane Austen the Reader*

a&b

The Jane Austen Remedy

It is a truth universally acknowledged
that a book can change a life

Ruth Wilson

Allison & Busby Limited
11 Wardour Mews
London W1F 8AN
allisonandbusby.com

First published in Great Britain by Allison & Busby in 2022.

A CIP catalogue record for this book is available from
the British Library.

First Edition

ISBN 978-0-7490-2930-2

Typeset in 11.5/16.5 pt Adobe Garamond Pro by
Allison & Busby Ltd

FSC
www.fsc.org
MIX
Paper from
responsible sources
FSC® C171272

The paper used for this Allison & Busby publication
has been produced from trees that have been legally sourced
from well-managed and credibly certified forests.

Printed and bound by
CPI Group (UK) Ltd, Croydon, CR0 4YY

This memoir is dedicated to Jane Austen,
her novels and her heroines.
They have given me unexpected delights of heart and mind
throughout a long reading life.

Author's Note

A memoir of any sort can be a revelation to the writer as well as to the reader. The experience of writing becomes part of the story, a creative act that might be considered either brave or foolish, perhaps both. It is possible that the relationships I examine in this reading memoir will be misunderstood. It may be that at times my memory falters. So it has been helpful to me – and might be useful to readers – to recall the warning issued by the narrator of Jane Austen's novel *Emma*: 'Seldom, very seldom, does complete truth belong to any human disclosure; seldom can it happen that something is not a little disguised, or a little mistaken.'

Introduction

Love and Happiness

Perfect happiness, even in memory, is not common . . .
JANE AUSTEN, *EMMA*

I was approaching sixty when questions about what it means to be happy assumed a special significance in my life, setting me on a new path that led to a careful re-reading of Jane Austen's six novels. On a crisp winter day in 1992 I was sitting in my car, waiting impatiently at a traffic light; without warning the red circle started to spin crazily, and again without warning I was hurtled into a vortex of incomprehension. Momentarily I lost my bearings, but I managed somehow to make my way home and climb the stairs to my apartment, where I lay in a darkened room for twenty-four hours. The following day the condition was diagnosed as Meniere's syndrome; the symptoms include hearing loss, nausea and vertigo.

The experience was disconcerting and left me shaken; but more disconcerting still was my experience a few weeks later, at a surprise party that had been arranged for my birthday. I entered a room to find sixty people, their faces covered with silver masks. I realised that behind the masks there were many good friends and loving members of my family, but as they clapped and cheered I was overcome by a strange antipathy. As the scene dissolved into a silvery nightmare, I felt like a character in Jean-Paul Sartre's novel *Nausea*; overcome by a sensation that was palpably physical and eerily metaphysical, too. I was shifting in and out of my body as I went through Austenian motions of civility and courtesy. I greeted guests and made conversation, I responded to kind words, but I was in some place else. I was watching myself and wondering who I was. In a revelatory surge, I had stumbled into a moment of truth: I was out of love with the world and I was not happy.

I am often compelled to revisit that existential turning point. It was awful in the sense that I am filled with awe whenever I remember it: the awe of experiencing the astounding connection between body and soul. Because I think that my body was telling me that my soul, however such an entity is conceptualised, was ailing. My physical symptoms represented a state of mind; I felt insufficiently loved, less than happy, and touched by grief: for myself, for what I felt I had not achieved, for the years that lay ahead.

But how to explain it? I had lost no one. I had reached the age of sixty with my family intact and my days filled with projects that interested me. It might seem that my life, like that of Jane Austen's heroine Emma, united some of the best blessings of existence. And yet, I was experiencing something more devastating than the distress and vexation that Emma encounters on her way to self-knowledge. I felt utterly lost. I sought professional help and was comforted by the assurance that Meniere's syndrome sometimes mimics depression. Medication was prescribed, I gave up eating salt, and I resumed my busy routine.

On the surface, life continued to be ordinary. I managed to function well enough on a number of community committees and as a consultant for the implementation of classroom oral history programs, despite intermittent symptoms. When a family legacy came my way, I bought a small cottage in the Southern Highlands, a two-hour drive from Sydney. I reminded myself that, even as a child, I had always enjoyed my own company. Aware that I had spent my adult life deferring, like so many women of my generation, to the assumed male authority of the household, I decided to put the cottage in my name alone.

Everyone recognises Virginia Woolf's phrase, 'a room of one's own'. I had surpassed Woolf's aspirations. Suddenly I had not only a room, I was the fortunate owner of a whole house. And, as Germaine Greer averred in *The Female Eunuch*, a book that changed the way I thought about my place in the world, it was money that had made the difference between unhappiness and something else. Jane Austen knew this all too well, as the poet W.H. Auden intimates in a verse that conveys with mock horror his shock that an English spinster appears to advocate mercenary marriages.

The Bloomsbury legend, as Virginia Woolf became known, was herself damaged by a grim patriarchal background, but she famously showed the world of women that genius can accomplish writing miracles. Her fiction is full of women engaged in the struggle. From Clarissa in *Mrs Dalloway* to Mrs Ramsay in *To the Lighthouse*, women waver between acquiescence and independent action. In *A Room of One's Own*, Woolf took Jane Austen as her example in a lecture to female undergraduates. She lifted the author's shimmering veil of associations and imaginings to reveal how astutely Jane Austen understood the role played by the patriarchy in normalising the subordination of women, and how effectively she camouflaged that knowledge.

It seems to me, however, that Woolf, for all her interest in women and fiction, closed the door on an equally deserving and much larger section of the female population: women like me who don't necessarily write fiction. All women need their own space to inhabit, their own air to breathe.

I was less endowed with imagination than Jane Austen but more fortunate than she when it came to 'pewter', as she and her wealthy brother, Edward, referred to money. My family legacy was a miraculous gift, providing me with a refuge from the city at a time when I suspected that recurring physical symptoms might signal an unacknowledged form of emotional distress.

Thirty years later I read a novel called *Secrets of Happiness*. The American novelist Joan Silber creates six narrators who struggle to find moments of happiness among the pressures and tensions of everyday life in contemporary western society. Abby, my favourite character in the book, comforts her grieving son with a verse by Langston Hughes. The American poet exhorts us to hold fast to our dreams lest they should, like a broken-backed bird, die before they can take flight.

No words could better capture the mood of my life when I retreated from the city.

My cottage came to represent a piece of real estate in which my state of mind might be remedied. It stood at the top end of a steep and winding road, in a location comparable in size to Meryton where the Bennet family lived; also to Emma's Highbury, 'a large and populous village almost amounting to a town. . .' I started to spend my weekends there, getting to know a community like the one Austen described to her niece Fanny as 'just the thing' to be of interest to a fiction writer – or, in my case, a fiction reader. I was hoping for a remedy: a panacea for a malaise that I could no longer dismiss.

I had thought I was doing well enough, but as I was arranging the photographs that recorded a gathering on my seventieth birthday, I noticed that I was not smiling in any of them. I wondered why, for someone so privileged, I looked miserable. Was I becoming a misanthrope? I asked myself. The expression on my face seemed to embody Elizabeth Bennet's observation to her sister Jane: 'There are few people whom I really love, and still fewer of whom I think well . . . The more I see of the world, the more am I dissatisfied with it.'

I am reminded as I write now of Kazuo Ishiguro's *The Remains of the Day*, a novel about a butler who looks back on a life lived in the shadows of other people's expectations and his own sense of duty, eschewing risk and declining to embrace life on its own terms. I remember asking myself then how I wanted to spend the remains of my own days, perhaps not in those words. I knew one thing for certain: I wanted something to change. There and then I decided to stake a claim to my space, to make my cottage in the Southern Highlands into my permanent home, to spend my time trying to understand my malaise, to find a happier way of being.

After fifty years of marriage, it was a difficult, complicated and emotionally painful decision. My husband was, I think, bewildered. I had never discovered a way to convey to him the intensity of my own feelings, the waves of frustration and regret that swept over me periodically, strong feelings that men are prone to dismiss as female hysteria. I longed to make decisions without being challenged, to be the one who sometimes had the last word, especially in matters that were chiefly my personal concern. I was tired, I realised; I was especially tired of being surrounded by people whose values I could no longer pretend to share. I had no idea how it would turn out for any of us as a family, but it was, I thought, time to take my turn; a last chance to examine what had become of a girl's once-upon-a-time great expectations of life.

I had been having recurring dreams in which sounds formed in my throat, but words failed to emerge. They were trapped in my larynx, struggling to be heard. My voice, which my elocution teacher had taught me to value as a musician would value a cherished instrument, had gone missing.

I wanted it back.

It occurred to me that my greatest love outside family and work had always been a love of reading fiction; of all the novels I had read, Jane Austen's were my benchmark for pleasure as her heroines had been models for the sort of woman I wanted to become. A nostalgia for those books swept over me. So I decided to think of recovery as a rehabilitation of my reading life, and to start by revisiting the six novels. I wanted to re-read those passages that had made Austen's fiction important to me: the bons mots, the well-worn quotations and the lively conversations. I didn't know it then, but I was embarking on an untested approach to reading. I was making Austen's novels a starting point for exploring the satisfactions and dissatisfactions of my own life, framed and illuminated by her fictional universe.

I had not been idle. I cast my mind back now to the years of my fourth and fifth decades, when I had plunged into a period of learning and doing: a postgraduate degree, participation in boards of management, coordination of intergenerational school programs, journal publications and a book about the art of interviewing. The curriculum vitae looked good, my endeavours had brought me rewards and even an award or two. But like the narrator in Nora Ephron's book *Heartburn* I failed to grasp the irrelevance of what I was so busy doing at the time. When I contemplated the prospect of facing life on my own I connected with Isabel Archer in *The Portrait of a Lady* by Henry James. She undertook a solitary midnight meditation to calibrate her moral compass and consider where her destiny lay. I was inspired by her example, although I never reconciled myself to her decision to remain with a husband whose nature repelled her. But that was Isabel's own fictional business.

I would do it differently; I would re-examine my lived life in the context of my reading life, hoping that I would better understand and hopefully transform my perplexed state of mind. So I decided to read all six of Jane Austen's novels with greater intent; reliving the past pleasure but also opening my mind to other possibilities, bringing the full complement of my feelings, thoughts and lived experiences to the act and art of reading.

Austen's fiction is sometimes concerned with improving the estate. So, I renovated my cottage at the top of the hill. It wasn't as challenging as the task that Mr Rushworth faced at Sotherton, in the novel *Mansfield Park*, but I started with colour. I had the walls painted yellow, the colour of sunshine, inside and out. A craftsman in a nearby village copied a Frank Lloyd Wright design for glass panes and inserted them in a frame to make a welcoming front door. I chose a tall slender lamppost to light the entrance at night. A friendly gardener helped me plant beds of cream and green hellebores under the mature rhododendron trees and masses of graceful bluebells under the birches. From a newly built elevated reading room with vast windows I looked out on a maple grove and up a thickly wooded hill. Like Emma, I rejoiced in the 'exquisite sight, smell, sensation of nature, tranquil, warm, and brilliant after a storm'; the difference was that Emma's storm was past, and mine was still raging inside me.

My life seemed to have been following a decade-long pattern. It turned out that I would live in the cottage that I called Lantern Hill, after a favourite childhood book, for almost ten years, during which I discovered just such a small piece of canvas in regional Australia as the one that served Austen as she sketched her typically English comedies of manners. I lived alone but I was less lonely than I had been earlier in my life. People made judgements; I didn't heed them. Some asked questions; I didn't answer them. Others – mainly women – understood, because they, too, had experienced the unbearable loneliness of marriage. And the only friends I retained were people I cared for and about.

I filled my days with reading, sometimes alone, sometimes in the excellent company of other Austen readers. These were different ways of reading, and each had its rewards. My three daughters remained, as always, the closest and most beloved friends of all, my latter-day heroines. During this period, they taught me as much as they had, I hoped, learned from me.

For the first time in my mature adult life I took a risk.

It was often daunting, but I soon felt that being mistress of all I surveyed had its compensations. I thought that 'to sit in the shade on a fine day, and look upon verdure' as I opened the first of the six novels I intended to re-read might be, as Fanny Price concludes in *Mansfield Park*, 'the most perfect refreshment'. I didn't guess that, by re-reading Austen's fiction at the age of seventy, I would be consoled in ways that would lead me to the best years of my life.

Chapter One

All About Austen

How quick come the reasons for approving what we like!
JANE AUSTEN, *PERSUASION*

My arrival in the regional town of Griffith in 1932 was dramatic for my parents. Not, perhaps, as dramatic as the opening of the Sydney Harbour Bridge that same year; charging out of the crowd on horseback, an Irish military man of dubious reputation managed to slash the ribbon and declare the bridge open before Premier Lang could do the honours. That was a political act, whereas the drama associated with my birth was more to do with geography. The doctor who was to deliver me lived in the neighbouring town of Leeton, about thirty miles away. Because he was delayed, my father – a doctor – delivered me himself.

The birth was, apart from that, uncomplicated, and I have stayed on for longer than I ever expected. The worst things that life has inflicted on me so far have dissolved into bittersweet memories that I recollect with wonder as I glimpse unexpected connections between my everyday life and my reading life. That's what happened when I first read Jane Austen's novel *Pride and Prejudice*, and it is also how I came to be a lifelong reader throughout a life that has been ordinary – if never having had to worry about food, shelter and security can be regarded as ordinary in a world where there is widespread want, homelessness and oppression. So it has been extraordinary as well, for the unexpected ways in which good fortune has commingled with and helped me through darker moments. For some years I have recognised that the love of reading has been one of the unexpected blessings in my life. Reading has defined my life and become a habit that is woven seamlessly into the way I think, feel and imagine.

I suffered the usual setbacks when I started to read. I was four years old and bewildered when first asked to copy letters from a blackboard onto my slate. My mother had enrolled me in the local convent because I was lonely at home and too young to accompany my brother when he started public school. I joined a class of children who had already mastered the alphabet, so the nun in charge enlisted the help of a young girl who was training to be a lay teacher. She was kind, gentle, encouraging and endlessly patient. Together we looked at letters and she gave them names; she explained that the written letters talked themselves into words, and although it took time I eventually found myself able to decipher the letters and mouth the words without help. By the time I was old enough to join my brother at the public school I could write and read a simple sentence so I was put into the first class.

This seems to me now to have been a poor decision. It was made by the school principal and it had repercussions. It meant that I never learned to mingle with other children in the big open kindergarten space that I passed every day of the week. I sometimes looked inside that room and wondered what it would be like to play at the miniature tables and chairs or to wander at will into areas in which toys and books were scattered everywhere. The principal's decision meant also that I had no friendship base in the formal classroom where I sat every day at a desk and tried to understand what was going on and what I was supposed to do. At lunchtime, I drifted alone around the dusty playground, watching the games of children whom I didn't know.

One day, I ventured to the furthest edge of the playground and was stopped in my tracks by the sight of an avenue lined by cherry plum trees and a procession of laughing children. They were following a girl and a boy who were wearing cardboard crowns covered in gold paper. Down the avenue they proceeded, beneath a canopy of green leaves and swooping branches. Occasionally one of the children stooped to pick up a ripe cherry plum. According to some unwritten law, the fruit was always handed to the King or Queen, as I presumed the crowned leaders to be.

I was entranced by this enactment of a fairy tale, and noticed another solitary girl similarly engrossed in the scene. We edged closer to each other. I am not sure who spoke first, but it didn't take long.

'My name is Ruth,' one of us said.

'So is mine,' replied the other.

We were in the same class but had not previously exchanged a word. We walked back to the classroom arm in arm and asked the teacher if we could sit together. She agreed, and for the remainder of the year we had plenty of opportunities to enjoy our friendship and share an abundant treasure trove of fairy tales.

My taste in reading always has and still does accommodate fairy tales. I made their acquaintance in the company of Hans Christian Andersen and the Brothers Grimm. I met a different version in stories that our father read to my brother and me at bedtime. They helped prolong Scheherazade's life night after night. I find their traces in Jane Austen's novels, and in the work of contemporary writers as well. Angela Carter retells the story of Little Red Riding Hood in her collection of fairy tales called *The Bloody Chamber and Other Stories* with a powerful feminist consciousness of sexual politics. But if I were asked exactly how, when and where I began to think of reading as something that transported me beyond fairy tales and wishful thinking, beyond diversion, escape, entertainment or distraction, beyond even the postmodern charge to tell truth to power and similar political imperatives; if I were asked when reading became a source of nourishment and imaginative expansion, I would answer without hesitation that my reading life truly began with *Pride and Prejudice*.

The spell was cast the day I opened Austen's most radiant novel. Sixty years later I thought of it as book magic, as I experienced the warmth of a glowing fire in my Southern Highlands home and remembered my Austen initiation on a contrastingly hot school day in summer. Then I was reading the book because it had been recommended by an English teacher whom I admired and respected. That is often the way, as the writer Rebecca Mead tells readers in *The Road to Middlemarch*, a book that celebrates her life with George Eliot. A retired English teacher with whom Mead read as a student was a crucial influence on her life. Together they prepared for her entrance examination. They analysed the Metaphysical poets and dissected Shakespeare's tragedies. Inspired by the novel *Middlemarch*, Mead determined to change her life.

Jane Austen's novels performed that service for me. They changed my life because they changed what I wanted to read and the way I connected with characters and ideas in fiction. More significantly than any other of the many novels that I have read and loved, Austen's novels set the gold standard for the books I would choose to read from then on. They were what the Latin poet Horace called '*dolce et utile*', sweet and useful. They shaped the course of my future: because of them, I became a lover of language, a teacher of literature, a parent-reader and, in a broader sense, an educator. My inner life has been nourished, illuminated and comforted by the empathetic voices, the complex characters and the challenging ideas in Austen's novels – and they have changed, as I have done, over a lifetime. It really did not matter so much, I discovered through reading her novels, whether my parents fulfilled every need that I craved. What they lacked was often found in the pages of a book.

A character in Michael Cunningham's novel *The Hours* wonders what book to give a sick friend, and resolves to give him one that will help him understand his place in the world, prepare him for change, and, indeed, 'parent him'. If being parented means being encouraged to explore and reflect on your own life and relationships, then Austen's fiction has helped me to feel that I was parented well.

I found my first copy of *Pride and Prejudice* in the school library. In those less sophisticated times, the 1940s, the library was just an ordinary classroom that had been fitted with cupboards and shelves. I am not sure how the books were arranged, but I doubt that the Dewey system was used by any of the English teachers who were responsible for keeping the books in order and who undertook voluntary library duty during the lunch hour. I was directed to the single library copy of *Pride and Prejudice* by Mrs Eason; she was my class teacher and she was on library duty that day.

My imagination was roused and stretched and shaped by what went on in Mrs Eason's classes. She inspired a fascination with grammar. She shared stories of her own experience of reading and literature. She initiated me into the 'terra incognita' of literature, where, as Yann Martel, a master of magic realism, puts it, we are given more lives. She told us about Shakespeare and read to us from her own copy of *Tales from Shakespeare* by Charles and Mary Lamb. She had played the role of the spirited Rosalind in a university production of *As You Like It*, and she recited some of her lines, but my fancy was also taken by Jaques, and I was thrilled by his idea that 'all the world's a stage'.

Our teacher recited the seven ages of man in full, and I was especially interested in the infant and the schoolboy:

At first the infant,
Mewling and puking in the nurse's arms.
And then the whining school-boy, with his satchel
And shining morning face, creeping like a snail
Unwillingly to school.

These were ages within my own range of experience. The speech offered me new words to think about and listen to in my head. I did not understand why 'mewling' and 'puking' were words to associate with babies, but they did not *sound* pleasant to someone who, as the younger child in the family, had never held a baby in her arms. They did not even taste or feel pleasant, I thought, sensing a poet's hypersensitivity to words as physical sensations: 'as sounds to be plumbed, as weights on the tongue', Seamus Heaney wrote of words that appeared in the poetry of Geoffrey Hill.

The whining schoolboy, unwilling to go to school, was also quite outside my experience. My brother, only twenty-two months my senior, was my model, ever a bright and willing student. For both of us, school was a positive experience. Our days from the ages of five to sixteen were spent at the local public school, in a series of buildings that sprawled across a large expanse of land. They accommodated each stage of our education, from kindergarten to high school. Infants, primary and secondary departments adjoined each other along a stretch of road opposite a dense swathe of bushland, junior levels at the lower end and, at the other, a pseudo-Georgian red-brick building that housed senior secondary-school classrooms, a science laboratory, the staffrooms and the principal's office.

School was only a twenty-minute bike ride from our home. I grew less and less lonely as I grew older, and I loved that morning bike ride. At times the weather was chilblain-frosty. Once, I remember, during a plague, it was thick with clouds of locusts blowing about in the hot wind. At its best, our climate was dry and crisp. That's how my father fondly described it.

I loved everything about my country town in New South Wales's Riverina region, not least its topography: Griffith is set on a low flat plain with a craggy rise called Scenic Hill at its edge, under the canopy of an expanse of sky that seemed to have neither beginning nor end. I loved its history, too. The idea of living in a township that had started life as Bagtown only twenty years before I was born seemed somehow auspicious, just as the Harbour Bridge had been. 'In the beginning,' my father recited from the prayer book we read on Friday night; and later, lying in bed, I thought, 'In the beginning, there was Griffith, and now I live here.'

The cluster of cement-bag humpies that housed workers on an irrigation construction site was eventually referred to as 'old Griffith' and abandoned, while Griffith proper, a few miles away, was declared a town in 1916. By the time I called it home, the town had undergone a series of improvements; thinking about that now, I am reminded that the idea of improvement as a condition of progress, whether of place or person, threads its way through Austen's novel *Mansfield Park*. But I would not enjoy thoughts like that until Jane Austen and I met, as destined, in the pages of her fiction.

I enjoyed ambling along the main street of the town, a wide tree-lined avenue with parkland on one side and shops on the other. It was in the park that I joined a throng of children who had been invited one Saturday afternoon to line up at trestle tables to receive drinks and chocolates to celebrate the coronation of King George VI. Wide beds planted with large trees took up the centre of the avenue, with plenty of spaces left for vehicles, whether horses and sulkies or box-like motor cars.

The first writing prize I ever received was for a high-school essay called 'Shop Windows'. I described a stroll down Banna Avenue, and the delights of gazing at cakes and pies in the pastry shop, bolts of brightly coloured fabric in the draper's emporium, and piles of Enid Blyton and *Girls' Crystal* magazines propped up at the front of the newsagent's display. The essay was published in the school magazine, *Oasis*. I couldn't wait to show it to my mother, whose sometimes-gloomy moods were invariably lightened by any success my brother and I had at school. Her reaction was not quite what I had anticipated. She was pleased, even proud, but a little disturbed, too. If people read that I drooled over custard tarts they might also think that I was hungry, which – and it was an accusation – would bring shame on the family.

I was too excited by winning the essay competition to pay attention at the time. But much later in life, as I began to understand the ways in which reading plays games in the brain, memories of my mother's ambivalent reaction also helped me to understand something about her disposition, and something important about the complexity of the reading process. Turning to theories to explain everyday activities can be tedious, but in the case of how we learn to read, the ideas of Louise Rosenblatt in an essay, 'The Transactional Theory of Reading and Writing', smack of common sense as well as theory. She explained reading as a transaction between readers and the black marks on the page. My own reading eyes were opened by Rosenblatt's simple statement that all readers draw on 'a reservoir of past experience' as part of the transaction.

Once I explored my mother's reservoir of experience I understood. I had learned over the years, from stories about her life as the youngest of seven girls, that my mother grew up in a household that struggled to put food on the table. The only time they ate fruit was at the Friday Sabbath meal, and then the girls shared the few oranges their mother could afford. My grandfather, Isaac, was too religious to be a good provider. He spent much of his time in the synagogue, praying. My grandmother, Hannah, was proud; so much so that she instructed her daughters not to reveal their poverty to strangers. Clearly, my mother's memories and associated emotions were triggered by my prize-winning essay.

My own upbringing provided me with a reservoir of quite different memories that I would, in time, bring to my own reading adventures. I was fortunate to live in a comfortable house and to sit down to plentiful meals. I was always made aware and grateful that my father's family had risen from immigration and penury in one generation. In the early years of the twentieth century, they had migrated from Palestine – then part of the Ottoman Empire – to Western Australia: first my grandfather, who worked in a general store in Geraldton, and then, when he could afford their passage, his wife, two daughters and infant son. A fourth child was born in Perth. In the fullness of time, they managed to send the oldest girl, Cecilia, to the Conservatorium of Music, and Ada, who was born in Australia, to study pharmacy. The only son, my father, fulfilled every Jewish parent's dream and studied medicine. In their family, as in Jane Austen's, one child, Rosie, was born with an intellectual disability; she was eventually sent to live in a succession of institutions and group homes, but never rendered invisible in the family history, as Jane Austen's brother, George, was.

My father came to Griffith as a locum, to fill in for a doctor who was on holiday. He was welcomed as a young bachelor. He was good social value, a competent sportsman in possession of a good singing voice. He loved country life so much that he decided to stay. He returned to Palestine to find a wife, brought her back to Australia from her home in Jerusalem, and built a private hospital in Griffith.

We lived near the hospital, in a red-brick house with symmetrical wings on each side of a wide, sheltering portico. There was a formal garden at the front, with two large circular beds planted with rosebushes and bordered with pansies. A silky oak and several jacaranda trees screened us from the neighbouring house on one side. I dreamed of climbing those branches and concealing myself in their foliage to hide from the ogres whose names I heard with increasing frequency in my parents' conversations as I grew older.

By the time I was seven, Hitler and Mussolini had become regular visitors to the nightmares that disturbed my sleep, but the days were sunny enough for any child. It was my job to pick fruit as it ripened in the small citrus grove behind the house, and to fill a large straw basket with oranges, lemons and grapefruit. Behind a high, latticed gate a hanging yard with clothes lines stretching from post to post gave me plenty of room in which to play with imaginary friends. A dirt tennis court and cement swimming pool catered to my father's and my brother's love of sport. The house was harmonious outside and spacious within. The fact that it had been designed by an architect, in a place and at a time when domestic architecture was rare, was a matter of pride to both my parents.

The town itself hints at the spirit of the American architect Walter Burley Griffin, who designed Canberra. Burley Griffin conceived a plan for Griffith that was only partially fulfilled. Traces remain even today of the original design, which featured a distinctive radial pattern with wide tree-lined streets, ring roads and parks. The main irrigation channel was conceptualised as the key landscape effect of the city, a 'sweeping curve around the central portion', but that wasn't quite the way it turned out. The railway had been planned as the focal point, and on the way to school in the morning I often leaned on my bike, waiting for the gates to open, when the train was in shunting mode.

The role of the river system, especially the Murray and its tributary the Murrumbidgee, was central to Burley Griffin's plan. It remains a timely reminder of the significance of the river system for the Wiradjuri people who inhabited the slopes and plains of the catchment area long before Captain Cook disembarked on the coast of Australia. In Tara June Winch's prize-winning novel *The Yield*, an

Indigenous character called Poppy compiles a Wiradjuri language dictionary. Among these is the word *bila*, for a river. Everything reaches back to the *bila*, Poppy explains – all life and, with it, all time. Was it more than chance, then, that Burley Griffin, a white man, dreamed the same dream for towns of the aptly named Riverina, a region dominated by water flowing through a network of rivers and tributaries?

In a strikingly different spirit, Griffith and its sister town Leeton articulated, if only in embryo, a vision of white European architecture as well. Leeton was more successful than Griffith in fulfilling these intentions, boasting, along its avenues, examples of Art Deco that have survived later urban refurbishment. A handful of buildings in my own town made gestures to the style. The Rio Theatre was the less prestigious of the two picture shows, as we called them then, that brought popular entertainment and screen stars into our lives; it was Art Deco only in the stepped geometrical outline that capped the building.

In this theatre, to the burning shame of all who lived there and then (including myself and my family, all of us painfully and personally aware of the racial prejudice perpetuated against European Jewry), it was accepted without question that the Indigenous population should be seated separately, at the front of the theatre, on canvas chairs rather than in the upholstered seats enjoyed by other patrons.

But the Rio Theatre was also the site of my earliest successes in life. I was shy with strangers; tongue-tied was the word people used in those days. Cast as a tree in a school play that we were preparing for the Christmas concert, I listened attentively to every word spoken during rehearsals until they lodged themselves in my memory. The familiar story of the understudy who strikes it lucky came true when the girl who had been given the main part fell ill. I felt no sympathy; I simply struck while the iron was hot. I, who rarely spoke up in class, assured the teacher that I knew the lines. I delivered them to her surprised satisfaction, and two nights later I had my first experience of being applauded on the stage of the Rio Theatre. It was exhilarating.

To my delight, it was just the beginning of something new and intoxicating in my life. The cavernous Rio stage and its wings and its smell of dust eventually felt like a second home, where I acted in school plays year after year. Much as I enjoyed the plays, my happiest memories were my solo performances, when I recited to music. I discovered the genre of the musical monologue in my father's tales of his early life and in his memories of his favourite sister, the one who went to the Conservatorium of Music. As a schoolgirl, she had accompanied herself as she recited to her family. The most popular piece in her repertoire was a melodramatic story of passionate love, theft and murderous revenge set in exotic-sounding Kathmandu.

Somehow, I came by the sheet music of 'The Green Eye of the Yellow God' by J. Milton Hayes, learned the words and persuaded Judith, a senior student who played the piano for school assemblies, to accompany me in a performance at a school concert. I sensed that I was giving a gift to my father. He was still mourning the premature death of his musical sister who, with her infant daughter, had been incinerated when the bus in which they were travelling in Palestine collided with a train. The windows were barred to protect passengers from the stones that were thrown at vehicles that carried Jewish passengers through Arab villages, so Cecilia and her daughter, Dalia, were trapped inside the burning bus.

I knew that my father was thinking of his sister when he asked me to recite the verses at home. Even without the music, without the staccato notes and thumping chords, the words carried their own message of high drama. Standing on the stage of the Rio Theatre and accompanied by Judith, I was as thrilled by my own performance as the audience seemed to be entertained by the melodrama.

The Lyceum Theatre, unlike the Rio, was dedicated to the silver screen. It was the elite picture show; as far as I remember, it welcomed no Indigenous patrons at all. My film-addicted parents patronised it at least twice a week – as frequently, in fact, as the program changed. The Art Deco touches were more elaborate than in the Rio. Inside both the foyer and the theatre, where we sat on upholstered seats, dimly lit glass bowls were held aloft by slender female figures. It was here that my mother, my father and I sat through two viewings of the film *Pride and Prejudice*, starring Greer Garson and Laurence Olivier, in a single week. That was during the year I turned fifteen.

I don't think my parents would have guessed my thoughts as we sat together in absorbed silence. Even as I followed the story, I was considering whether my mother, with her nervous headaches, wasn't just a little like Mrs Bennet; and my father – well, one could only wonder at how a fictional character with a tendency to poke fun at those less quick-witted than himself could be so familiar. I doubt that, watching the film, I detected the larger ironies with which the heroine must wrestle. These would only become apparent later, when I read the novel. For the time being, Mr Bennet's abundance of wit and the humorous spirit with which the family greeted Mrs Bennet's fluttering nerves did little to disrupt what were, in my mind, the domestic delights of life at Longbourn.

When it came to the daughters, who were so much closer to my own age, I was especially curious. Now I wondered how my parents perceived me in relation to the Bennet girls. If they imagined me as any of the five daughters, I would have liked it to be lovely Lizzy or perhaps gentle Jane. Although there was little reason to associate me with either, I really hoped it was not Mary; she, like me, had a bookish bent. I could see that both Elizabeth and Jane shone in comparison with the shallow and silly younger sisters. I thought they were amusing, but I was unsure about Mary. Although her hair was pulled back into a tight bun and she wore glasses with round wire frames – to give her, I suppose, a studious and plain look – she did not evoke my scorn. Perhaps I identified with someone who was less popular and pretty than her peers. But still, I thought, anyone would prefer the company of Elizabeth and Jane.

The year of our family viewing was 1947, so the film, released in 1940, must have made a late, or perhaps even a second, appearance in our town. Already the dark cloud of the Second World War that had hung over my childhood was becoming a memory. It was all opportunity and optimism in the wider world that beckoned us from everywhere, including the English classroom, in which a wise teacher introduced us to Jane Austen. He did it by way of *As You Like It*, the Shakespeare play we were reading and discussing in class. I had already been introduced to Rosalind by Mrs Eason; when I commented to Mr Connor that Rosalind reminded me a little of the heroine I had seen the previous night in a film called *Pride and Prejudice*, he pointed out that Elizabeth Bennet actually originated in a book of the same name. He promptly added the novel to our reading list.

That is how I came to spend my lunch hour one day in 1947, sitting at a desk in a classroom-cum-library, and reading, for the first of many times, the book that gave its name to the film. Not even reciting speeches from Shakespeare in my elocution class and at home for my father's pleasure had prepared me for the first sentence of this novel. Like multitudes of readers before and after me, I read it several times. I heard it in my head. This was language, prose language, used as I had never heard it:

> *It is a truth universally acknowledged, that a single man in possession of a good fortune, must be in want of a wife.*

Later, at home, I read the sentence aloud, as I had been longing to do ever since I scanned it silently in print. I savoured the sound. Simple as the sentence seemed to be, it was grammatically quite complicated. I recognised it as a periodic sentence, because we had been reading Dr Johnson's essays in class and had been trained to spot something called suspended syntax, a strategy that delays the complete sense of a sentence till its very end. So, after a couple of readings out loud, I heard the suspense and drama created by positioning the main, arguably absurd, proposition at the end of the famous sentence. Of course, I didn't know the sentence was famous then, but I was already on the way to discovering the key to an enduring literary triumph. The success of one of the most frequently quoted first sentences in literature is partially dependant on the author's mastery of the language of grammar and the language of meaning. She managed to take my breath away by boldly blending the climax of a periodic sentence with the anticlimax of the proposition that wealthy men are necessarily in want of wives. Even at the age of fifteen I knew that could not possibly be true, let alone universally acknowledged.

I was a teenage girl in the 1940s: thoughts and images of marriage abounded in magazines and conversations with girlfriends. Nowhere, it seemed to me, could it be said that men, blessed with a good fortune or not, were in want; that seemed to be women's lot. I recalled the question debated by Alice and the March Hare in the first book I had read quite by myself. Is saying what you mean, I wondered, the same as meaning what you say? The more I listened to my own voice, the more dubious I became. Who was telling this story? Jane Austen, whose name was on the cover, or someone else whose life had its origins inside the covers of the book? Reminded again of Alice, I grew curiouser and curiouser.

* * *

As I re-read the novel by the fire in my yellow cottage, I was surprised to be jolted from past reading recollections to present circumstances. I was getting to know the community in which I was now living – mainly through the Friends of the Library and the Jane Austen Society, but through neighbours and their friends as well. How many women had I met with Austen-like designs in my new habitat? I asked myself. Well, two at least among a small number of new acquaintances. A divorced lady who rented a house in my street had set her heart on finding an unattached male somewhere among the bridge players at the local golf club. She sought male partners with an Austenian determination. And I had met a widowed lady who joined the gardening club and discovered, to her delight, a male gardener whose wife did not share his horticultural enthusiasm. The widow set her gardening hat at him as readily as any Austen character might do. I turned to the scene in which Charlotte Lucas waylays Mr Collins in the lane, away from Bennet eyes, and read it aloud. Meryton and Regency times seemed quite near, in space and time.

I had learned the advantages of reading aloud in my weekly elocution lessons with another of the teachers I remember with unbounded affection. Miss Cassie Brain taught me over the years to concentrate on thinking about where to pause, which word or phrase to emphasise, as well as how to breathe deeply and silently, to pace and pitch my voice and to modulate my tone. They were sublime afternoons that flew like no others, spent practising and developing my vocal skills in order to enrich my understanding and enliven the delivery of the poems I recited many times over in my gifted teacher's modestly furnished sitting room.

'Ah, Jane, you sorceress,' pronounced the novelist Edith Wharton after listening to the novel *Sense and Sensibility* read aloud. I was surprised to find evidence in Jane Austen's letters that the author, too, paid attention to the skills required to read her novels aloud. 'Our 2d evening's reading [of *Pride and Prejudice*] to Miss Benn had not pleased me so well,' she wrote to her sister in February 1813, 'but', she added, 'I beleive [*sic*] something must be attributed to my Mother's too rapid way of getting on – & tho' she perfectly understands the Characters herself, she cannot speak as they ought.' Habits of reading aloud are recorded in other private letters that were later published for all the world to read. The novelist Edward Bulwer-Lytton wrote to his mother that her failure to enjoy Austen's novel *Emma* might be because it was badly read aloud to her. And it's not only Jane Austen's novels that have been treated to vocalisations. The reading memoirist Rebecca Mead reports that the artist Vanessa Bell painted while her sister Virginia Woolf read aloud from the great nineteenth-century realist novels. '"I can still hear much of George Eliot & Thackeray in her voice," Vanessa wrote.'

Thinking about Austen's novels in vocal terms tempts me to use music as a touchstone for talking about her language, although it was a great disappointment to me that I lacked what is called a musical ear. The confusion I experienced during my early piano lessons when asked to distinguish between relatively close high and low notes led to my being classified as tone deaf. But it was not so when it came to reading prose fiction. Once I had been introduced to Austen, I discovered just the opposite. It was as though I had an inbuilt mechanism that recognised 'true' notes and tunes in what I was reading, even if I wasn't sure why that was.

Perhaps I had a natural aptitude, perhaps Miss Brain's lessons had prepared me, had educated me already, to pick up what was true and what was false; and Jane Austen's prose was the testing ground for identifying the many ways in which language works to create what I seemed to recognise, once and for all time, as fictional truth. In Austen's novel *Emma*, Mr Knightley asks the heroine, 'Whom are you going to dance with?' She replies, 'With you, if you will ask me,' and, as Virginia Woolf observed, that was enough. Charlotte Brontë disparaged Austen's romantic imagination. She read *Pride and Prejudice* and asked what was to be found: 'A carefully fenced, highly cultivated garden, with neat borders and delicate flowers; but . . . no open country, no fresh air, no blue hill, no bonny beck.'

What does Brontë know of the literary imagination that makes the few words exchanged by Emma and Mr Knightley as romantic as anything Mr Rochester says to Jane Eyre? When I read Austen's passage aloud I hear it as a short and perfectly pitched solo melody, inserted lovingly into a longer sonata movement, a response to a musical proposition.

When I discovered the possibilities of language as Jane Austen used it, both on the page and in my ears, a new door to fiction opened. Just as suddenly, another closed. Gone were the days when I waited impatiently to speed-read my way through the short stories included among gossip about socialites and film stars that my mother looked forward to reading in the magazines tossed over the fence and onto our front lawn every week. I didn't have the vocabulary to name clichés and stereotypes, but I knew that something about the writing and the characters was, in Hamlet's words, 'stale, flat and unprofitable'. My taste for them dissolved overnight.

Gone, too, were the days when I derived quite so much pleasure from the heroines of my younger reading days. Until then, I had cried many times when tomboy Judy, punished so unfairly by her stern father, died in Ethel Turner's *Seven Little Australians*. I had rejoiced often when my favourite L.M. Montgomery heroine, Jane, who spent holidays with her estranged father at Lantern Hill, rebelled against the dictates of her controlling grandmother. I could not get enough of the wind that tossed my hair, transformed from a curly dark frizz to a straight blonde mane, as I rode my horse across the paddocks of Billabong station with Norah, a long-legged, athletic Australian ideal of girlhood created by Mary Grant Bruce. After meeting the Bennet family, the girls I had known so well dwindled a little; now they were like friends whom I still loved and valued, whose place in my memory was non-negotiable and enduring, but whose company I had outgrown. I remembered them fondly but rarely wished to revisit them.

Perhaps it is just that I was becoming a grown-up reader. Although I didn't yet know it, I was falling under the spell of social satire disguised as comedy, in particular as comedy of manners. Meeting a girl like Elizabeth Bennet in fiction, I was forming an ideal of femininity that novelist F. Scott Fitzgerald regretted a century later for its influence on his own wife. It occurs to me that Fitzgerald's female ideal – the flappers of his wife Zelda's generation – might have had some of Elizabeth's vivacity and independent spirit, but turned out to be more fun to court than to marry.

One of the quotable quotes that flowed from Virginia Woolf's pen is her assessment of George Eliot's *Middlemarch*: 'the magnificent book which with all its imperfections is one of the few English novels written for grown-up people'. Perhaps readers pay a price for growing up. Taking my cue from Woolf, and drawing on my own experience as a reader, I think of Jane Austen as a writer whose novels never stop helping readers to grow up.

Chapter Two

The Austen Antidote

An excellent charade indeed! and very much to the purpose.
JANE AUSTEN, *EMMA*

I have been familiar with the idea of an antidote for as long as I can remember. My father, being a medical practitioner as well as a parent, was quick to administer antidotes to his family as well as his patients. He would, for example, order a dose of Epsom salts to get rid of a bad mood. So for me, antidote has always suggested something nasty, something medicinal, like the poison it is meant to counteract. The most astute of early Austen readers spoke of her as bringing a dose of 'medicinal realism' (as Barbara Benedict and Deirdre Le Faye observe in their 2006 introduction to *Northanger Abbey*) to the volumes of romantic and gothic fiction that they regarded as trash, filling the shelves of circulating libraries with unwanted temptations for young female readers.

Actually, Jane Austen herself uses the word 'antidote' counterintuitively. It creeps into the novel *Emma* via a charade with which most of her readers would have been familiar. In the first volume of the novel, the mischievous, charming but irritatingly presumptuous heroine persuades her ingenuous protégée, Harriet, that Mr Elton, the village curate, has formed a romantic attachment to her. As evidence, Emma gives her version of the charade that the pompous young clergyman has contributed to Harriet's collection. Harriet plans to transcribe it into 'a thin hot-pressed paper . . . ornamented with ciphers and trophies'.

The contribution is neither original nor clever, but it represents a prevailing view of the relationship between men and women:

My *first* doth my *affliction* denote [woe]
Which my *second* is *destin'd* to *feel*; [man]
And my *whole* is the best *antidote* [wo'man]
That *affliction* to soften and *heal*.

Harriet has no idea how to make sense of the four lines. No wonder. It calls for a stretch of the verbal imagination (of which Harriet has little, if any) to grasp how the two syllables relate to the whole word. That done, it is simple: the charade spells out the view that women exist as an antidote, they are here to soothe any pain that a man might experience in his life. Emma is convinced that Mr Elton is thus paying a tribute to Harriet as the ideal woman.

Once I had worked out the message, the sheer absurdity of the proposition made me laugh. This was at a time when I was feeling my wings as a university undergraduate, and I tended to laugh a lot; life was so full of promise. I had gained in confidence in my senior high-school years. I had no reason to feel at a disadvantage to the male species. I had performed better than any male in my class in my final-year examinations. I was widely read for my age and starting to enjoy history more than I had when facts were the substance of our classroom lessons and memorising was the key to success. At university I was developing a historical perspective, learning to draw inferences from the past to illuminate the present and speculate about future possibilities. I meant to do well and, although I was sometimes shy, I had the intellectual assurance of a postwar young woman, taking it for granted that I would find a career to my liking.

I was not, however, averse to the idea of marriage. The circumstances of Elizabeth Bennet and now a second heroine, Emma, were propitious. Everything in the novels suggested that they and their prospective husbands regarded each other with mutual respect and approached marriage as equal partners. I was aware that women had moved into new and previously male-oriented roles during the war, when the Land Army girls who drove tractors on the farms came to town in their shorts and shirts. They laughed loudly as they strode down Banna Avenue or sat drinking in the milk bars whose Greek owners had concocted suitably Australian names such as the The Bouquet and The Garden of Roses. I thought these young women might be like Elizabeth Bennet, who delighted in ranging across muddy fields in her long dress. I was starting to notice that fiction conjures up associations, and when I read about Elizabeth Bennet's tramping I thought about the girls in their farming outfits and wondered if they would be as much at home in the sitting room as Austen's heroine proves to be.

Of course, there was a lot about the Land Army girls that I didn't know, and I didn't think to ask questions. I would not, for example, have wondered why the same girls were not allowed at that time to drink with the men in the bars of the town's three hotels. In my own mind, if I thought about the subject at all, I did not contemplate an adult world in which women's lives were subservient in any way, although clearly they were often different. If women did the housework, I thought, remembering a history lesson delivered by an unusually interesting history teacher, it should be by their own choice and negotiated on the basis of an equitable division of labour. Predictably, that same teacher didn't last long in our school without a warning from the Parents' and Citizens' Association to leave his political opinions outside the classroom door.

The charade in *Emma* made me think that I was fortunate to be born into a more enlightened world. It sheds light on the gender politics of Austen's time. And it is a telling example of how effectively Austen used her fiction to poke fun at ideas about the deferential relationship of women to men and the inferior role of women in society; to highlight the ways in which prevailing beliefs are dressed up in fine words and pretentious expressions. I learned the charade by heart when we were studying the novel; I was fascinated by the ease with which it mocks the idea that informs the verse as well as the fictional character who contributes it to Harriet's collection.

In the context of Austen's own life, it astounds me even now that the novelist found a way to do this, living at a time when it was taken for granted that, as the charade implies, a good woman was indeed an antidote for the woes and worries of a good man. As spinsters, Jane and Cassandra Austen were at the beck and call of their brothers; they sewed their shirts, nursed them when ill, attended their wives in childbirth, amused their children and depended on their favours. The charade is more than the sum of its individual lines; it is a reminder of those cultivated and sometimes childish men of letters who wrote of an Austen heroine as if she were an antidote in a general sense, a spoonful of sugar to make life's medicine go down.

Jane Austen as an antidote is a thread that runs through her own story. The family memoir that was produced in 1871 not only presented the novelist to her reading public as a saintly figure, but it also promoted the novels as an antidote to what was amiss with modern life. The myth of Austen's saintly modesty fooled a generation or two of men of letters. Virginia Woolf mocked the adulation of Austen's conservative male readers. 'There are twenty-five elderly gentlemen living in the neighbourhood of London,' she wrote jokingly, 'who resent any slight upon her genius, as if it were an insult to the chastity of their aunts.' The politician Benjamin Disraeli boasted that he had read *Pride and Prejudice* seventeen times. Robert Louis Stevenson, who created male archetypes such as Dr Jekyll and Mr Hyde, seems the least likely person to get down on bended knee and propose to Lizzy Bennet, but he claimed he did so every time he read *Pride and Prejudice*. The hard-boiled novelist Martin Amis, writing in the twenty-first century, confessed to at least five or six readings of the same novel. With similar hyperbole he pinpoints the moment at which love blooms for Mr Darcy as a moment when it also blooms 'for every male reader on earth'.

There was even a celebrated scholar who consumed a portion of an Austen novel every night in bed, until he went to sleep; it was suggested that it 'composed him like gruel'. Reading Austen's fiction was never like that for me. The heroines of *Pride and Prejudice* kept me well and truly awake, and provided me with richer fare than literary gruel. For my part, I was presented with an antidote to the disappointing idea that the best novels were written by males, about males, and even for males. I rejoice now that one female writer and a handful of female protagonists had caused my imagination to flourish and made me a reader for life. The language that Austen's heroines spoke was not only pleasant in my ears; it was an antidote to the clichés of sentimental stereotypes.

A love of the sound of the English language was at the core of my passion for reading. It may sound incongruous, but an unlikely influence in this addiction was my paternal grandfather, with his thick European accent and very un-English habits of speech and social behaviour. His eccentric personality played a pivotal role in developing my verbal imagination. I don't know how, where or when he learned English, and, in fact, we were never quite sure where he came from. When he died, we found his passport, which recorded his birthplace as Bobroysk, Russia, his height as five foot ten, his eyes as dark grey and hair as grey. But during his lifetime he insisted that he was subject to, and the subject of, no country in the old world. I can hear again the deep, heavily accented voice in which he wove simple but exciting stories around the courage of his parents as they fled from a pogrom presumably but improbably by train, since according to his account his mother miraculously gave birth to him on a train between Poland and Russia; his momentous decision as a young boy to make his way to Palestine on overhearing his parents' decision to send him away to study religion; his hand-to-hand combat with ferocious bears in the dense forests he passed through; and an intimate account of his romantic meeting with my grandmother, who had emigrated from Russia with her parents and brother during what is known as the second migration of Jews to their ancient homeland. By the time I was sitting on his knee to watch more closely as he deftly removed a thin tissue of paper from his brass tobacco box and expertly rolled yet another cigarette, he spoke surprisingly good English. He could hold an audience in thrall. He entertained family and friends with stories of his early life that both defied and delighted the imagination, and with his love of storytelling went an endless supply of riddles and word puzzles.

Grandpa, as my brother and I called him, was given to telling stories at the drop of a hat. Some were addressed to general matters of life while others matched specific circumstances. He was always eager to comfort mourners, for example, with an exemplary tale of travellers, each of whom, when given the opportunity to exchange a personal suitcase of woes for someone else's, refused to part with the familiar one. Of course, my grandfather did not tell the tale so baldly; he embroidered it with details, personal and geographical, and accompanied it with philosophical commentary on the meaning of life and the inevitability of death. From memory, his parables were welcomed and seemed to bring comfort, even if only by way of bemusement, to his listener.

My most cherished memories of storytelling spring from the regular Saturday night ritual that completed our observance of the Sabbath. In the dim light of a single candle, my grandfather and my parents sang plaintive songs in Yiddish, the language that was, for all of them, their mother tongue. My father's favourite song was a lullaby he remembered from his infancy, when his late mother, of whom he spoke with great fondness, sang him to sleep with the promise of almonds and raisins in his dreams.

My mother was born in Jerusalem and had learned a classical and sacred model of the Hebrew language from an ultra-Orthodox father who belonged to the priestly tribe called the 'Cohanim'. She recited beautifully cadenced passages from the prophet Isaiah. Her light bell-like voice also suited the sweet melodies that had been composed to accompany lyrics in the modern Hebrew language, revived only shortly before she was born. The words were celebrations of the miracle of life in a Jewish homeland. I wonder now, although it did not occur to me as a child, whether being transplanted from the old city of Jerusalem, with its exotic and turbulent history, its thronging crowds and colourful markets, to a dusty town in the Murrumbidgee Irrigation Area might in some way account for the throbbing headaches that sent her, like Lady Bertram in *Mansfield Park*, to the couch for many hours of the day.

As far as I was concerned, the highlight of the evening was my grandfather's rendition of songs through which he wove biblical stories of stark and compelling drama. Fragments of them remain in my unreliable musical memory. One of my favourites was about a little girl, Sara, who was transported to heaven, like the prophet Elijah – perhaps even with him, I can't recall – in a chariot of fire. My grandfather followed the song with a description of the girl – of course, she resembled me, with her long plaits and brown eyes – and Grandpa delighted me with an imitation of the snorting of the horses that pulled the flaming chariot, impatient to get home to heaven.

The drama of that song was matched by a suite of songs that depicted the plight of the boy Joseph in his coat of many colours. Following an account of the jealousy roused in Joseph's older brothers by their father Jacob's gift of the coat came a syncopated oriental beat to accompany words that told of the discovery and rescue of Joseph from the pit where his brothers had disposed of him by a band of passing traders in their caravans. The climax was reached as the caravan bearing Joseph on its way to Egypt passed by his mother's tomb. 'Rachel, Rachel, Mother Rachel,' he cried out piteously, and each time I heard it, my tears flowed.

As I remember it, though, time spent with our grandfather was also full of fun and activity. When he visited us from Sydney, where he lived with several cats in a room above a commercial city garage, he did more than tell stories. He taught me to ride a bike, and he played energetic ball games with my brother. When we came inside the house, he quizzed us. 'What is black and white and red all over?' he would ask. And we would giggle when he gasped in amazement, as he always did, when we answered correctly in unison, 'A newspaper.' And once again he would warn, 'If you expect to rate as a gentleman, don't expectorate here,' wagging his finger at my brother. I could never understand how he came by such a funny sentence. On a visit to Sydney when I was older, I read the words on a public notice in the tram that he would have taken from his sparse room near Central Station to his chess club, located in one of the city's grandest department-store buildings. I marvel now that he, for whom English was a language learned later in life, came to relish the word play that never failed to puzzle and delight us as children.

So, unlikely as it may be, word play in English was something that was shared by my family – descended from Eastern European migrants via the Levant and transplanted in its first Australian-born generation to a rural town in Wiradjuri Country – and Jane Austen and her family, who inhabited what is called the pseudo-gentry in Regency England. And the seed planted in me by my grandfather meant that I was receptive to the sophisticated use of riddles, conundrums and charades that I would encounter when I moved from the deceptively simple pleasures of *Pride and Prejudice*, which served as an antidote to adolescent doubts, to the antidote provided by the challenge of fictional puzzles in the novel *Emma*: a likely cure for a complacent mind.

It is clear from accounts of Jane Austen's early life in her father's parsonage in the county of Hampshire that her whole family delighted in challenging each other in their leisure with verses written to order and with lighthearted riddles. Mrs Austen's verbal humour shows through a little verse inspired by the vowel sound in the word 'rose':

> This morning I 'woke from a quiet repose,
> I first rubb'd my eyes & I next blew my nose.
> With my Stockings & Shoes I then cover'd my toes
> And proceeded to put on the rest of my Cloathes.

I am not surprised that the younger of her two daughters shared her comic spirit. But when comparing their verses, it is evident that there were already signs of a more sophisticated imagination in the younger writer's verbal deftness and versatility.

You may lie on my first, by the side of a stream,
And my second compose to the Nymph you adore
But if when you've none of my whole her esteem
And affection diminish, think of her no more.

I relish the canny shift by means of which the versifier turns the syllables into the word *banknote* as the solution to the charade. Already Austen was learning to spice observation with irony.

There must be something about the Lyceum Theatre because that's where we were, my parents and I, when I had my one and only strong urge to write a poem. This was two years before I was to have my fateful encounter with *Pride and Prejudice*. I have no recollection of the film we were watching, but it was interrupted by the announcement that the war was finally at an end. The victory in Europe had been celebrated in the month of May 1945, but general relief was restrained because of the continuing struggle in the Pacific. Now jubilation was unalloyed. No one was thinking about the moral implications of the bombs dropped on the cities of Hiroshima and Nagasaki in Japan – not at first, anyway. Those thoughts would have to wait until after we had celebrated the end of fear and the homecoming of brothers and fathers.

The only long poem I ever wrote was composed on that night. Much as I have always enjoyed reading poetry, I myself have never been able to produce anything worth keeping, despite occasional scraps I have stored away in a large box labelled 'Writing thoughts'. But on a date that is remembered as VJ Day, signifying Victory in Japan, the relief of knowing that our family would be safe from persecution – we did not yet know about the worst excesses of the death camps – prompted me to express my feelings poetically.

But the story has run ahead of itself. First, following the glorious news, came an unbidden recollection of a schoolfriend called Daphne, and with that came a wave of pity and regret. Daphne had sat next to me in fourth class at primary school. She was clever; much cleverer than I could hope to be, I knew, as she effortlessly answered questions that stumped the rest of the class. She was artistic, too. She often sketched while listening to a lesson, and to my amazement a prancing horse would always emerge lifelike from her pencil strokes. I learned that she was a middle child in a close-knit family of eleven brothers and sisters. They lived on the outskirts of town, where a small group of families like hers existed on the edge of poverty.

One day, Daphne arrived at school with red eyes and told me that her older brother, Ernie, who had enlisted as soon as he was old enough, had been killed in action. She was crying for her mother as well as for her brother. She often spoke about her mother with gratitude and admiration for the way she took care of them all. Her mother's hair was always put up in a perfect bun, Daphne told me, even in the early hours of the morning when she was stirring the porridge for breakfast. The daughter was certain that her mother knew everything. And sure enough, she had known that Ernie was going to be killed. A week earlier a framed photograph of Ernie had fallen off the wall. Yes, her mother had realised then that it was only a matter of time. Yesterday the telegram had been delivered. And now she was crying, for the first time ever as far as Daphne knew. She couldn't stop crying for her dead son.

I hadn't seen Daphne since we moved up from primary school. She, who certainly qualified for the A class, had voluntarily transferred herself to the class that studied domestic science and home economics in a separate school building, where she learned to dust furniture, polish floors and cut the crusts off sandwiches. The rooms were not all classrooms; some of them were stage settings for domestic life in the sort of households where girls might expect to be employed. What use would Daphne have for subjects such as Latin and French that were obligatory for A-class students? I can imagine that her mother asked herself this question and that, for her, the answer was unequivocal. Daphne's path and mine diverged geographically and socially once we were in different parts of the school, but on that night in August 1945 my memory flashed back to her pale and miserable face and the shock of her awful news.

Fleeting thoughts of Daphne on VJ night did not inhibit the exclamations, kisses and hugs that followed the announcement of peace. Afterwards, in my bedroom, I felt a renewal of the urge to record how I was feeling. I wish I could say that my emotions, recollected in tranquillity as Wordsworth recommends, had a memorable outcome. My poem 'Peace', written that night and polished a little with the help of my teacher, Mrs Eason, who remained my friend after I was no longer in her class, started with the line, 'Peace, peace, wonderful peace, has come to us this night'. It does not get any better. I did not keep it, and my memory of the first line is all that remains of its composition.

I was reminded again of my friend Daphne years later when I read the novel – novella really; only 132 pages in length, a read of half a day or night – written by the prize-winning author

Graham Swift. *Mothering Sunday* was first published in 2016, and it has the subtitle *A romance*. It is a novella not just because of its length; it does what novellas are supposed to do, depicting a defining moment in a life. As for romance, well, it has been described as a tale of life and lust, but for me it depicts a romance between a girl and reading as much as it is an erotic relationship between the son of the house and a domestic servant who, in the tradition of her times, is released from domestic duties on certain appointed Sundays, known as 'mothering Sundays', when housemaids were encouraged to go home to visit their mothers.

The novel is set in March 1924 and is wonderful for the transitions it makes from present to past and back again. Jane Fairchild is a housemaid, and the son of the house, just a year older at twenty-three. The book might also have been called a tragedy, because the son dies, apparently accidentally but possibly by his own will. His erotically charged relationship with Jane will never be sanctioned by his parents, to whom he is bound by strong ties of filial duty. But if a romance is about dreams fulfilled, that happens when Jane is given access to the household library by the master of the house in a momentary empathetic connection. This defining moment offers her an escape from the life she has been living – an antidote, in the spirit of Jane Austen, that proved to be the remedy she needed: free passage through the library door and a corridor to life as a novelist.

As a reader I wonder about the name Jane Fairchild. It rings a bell with Jane Fairfax, the character created by Jane Austen as a foil for her heroine Emma. Both Janes are potentially imprisoned by their circumstances, and both manage to find an alternative. Jane Fairfax chooses marriage, Jane Fairchild becomes a reader and then, by an unexpected twist, a writer of imaginative fiction. If Austen had been writing in the late twentieth century, like Graham Swift, perhaps Jane Fairfax, too, would have chosen a more independent future. I personally never envied her a future with Frank Churchill; but, then, I had already met Mr Wickham in *Pride and Prejudice* and Willoughby from *Sense and Sensibility*, so I had the measure of a charming cad when I met him in a novel. As far as my friend Daphne is concerned, I have no idea what became of her, but I wish now that her mother had realised the possibilities that enrolment in the A class might have offered.

Daphne's story resonates more happily for one of Jane Austen's heroines. I am reminded of how young Fanny Price in *Mansfield Park*, disadvantaged in a completely different way, is enabled to transcend the setbacks of birth partly because she has learned how to read. Her cousin Edmund, the only truly empathetic relative in her adoptive home, is the enabler:

> He knew her to be clever, to have a quick apprehension as well as good sense, and a fondness for reading, which properly directed, must be an education in itself . . . he recommended the books which charmed her leisure hours, he encouraged her taste, and corrected her judgement; he made reading useful by talking to her of what she read, and heightened its attraction by judicious praise.

Reading as an education: this was Edmund's remedy for the unpleasantness of Fanny's situation. I wish that Daphne could have found a mentor like him, someone who would recognise her potential as Edmund recognised Fanny's.

My feeble attempt at poetry did not affect my love of English lessons. We were not often required to write poems in class, although some students chose to do so. One of my classmates, Dianna, was a born poet. We both took English Honours in our final year and engaged earnestly with each other in class, over a wide reading program that focused on English and American writers. It included an abundance of twentieth-century poets, dramatists, short-story writers, essayists and novelists. Dianna particularly loved the poets, while I favoured dramatists and novelists.

My bookshelves by that time housed a splendid collection of books drawn from the recommended Honours curriculum list. My father had invited my English teacher to a meeting to discuss my ambition to sit the Honours papers in my matriculation year and asked him for a list of the books I would need to cover the course. Unlike the heroine of the novel *Emma*, I embarked immediately and enthusiastically on the task of reading them. 'The list she drew up when only fourteen,' Mr Knightley reminds Emma's governess, remained just that, a list. He continued, 'I remember thinking it did her judgment so much credit, that I preserved it some time; and I daresay she may have made out a very good list now. But I have done with expecting any course of steady reading from Emma.'

When the book box arrived from Angus & Robertson, the premier Sydney bookstore, my father was almost as excited as I was. He had developed a love for literature himself. I have a few books that he must have studied at university, when he filled in a year while waiting to be old enough to enter the medical faculty. I have his copy of essays by Francis Bacon with copious marginalia

58

neatly inscribed in pencil. He had a remarkable memory, especially for poetry, with immediate recall of passages from Shakespeare, Milton and Wordsworth to fit almost any occasion. There are no notes in his copy of *Essays and Lays of Ancient Rome* by Lord Macaulay, but I loved reading aloud from the book, especially the stirring account of the hero Horatius and the valiant comrades who answered his call to save Rome from the Etruscan advance:

> Now who will stand on either hand
> And keep the bridge with me?

When I made my 'grand tour' of Europe with my parents in 1951, my father and I stood on the banks of the River Tiber, accompanied by a guide from Thomas Cook & Son. We took turns in reciting verses from the lay. 'You are like an apple cut in two,' commented the bemused guide.

I have liked to recite poetry aloud all my life, but reading prose has always suited me better, I think because of my obsession with human beings and the rhythms of language and social relationships. Dianna, my reading friend, worked with words in other ways. She was in love with the natural world and had an instinct for the rhythms of both words and the earth. Her father had shown her the erosion of soil on their citrus orchard and explained the damage done by irrigation and salination to the wellbeing of the earth in which their trees were planted. Like everything in nature, this knowledge inspired a poetic impulse in Dianna.

She and I talked about poetry thirty years later when a small group of us who had been at high school together met as adults in Sydney. We exchanged reminiscences and told each other of our marriages, our children and our current occupations. Dianna had trained as an early-childhood teacher, risen in her chosen profession, and was by then a college principal and educational consultant. She had married one of her Methodist Fellowship leaders, had several children, and was now divorced. She was in a new relationship that involved a lot of travelling and she was hoping it would work out well. A second divorced member of our group, May, had left school without completing her senior years. Before her marriage she had earned her licence to fly and helped her father, who had been a wartime pilot, to restore a single-engine plane left over from the war years. She told us that she had five children and I wondered whether she had become too independent to remain married.

Of those who were still married, Isabel was leading a women's magazine lifestyle: immaculately groomed, married to a businessman, she had completed an arts degree but hadn't worked since she was married. She arrived and left our luncheon venue in a chauffeur-driven car. Carmen was one of the girls with whom I had loved to chat as we rode our bikes home from school. She was working as a counsellor, had problems with a divorced son, but spoke glowingly of her husband, whom she had met at school. I thought hers sounded like a good marriage. Jennifer had always been a lively chatterbox, and here she was again, talking animatedly about herself as she had always done; more about her success as a mature student than she did about her marriage. And here, too, was the other Ruth; we had drifted apart in our latter school years, but met up again at university, where we both had an interest in theatricals. When she shared the details of her uneventful life – married to an engineer and teaching while bringing up four boys – it sounded like a solid marriage, but no trace remained of the fairy-tale parade of King and Queen under the cherry plum trees that we had observed longingly all those years ago.

I am sensitive to traces of fairy tales in the fiction I read; I am interested in how the fairy-tale elements blend with the realities of human existence. If we read her novels often and attentively, we see that Jane Austen sometimes pretends that life is like a fairy tale. But this is only an illusion. No one's life or fiction illustrated more tellingly than hers that fairy tales rarely last. The fairy-tale adoption of her brother Edward ended sadly with the death of his wife, a young woman who had given birth to eleven children. Jane Austen's own romantic fairy tale with her friendly neighbour's nephew collapsed before it went much further than a mild flirtation. Emma Woodhouse, like Snow White and Cinderella, is beautiful, clever and motherless. On the other hand, she is rich, her surrogate mother loves and spoils her, and her father idolises her. Austen's fairy tales are no more than hints and whispers; her courtship and marriage plots are preludes to a different reality.

Emma Woodhouse, whose life had offered nothing to distress or vex her when the novel opens, entered my world in the first Austen novel I read at university. Because my love of reading made English studies my priority when I enrolled at The University of Sydney in 1949, my relationship with Austen prospered. The novel *Emma* was introduced by Miss Herring, a lecturer who read the first sentence, aloud and twice, before she delivered her lecture. Here I was again, feeling as I felt when I read *Pride and Prejudice*: that I was on home territory. Following the theme of the first lecture, I gave myself over to discovering Emma as she discovers herself. I set about untangling the novel's parade of puzzles, which, with Miss Herring's guidance, finally settled into a design that brought order and elegance to the novel. By then I had taken up residency with Emma in Hartfield and plotted the village landscape in my head.

In my new life on campus, however, I was confronted with a more daunting landscape. My sense of direction has never been strong, and it took time to reorientate myself from the idea of easily accessed classrooms at high school to the larger landscape in which lecture rooms and theatres were located within a network of roads and enclaves. Now I had to navigate my way around a more expansive landscape of lawns, paths and imposing buildings, unsure of my bearings once I left the confines of the university quadrangle and its shaded cloisters. Eventually I found my bearings and was able to walk confidently down Science Road to the Wallace Theatre, where most of my lectures took place.

Two hundred or so students squeezed themselves between long rows of desks and benches, readying themselves for lectures about English language and literature. It was often impossible to find a seat, and some students stood at the back of the theatre; others sat on the raked steps that led down to the stage and lectern. We were a disparate lot of would-be scholars. Some, like me, were just out of school, sixteen or seventeen years of age. But many students were older, the final intake of ex-servicemen who had been offered a university education following the end of the Second World War. What they were feeling I cannot know, but I imagine that, along with their war-weariness, there was also a sense of new possibilities. I myself felt a new beat to life, and it filled me with anticipation for what was to come. Anyway, there we sat as one cohort, busily scribbling in our notebooks, all of us in our own worlds of concentration, contemplation or, in some cases, distraction.

From the beginning, English lectures were the highlight of my week. Thelma Herring, the first Austen expert in the English faculty, initiated us into the literary puzzle of the character Emma Woodhouse and the perfection of the novel *Emma*. After the introductory lecture she continued to read passages aloud, as I was already accustomed to doing. Her readings demonstrated both the elegant sound of Austen's language and the artful way the author plays with words and sentences to confound her readers. I responded spontaneously to her idea of *Emma* as a 'subjunctive novel' because the heroine only *seemed* to be blessed. The ground had been prepared for me to respond to Miss Herring's readings and connect with fiction in a more sophisticated way than I had done at school. I had always enjoyed my grammar lessons, and during the hours I had spent with my hometown elocution teacher I had learned a lot about how reading aloud intensifies the power of language.

In *Emma* Austen gives us a heroine who, in her customary and contrary way, resists the experience of reading. And reading emerges in the novel as an antidote for many failures of human nature: ignorance, lack of discrimination and moral awareness. Emma acknowledges the value of reading but rarely takes her enthusiasm beyond drawing up lists of books that she *intends* to read. Mr Knightley, her older friend and mentor who is destined, in the fullness of narrative time, to become her lover, suggests to her erstwhile governess that intention is not enough; that reading might remedy Emma's somewhat wayward flights of fancy. As the novel progresses, Emma does discover, through experience, that she lacks judgement, especially about others and their intentions. In a larger framework, reading Jane Austen's novels would offer me a remedy for some of the doubts, uncertainties and disappointments that have mingled with the better parts of any life.

I felt the happily-ever-after illusion of a fairy-tale marriage hovering over a YouTube conversation between two modern-day academics. Under the banner of 'The Austen Antidote', they wear their scholarship lightly. The fact that they are married adds a touch of whimsy to the encounter. Professor Looser has edited a small book with an Austen quotation for each day of the year. Her appealing volume is in a different category from the many productions that cater to Austen fans rather than to Austen scholars. *The Daily Jane Austen: A year of quotes* serves both cohorts of readers well. But Looser warns readers to think again about the notorious misquotation of Austen's work. Context is everything in fiction, as it is in life.

I was charmed by Looser's selection when she was asked by her husband, Professor George Justice, for the most 'beautiful' quotation for marriage from among the Austen daily doses in her collection. She chose the advice that Elizabeth Bennet offers Darcy after the resolution of conflicts that have arisen from the pride and the prejudices of both parties. With her customary sauciness, Lizzy suggests that he should 'think only of the past as its remembrance gives you pleasure'. It is a witty choice and I was momentarily taken aback by my ambivalent reaction.

It struck me with an unexpected flash of insight that such advice must surely be taken with a grain of salt by women of my generation. For some of us, happy memories are not the first that come to mind: an earlier optimism about love and marriage was sorely tested by the realities of married life. In search of happy memories, I would have to go further back, to the days of courtship. Like Catherine Morland in *Northanger Abbey*, I arrived at a time in my life when something happened to throw a hero in my way. He arrived in the form of a dental student to whom I was introduced in the university quadrangle. His quick quips satisfied the natural inclination that I shared with Elizabeth Bennet, the love of laughter.

I have been married to my hero, mostly on but sometimes off, for close on seventy years. The beginning of our romance was slow to start on my part, but then it became as precious as Anne Elliot's feelings for Captain Wentworth. I had never felt so comfortable with anyone outside my family. I had never laughed so much; and I had never felt so loved. I was young and I enjoyed the experience of being pursued. So it became a time of laughter, shared dreams, a belief in the enduring nature of a love affair and a feeling of empowerment. I was in an unexpectedly carefree place. Gradually, the worldly aspirations that I had contemplated as my future – perhaps as a scholar or more likely as a performer – started to fade.

I had drifted into the world of the 'hidden persuaders', as journalist Vance Packard termed the advertisers who used psychological techniques to manipulate the public. These social influencers glorified the role of women as wives and mothers, and I had been 'schooled' to regard marriage as the natural conclusion of girlhood and the gateway to the adult phase of life. It turned out that 'marriage is as marriage does', to borrow a cliché that came back to bite, as clichés tend to do. It was not just personal. When life settled after the war, the world went back to the old normal, and the apparent readjustments of gender relationships fell away. Now I can recall the early years of marriage as a transition period, during which I adjusted, almost overnight, from the enjoyment of being with a man who was in love to the reality of deferring to a male who was in charge.

At the time I was barely aware of the shift backwards in time, to cultural assumptions that were not so very far removed from Mr Elton's charade. I had read Jane Austen and absorbed her ideas about companionate marriages, but when the crunch came, when children arrived and the male was the breadwinner, I succumbed as unconsciously as many others to the hidden persuaders lying in wait in every magazine: the advertisements, advice columns and even women's reportage that gave gold stars to the woman who made her husband happy. Not then but later, I asked myself, what of the vaunted absurdity of Mr Elton's riddle? Despite my presumptions of autonomy and independence, despite the university education that I, unlike my mother's generation, could take for granted, I found myself at a disadvantage, less and less able to sustain my own voice, let alone raise it to protest, as the pleasures of motherhood dimmed when compared with the absolute freedom of the male breadwinner. It was not necessarily a matter of being wronged; rather, it was a confrontation with the reality, a consequence of being born on the wrong side of feminist history.

Plenty of marriages of my generation featured stay-at-home wives and *Mad Men* husbands. I do not imagine that there are many happy memories to be harvested there, especially for female spouses who spent lonely nights waiting for the male of the house to return from late-night activities that might or might not be work-related. Too many such wives lived out their days preferring not to know which way the wind blew – or pretending not to know, if that was what it took to keep their marriages afloat.

All around me at that time, in the 1950s and 60s, women were working out ways to deal with the unexpected hand that life had dealt them. Most of my female friends had enjoyed a university education. Most of them had subsequently married. Very few wanted to contemplate divorce. Some couples did seem relatively happy just as they were; others flirted with each other's partners and laughed off a sort of benevolent neglect by their own. Some women immersed themselves in their children's lives. Then there were those whose sense of emotional deprivation led them to take desperate measures.

One of my closest friends, Deirdre, stopped fussing about keeping an immaculate house and full biscuit barrel. She did not neglect her children, but she used the time they were at school to immerse herself in affairs of the church of healing to which she belonged, and in a fantasised affair of the heart with the minister. A second friend compensated for her dissatisfactions by comforting another woman's discontented husband. I am not sure whether infidelity was the cause or the symptom, but it was all around. All these possibilities were discussed as we stay-at-home wives engaged in long telephone conversations or when we gossiped over cups of instant coffee at our kitchen tables.

I knew that I was unequivocally monogamous by nature. So, I blotted out unwelcome thoughts and did lots of housework in the morning. In the afternoon, before the children came home from school, I read contemporary fiction that spoke to my state of mind. Margaret Drabble's *The Millstone* challenged me to be braver, but Penelope Mortimer wrote a book that resonated more authentically with who I was in the 1960s. Her title is inspired by the nursery rhyme, 'Peter, Peter, pumpkin eater / Had a wife and couldn't keep her'. The heroine of *The Pumpkin Eater* found herself in the linen department of Harrods in London, dampening the cloths 'with extraordinarily large tears'. Edna O'Brien, the Irish novelist, wrote that 'almost every woman I can think of will want to read this book'. I, for one, read it many times.

I also cried secretly in my bedroom, attended popular cooking classes, and spent many hours preparing for dinner parties and following recipes for dishes laden with cream and butter. We entertained in a pretty dining room with red velvet curtains and reproduction Georgian mahogany furniture and porcelain cigarette receptacles artfully placed along the table. Perhaps it was because Jane Austen and her companionate marriages seemed so far from my current reality that I came to neglect reading her novels for the time being.

I also came, almost imperceptibly, to feel like a second-class citizen in the republic of marriage.

In one of my most memorable theatrical experiences, the actor in a one-woman show circled around the human dilemma of marital fidelity. Joyce Grenfell, a gifted monologist, visited Australia in 1963. I had heard her monologues on the wireless and knew that she was a relation by marriage to Ruth Draper, an older monologist of whom my elocution teacher spoke with admiration and delight. Grenfell apparently was even better; comparing the two artists, a critic remarked that Grenfell's monologues were 'the best thing of their kind since Miss Ruth Draper, the difference being that Miss Draper's are too long and Miss Grenfell's are too short'. Grenfell was especially well known for her nursery-school monologues. She spoke in the voice of a teacher, capturing the full range of emotions required to do the job: patience, gentleness, humour, exasperation, frustration, determination and a whisper of repressed anger. Her virtuoso performance was informed by an Austenian gift for observation and ironic representation. Nothing about this engaging teacher was spared: the virtues were acknowledged, but her delusions were skewered with equal precision.

We were a group of friendship couples in our thirties, sitting together to watch the performance at the Theatre Royal. Before interval, Grenfell delivered two or three familiar pieces to enthusiastic laughter. After the break she spoke in a different voice. Sitting in a chintz-covered armchair, she hugged a paisley stole around her upper body and wistfully recalled episodes from a married life. So much love, so much joy in the courtship; so much uncertainty and loneliness in what came later. No expression of regret or bitterness at all; nothing but acceptance and undiminished affection as she pulled the large scarf more tightly around her shoulders.

It was not the absences that she chose to dwell on, she reflected. It was the recurring return to hearth and home that she celebrated, somewhat ruefully it seemed to me. I wondered what the men in our party, including my own husband, were thinking. Would they take it as a form of permission, even an act of affirmation, that women willingly accept the role portrayed so sympathetically in the monologue? I wondered about the women, too. I recalled an older woman of my acquaintance who was regarded as a strong matriarchal figure in a model family. A scene flashed across my mind. She was holding forth at an afternoon tea, assuring a group of women that she could cope with her husband's taking his hors d'oeuvre 'out' because she knew he would return home for the main course. She also serves who only sits and waits?

At the end of the performance, the applause was more muted than it had been before the interval. I wondered if other women in the audience shared my disturbing thoughts. At supper the conversation skirted around the skills of the performer and settled on the sharp observation and psychological insight that Grenfell brought to her rendition of the teacher. No one raised the ambiguities implicit in the main piece. Driving home I considered debating the issues raised in the monologue, but I extrapolated from the proposition offered by the narrator of the novel *Persuasion*: 'Husbands and wives generally understand when opposition will be vain.' I left the subject alone.

Marriage was one topic, among many, that I had discussed with my friend Dianna during the period in which we found each other again. At school our friendship had been confined to the classroom and our discussion of the books we were reading. As adults, I think we both realised how much we enjoyed each other's company, so at times we met separately, outside our class reunions. She was an attentive listener and offered affirmation or advice whenever I told her about my recent professional transition from teaching English to developing intergenerational oral-history programs that encouraged learning as the educator Roslyn Arnold describes it in her book *Empathic Intelligence*. Similarly, I was fascinated by the innovative program she had developed to teach numeracy to young children. She confided that writing poetry was her way of working out the mysteries of existence, and she had found inspiration and sometimes solace in her compositions during a life that had been professionally rewarding and personally turbulent.

When I began to re-read Jane Austen, I shared some of my

favourite 'marriage passages' with Dianna. We agreed that, as post-war wives, we had hoped for companionate-marriage relationships and sighed over the failed possibility of a 'union that must have been to the advantage of both'. In the case of Elizabeth and Darcy, *her* 'ease and liveliness' might soften his mind and improve his manners, while 'from his judgment, information and knowledge of the world, she must have received benefit of greater importance'. We had both hoped for a reciprocal relationship in which the strengths and weaknesses of each partner would provide a counterbalance. We both resented the idea of playing second fiddle in any human relationship. Dianna and I shared our dream that our daughters would benefit from the resistance we felt to the inequity of marriage realities. Neither of us believed, as Charlotte Lucas did, that happiness in marriage should be accepted as 'entirely a matter of chance'.

Sadly, Dianna's hopes for an enduring second relationship fell apart when her memory started to fail in about 2010. The last time we met in the city I accompanied her to Town Hall Station and made sure that she caught the right train. It was obvious that her senses of place and direction were declining. Shortly after that final meeting she sent me a letter to say she was leaving Sydney to live near her daughter in Melbourne. She enclosed a poem that she had written. It was called 'Brain':

It used to be secure
A steady peg on which to hang

Important things.
A base from which old thoughts
Could be reviewed
Reflected on.

A staunch resource of gathered acts and deeds
Enduring parts of me:
Ideas, beliefs and theories, tested, tried,
Skilled actions, jobs well done,
That hold my whole together.

A little less assured, these days?

Dianna's path through life made her a guide worth following, I thought, as I put the verses somewhere safe. She herself had acknowledged the poet W.B. Yeats as her guide. She once quoted the final lines of the poem 'He Wishes for the Cloths of Heaven' as her romantic mantra:

I have spread my dreams under your feet;
Tread softly because you tread on my dreams.

We sighed in unison, ageing romantics that we both were at heart. When I received her poem, I hoped that her gift for poetry would be an antidote to the patches of emptiness that were bound to invade her life as the condition progressed.

Standing on the pavement in a queue outside a suburban branch of Barclays bank in 2017, I had occasion to think once again about how Austen's fiction had served as a remedy in my own life. A happy chance placed me in London when the historic ten-pound note with Austen's image was released by the Bank of London. I was visiting my son, who had lived there for most of his adult life, and it was with a sense of my good fortune that I joined the long queue of Austen lovers and amateur currency investors waiting patiently outside the bank to buy up a few notes for posterity. There I fell into conversation with the woman ahead of me in the queue. She had never read an Austen novel but thought that a bundle of the newly minted banknotes with the famous author's portrait might be a good investment.

My new acquaintance had seen more than one television series of Austen's fiction and was eager to hear about the differences. Recalling our conversation now, I am reminded of Jane Austen's friend Martha Lloyd, so I'll give her that name. I hope that after our conversation she might have become, like Martha, a dedicated reader of the novels. At the time, she was curious to know what it was about Austen's fiction that mattered so much to readers like me, and why I would want to stand in a queue for the banknotes.

'Well,' I said, 'they'll be a reminder of a fascinating story of coincidences really. When Jane Austen was a young girl, she wrote a little verse that was also a puzzle in which two syllables make up the word "banknote". Austen didn't much like the conduct books of her time; she worked out more subtle ways of talking about manners. Her verse suggests that a girl who marries for money alone is not worth marrying. The relationship between marriage and money is an idea Austen plays with many times over.'

'So you want the notes because they remind you of the coincidence?' Martha asked.

'Yes, that coincidence and another one as well. In 1803, Jane Austen sold a manuscript called *Susan* to a publisher. Years passed without it being published. Shortly before her death, when she was only forty-one, her brother Henry negotiated to buy it back for the same amount that she had received for it: ten pounds. And now she is the first woman to have her image on the British ten-pound note. I think that's a noteworthy coincidence, if you'll excuse the pun.'

Martha laughed. 'Some schadenfreude there, I should think.'

By this time, a young couple behind us invited themselves into the conversation. Surprisingly it was the husband who spoke up. He had read *Emma* at school and really enjoyed it. I shall call him Henry, for Austen's favourite brother.

'After I read *Emma*, I tried *Pride and Prejudice* and liked it just as much. Which one do you prefer?' he asked me.

'Actually, I can't really compare them,' I said. 'I like them both for different reasons, and like so many Austen readers, my favourite is usually the one I'm reading at the time. I can tell you what I like best about each novel. In *Pride and Prejudice*, the heroine learns to read other people, while the heroine of *Emma* learns to read herself. I suppose they are different aspects of why it is important to read well. The banknote tells everyone that Jane Austen is all about reading. The quotation on the new note says: "I declare after all there is no enjoyment like reading".'

'What a perfect quotation!' Martha enthused.

I shrugged. 'Well, it's problematical. The character who says the words is only pretending to like reading so that she can impress a man she is after!'

Martha's eyes widened. 'Whoever it was that chose the quotation made a blunder then?'

'Yes – and, ironically, blunders fascinated Jane Austen.'

Henry said, 'Once our teacher pointed that out, I read *Emma* again to discover all the blunders I had missed.'

'That's a good idea,' I told him. 'We're talking about reading, but really *re-reading* is the key to Austen's fiction.'

'So, if you had to sum it up for someone like me who has

not read any of the novels,' Martha said, 'how would you convince me that reading one of Austen's novels is better than seeing the movie?'

I considered this for a moment. 'I suppose the advantage of reading is that it makes you think for yourself. In the movies, the director and the actors do so much of the thinking for you, and they are often exploring or even imposing ideas that critics have written about. So if you haven't read the novel, you only get what others make of it. But reading them attentively – and especially re-reading them, as Henry did – teases your brain, challenges you to work out the significance of what is happening in the story. It also allows you to interpret the novel in relation to your own life. It encourages you to think about what you should value, how you might think about your friendships and the values of people you mix with. Reading makes your brain more lively, I think; a real antidote to boredom!'

By this time, we had moved to the front of the queue and, after purchasing our notes, we parted company.

Henry James is one of the more sceptical readers of Jane Austen's fiction. And yet his own heroines owe much to the transformations wrought in Austen's fictions. Isabel Archer's fevered midnight meditation in *The Portrait of a Lady* is the tragic analogue of Elizabeth Bennet's more measured meditation on Darcy's letter. But James, who was so perceptive when he wrote about George Eliot, got the plot and everything else wrong when he damned Jane Austen with faint praise. I suspect he was rather jealous of the revival of her sales. He diminishes her when he refers to her as 'delightful Jane' and, almost unbelievably, he dismisses her heroines for their 'small and second-rate minds', calling them 'perfect little she-Philistines'.

In an essay written in 1905, James makes use of and elaborates upon the domestic images of Austen in the garden and Austen bent over her sewing basket drawn from the family memoir published in 1871. With all her 'light felicity', he writes, 'she leaves us hardly more curious of her process, or of the experience in her that fed it, than the brown thrush who tells his story from the garden bough'. That's what women are good for, he seems to be saying, and occasionally something unexpectedly worthwhile comes of it. Picking his way among images projected by the family in order to preserve Austen's womanly reputation, he dwells on her work basket and her tapestry flowers to lead him into thoughts about the likelihood of dropped stitches 'picked up as little touches of human truth, little glimpses of steady vision, little master-strokes of imagination'.

Women of my generation have been used to hearing this sort of patronising tone, from males in general, and from husbands in particular. Our views of the world and human relationships have been dismissed as too feminine, too idealistic, utterly unrealistic. The dramas of life with which we engage are ridiculed as melodramas. But perhaps I am too protective of Austen in my reaction to James's slights. She really doesn't need defending. Perhaps I should be happy to let his words be, those little touches, glimpses and masterstrokes; let them stand for what they are on their own terms – antidotes to the manners of every age and to the excesses, vanities and hypocrisies that tend to be acted out in real life.

That's the thing about reading: our brains hold an archive of everything we have ever read. I have noticed that, in some mysterious way, reading memories surface from nowhere to connect with a random present moment. From Austen, Elizabeth, the Bennet family and marriage I wander into Margaret Drabble's and Penelope Mortimer's territory; I tune into remembered resonances with Graham Swift and *Mothering Sunday*, wander on to comparisons with Henry James and Isabel Archer, and then reflect on my own life and my own memories, pleasant and otherwise. That's the rather messy business that we readers engage in as we look for coherence in what we are reading. It is also how many of us come to terms with our own lives, making some sort of sense of our life stories as we read.

Perhaps it is because I read this way that I sometimes feel as though I was born with a novel in my hands. Now I tend to re-read my own life as a sort of 'long-form fiction', a term in current vogue. Educators worry that young people born into the internet generation will lose the ability to read anything longer than their tweets and texts. If this prediction proves to be true, it will be a sad loss of the opportunity to find first the wisdom and then the comfort that so many of Austen's readers describe.

Chapter Three

Pride and Prejudice:
In Sunshine and in Shadows ...

Which of all my important nothings shall I tell you first?
JANE AUSTEN, LETTER TO CASSANDRA, 15 JUNE 1808

When my brother turned five, he was given a birthday party. Because entertaining made my mother extremely nervous, this was a most unlikely event. But our parents had only recently returned from an extended overseas study trip for my father, so perhaps this was a special reward for having spent six months without them. My brother was thrilled to be having a party; he could hardly contain his excitement, and having received a caravan team of camels, beautifully carved from olive wood, from our maternal grandparents in Jerusalem, he proudly set them out on the sideboard for all his friends to admire. The party turned out to be everything he could have hoped: games in the garden and party treats at a laden table on the veranda. At the end of the day, we discovered that the camels had disappeared into the sunset along with the guests, and a shadow fell over the memory of the brilliant day.

No fiction writer understood this contrast better than Jane Austen. She weaves together the light and shade of human experience as seamlessly as life itself. This was a realisation that took shape in my mind over time, and with it came the understanding of how reading helped me to accept and to adapt to light and shade in my own life. *Pride and Prejudice* is in one way the sunniest of Austen's novels, although *Northanger Abbey*, when I discovered the charm of its heroine's useful optimism, made a similar claim on my affection.

Re-reading *Pride and Prejudice*, with its ebullient marriage plot, in the light and shade of my own house and garden allowed me a second chance to let my thoughts wander at will around people and events as they floated into my mind. I grasped then that the getting of Elizabeth's wisdom and the getting of Elizabeth's man are elements of the same story. I experienced Austen's extraordinary powers of observation as a reimagining of the conventional love story, giving it a novelistic sparkle without filtering out the underlying shadows. Sun without shade is like day without night, I thought when I re-read the novel; it leaves us susceptible to a sort of psychic sunstroke in which we might lose our emotional bearings.

Take Karin, for example. She was a friend I made in my adult life who paid a high price for eliminating the shadows from memories of her childhood. I met her when our children attended a small Rudolf Steiner school on Sydney's North Shore. She was extremely lovely to look at, petite and elegant. She became the sort of friend I had dreamed of when I was younger: someone who confided in me and a confidante to whom I could speak my secrets. We also talked about books, because when we met she was studying to become a literature teacher.

Karin had wanted to be a doctor early in life, then a musician, and she completed her secondary schooling at the Conservatorium of Music, specialising in the oboe. But on leaving school she also wanted to leave home, so she enrolled in a secretarial college. Again she excelled, and she soon found work as a secretary. Then she married and had a child. Not long after the birth of her daughter, she divorced her husband. In the years that I knew her, she involved herself in a succession of romantic relationships that invariably started with rapture and ended in disillusion.

When Karin enrolled at university as a mature student, we often discussed her assignments. I was struck by our differences when we debated the complex and puzzling passions and relationships of the women in D.H. Lawrence's novel *The Rainbow*. Gudrun and Ursula were, I think, aligned with Karin's temperament as Austen's heroines were with mine. Falling in love, my friend told me, was an irresistible force that entitled the smitten one to pursue the object of desire, no matter the circumstances. Of course, both I and the fictional Fanny Price have been called priggish for not going along with that philosophy of love. But, as Fanny was able to negotiate her friendship with Mary Crawford without adopting her opinions, so Karin and I managed to avoid pitfalls that might have threatened our friendship.

Karin's childhood, first in Europe and then Australia, had been complicated by her parents' separation and the fact that her father, who was Jewish, had abducted her older sister and taken her to England, leaving the younger child to be raised in Germany. Her non-Jewish mother realised that under Nazi racial laws Karin was at risk. A brother in Australia arranged visas for them to emigrate. Omi, as she was called by Karin's friends after the birth of her granddaughter, never stopped mourning the loss of her older daughter, who had become a celebrity on stage and screen. And Karin, I suspect, never stopped wondering whether her mother would have preferred her to have been the kidnapped child.

Just as my friend was climbing the ladder to professional success, her life started to fall apart. Anxiety, insecurity, panic attacks and a collapse of confidence led her to a psychiatrist. He asked her to recount her life to date. I can imagine her description of her childhood with Omi because I had heard it myself: games of the imagination, nature walks, concerts and art galleries. The psychiatrist's response bewildered her. I felt her distress when she repeated to me his response. 'You describe the sunshine in your life as a child,' he said. 'Where are the shadows?'

I was not as surprised as Karin. I had often asked my friend whether her father's decision to take her sister had affected her. She always dismissed the question as irrelevant. She implied that she had never thought of his choice of her sister as abandonment; it had simply never bothered her.

This refusal to acknowledge the shadows in her life might have reduced Karin's pain, but the price was high. She was reluctant to retrieve grief buried out of sight as she was growing up. She struggled for the rest of her life, resisting the experience of pain that is bound up in the human condition, but experiencing physical and emotional symptoms that inhibited her professional career. And although she dedicated herself to bringing sunshine into the lives of her friends, as she certainly did to mine, in the end her resistance to the interplay between light and shade in her own life influenced her judgement and left her depressed. Eventually she decided that her life was not worth living. Her story would have no place in a novel by Jane Austen, but it holds its place in my heart as a tragedy that might have been avoided if shadows had been acknowledged.

In 1797, when Jane Austen was twenty-one years of age, her family gathered in the evenings to hear a first draft of one of her mature novels. It was called *First Impressions*, and Mr Austen was impressed enough himself to try to have the novel published at his personal expense. The whole family must have been disappointed when the manuscript was returned, unread. Fourteen years later, after her father's death and a long and difficult period in which she, her mother and her sister were virtually peripatetic, Jane settled into a permanent home provided by her brother Edward. Here, at Chawton, in a cottage on his estate, she revised her existing manuscripts. *First Impressions*, a title already in use by then, became *Pride and Prejudice*.

It is unclear what changes were made, but the fictional story that emerged is set for the most part in Hertfordshire. It focuses on the Bennet family and their life among the lower echelons of the gentry, a scenario I transferred to the idea of my own family, who were certainly not among the social 'crème de la crème' of our town, something of which I was well aware by that time. I responded enthusiastically to the drama of a romance between the second-oldest of the five daughters, Elizabeth, and Mr Darcy, a gentleman of significantly superior social status. I was fascinated by how an intellectually superior heroine of lower rank handled the pride of a hero who considered himself to be of a higher calibre than her family and social circle. It took time to spot that the heroine also had a flaw: a prejudice or tendency to prejudge a contentious situation without properly considering the evidence on which a sound verdict might be based.

The novel was finally published in 1813, and its history has added to its mystique. A 'darling child', Austen called it, announcing the arrival of the finished manuscript in a letter to her sister, Cassandra. Then she added one of the many sentences that have become the topic of ordinary readers' conversations as well as a matter of scholarly contention:

> The work is rather too light & bright, & sparkling;–it wants shade; it wants to be stretched out here & there with a long Chapter – of sense if it could be had, if not of solemn specious nonsense, about something unconnected with the story . . . or anything that would form a contrast & bring the reader with increased delight to the playfulness & Epigrammatism of the general stile.

Austen's verdict has intrigued her most attentive readers. What does she really mean? Is it simply a parody of other writers of her time? Should it rather be read as genuine self-criticism, as suggested by Q.D. Leavis, the Austen scholar who, in her introduction to a 1957 edition of *Mansfield Park*, suggests that *Pride and Prejudice* was a success that 'she would not care to repeat'? Or is its significance better captured by Hilary Mantel, the twenty-first century novelist-reader who emphasises always the dark and deep irony in Austen's world view? I choose to read it as the sort of mock self-deprecation that draws attention to a hidden agenda of rendering reality in its true colours.

What I find remarkable now about Austen's bright and sparkling novel is its mix of fairy tale and sharply observed depiction of the society around her. In her re-reading of the novel, the writer Allegra Goodman discovered both social satire and a Cinderella-like Elizabeth Bennet who rises above her vulgar mother and her silly and thoughtless sisters. She admires the book because at the time of her re-reading she was mourning a family loss and needed as much cheerfulness as she could find.

As a born re-reader, I can trace my development in the ways that my responses to *Pride and Prejudice* have changed over the years. At different moments in time my reading has shone a torch on different bits of myself, my family and my friends, depending to some degree on what is happening in my inner life and my relationships, influencing what emerges from the text and settling for the time being in my imagination. My engagement with the novel is perfectly conveyed by a fictional character in *The Moonstone*, a nineteenth-century novel written by Wilkie Collins and credited with being the first detective story in English literature. Gabriel Betteredge, one of several narrators, describes his relationship to the book *Robinson Crusoe*: 'I have tried that book for years . . . and I have found it my friend in need in all the necessities of this mortal life. When my spirits are bad – *Robinson Crusoe*. When I want advice – *Robinson Crusoe* . . . I have worn out six stout *Robinson Crusoes* with hard work in my service.'

In other words, Gabriel tells us, some books can give us whatever we need at the time of reading. In his homely way, he expresses the nature of my relationship with *Pride and Prejudice* and explains why that novel became my friend in need as I was growing up. I cannot count the number of times I have read it, but Goodman, in her book *Pemberley Previsited*, remembers her first reading at the age of nine followed by each of her later re-readings. She describes them as an unfolding. 'Like pleated fabric, the text reveals different parts of its pattern at different times,' she writes. Like me, she has found older memories and experiences in the folds of the text at each new reading.

My first reading of *Pride and Prejudice*, at the age of fifteen, lit up my life. I sat reading it in my bedroom with the sound of Austen's language making music in my head. The elegance of the sound was a relief from the quarrelling that sometimes erupted between my parents. In my adolescent state I found in the Bennet daughters a sort of sisterhood with whom I could relax. I didn't identify with Elizabeth Bennet – far from it – but she gave me a model for the sort of girl I wanted, if not to become, at least to have as a companion. At that moment in my life, it was friendship that I wanted and needed.

Looking back, I am grateful for the ways in which my first reading of *Pride and Prejudice* gave me hope for an agreeable adult future. It was the liveliness of life at Longbourn that made an impression, not any underlying tensions. I needed to rise above the insecurities and anxieties that generally accompany adolescence. I am conscious now that I was not quite ready to dwell on the hovering shadows in my own life. I resembled Elizabeth Bennet in one way: I did by nature love to laugh. 'Follies and nonsense, whims and inconsistencies, do divert me,' she owned, 'and I laugh at them whenever I can.' Laughing at Mrs Bennet and her foolish younger daughters was a welcome distraction.

Austen's heroine encouraged me to develop a to-and-fro way of reading, because I compared my life with hers as I read. My feelings and thoughts moved from the story to my own experiences and memories, and back to the story. The underlying complexity of the novel might have evaded my conscious attention, but reading about Elizabeth evoked feelings and thoughts of which I had been unaware. Feminine intuitions about love and life took on a more tangible form in my mind as I read.

Earlier in my life, I had looked to my heroines to lead me into other, more interesting and much animated worlds than the one I inhabited. I followed, but I am not sure how deeply I engaged with, Anne of Green Gables, Norah of Billabong and Judy, who made me both laugh and cry in *Seven Little Australians*. Perhaps only Jo March in Louisa May Alcott's novel *Little Women* and its sequels provided me with anything like what I would eventually experience in reading Austen's fiction and what contributes to its enduring popularity: an exploration of what it means to be human, of the consequences of daring to make bold choices about how to live.

The influence of the transcendental philosopher Ralph Waldo Emerson filters into the fictional would-be author Josephine March. The Alcott family was part of Emerson's community of minds. Jo is suspicious of social constraints. She transgresses and transcends, not so much in her conduct but in the act of writing itself; Austen does the same. The American public intellectual Cornel West pinpoints one reason for Austen's enduring appeal; he calls her out as a child of her age, but one whose capacity to transform stories into an art form enables her to transcend her age and create fiction that is relevant to all ages.

In a different way, I, too, was a child of my age. Growing up was really a preparation for getting married. This applied to both females and males, but I doubt that males dwelled on it to the same extent. Films and magazine stories touted marriage as the 'happily-ever-after' ideal for their heroines. The slogan 'Marriages are made in heaven' was repeated endlessly without raising a laugh, as it would almost certainly do in the twenty-first century. Unlike cheap disposables that flood today's market, marriages were meant to last, to be permanent. But, although a child of my age, I was an adolescent, developing my own mind, and Austen offered women less-compliant female models. From the moment Elizabeth Bennet laughed when she told her friend Charlotte Lucas that Darcy had declined to partner her at a dance, she became my own heroine. What other heroine laughed at such an experience? Elizabeth was just the model I needed as I was thinking about mixed parties, school dances and the dreaded possibility of being a wallflower. It was exhilarating to share in the unique audacity of Austen's merry heroine.

I loved reading the conversations in the novel. They showed me an alternative to the conversational inadequacy of my everyday life. I had gradually made enough friends to feel comfortable at school. My friendships, however, were not rich or especially rewarding. I craved something closer – a soul mate, perhaps. I did not have a best friend like Charlotte, with whom Elizabeth could share secret thoughts. I connected with a fictional friendship that was complicated, that gave me food for deep reflection. Elizabeth's continuing regard for a friend whose decisions were not those that she herself would have made prompted me to think more deeply about the nature of true friendship.

As I recall my adolescent reading of the novel, I am more than ever aware of the subtle ways in which Austen leaves room for readers to think and feel about issues in their own lives. The brightness that shines over Longbourn is dimmed momentarily by the rain that falls, literally, when Jane follows her mother's instructions to journey to Netherfield on horseback. It is not a lecture or, as Austen playfully suggests, a serious chapter interpolated in the fiction, that is required to highlight the conditions of human experience. It takes a certain sort of mindfulness in a reader, a willingness to accept that life, like art, is a blend of light and shade. And each is allowed its space in Austen's fiction.

In the preface to his twentieth-century drama *Our Town*, Thornton Wilder described Austen's art as subtly elusive in ways that are almost impossible to identify. For me, one of the pleasures of re-reading Austen is to shake her novels again each time. I find that approach more rewarding, more respectful of the author and the work, than the process of taking them apart, as young readers at school are now encouraged to do. I sigh for their loss.

Shaking *Pride and Prejudice* in different seasons, I came to understand that the subtle means by which the writer controls light and shade in her fiction is also a way of representing the nuances of lived experiences. An illuminating moment connected the art of fiction with what I had learned from Miss Brain, my elocution teacher. She introduced me to the idea of vocal modulation during our first lesson, but it took me many years to transfer my understanding of what I had learned about voice production earlier in my life to the production of fictional narrative.

My speech training had begun one Friday afternoon when I turned off the main thoroughfare into a byroad just before the railway line to visit Miss Brain on my way home from school. I rode down a narrow street to a small block of flats. Propping my bike against the brick wall of the building, I walked across a narrow strip of lawn, pushed open a heavy glass door, and knocked on Miss Brain's solid timber door. A slender woman of about thirty greeted me. Her voice was a new experience, fitting with the words that Mrs Eason wrote in my autograph book some years later, quoting King Lear's description of Cordelia's voice as 'gentle, soft and low'.

The teacher ushered me into her sitting room and, after a short introduction, opened an exercise book. Her first entry, in a graceful script, read: 'modulation: light and shade, the art of varying tone and mood'. Then she explained that the voice, *my* voice, is an instrument. Elocution lessons were to be like piano or violin lessons; I would learn to use my instrument well so that I could give pleasure to my listeners. The quality of Miss Brain's welcoming voice has never left me. I hear it in my head whenever I think of the first hour we spent together.

During that introductory lesson, my teacher returned several times to the concept of vocal modulation as an art; similar in its essence to painting, a selection of colours – yes, I thought, *her* voice would have to be a warm colour – in tones that express feelings and convey meanings. I would learn about the organs of speech, she told me, the lips, tongue, teeth and the rest; how to exercise and control them, as well as how to breathe from my diaphragm, so that my own voice, especially when I read stories or recited poems and dramatic speeches, would be transformed into an instrument of personal meaning and interpretation. And she repeated her mantra that modulation was the goal of the elocutionist.

Later readers, we know, have responded to the modulation of light and shade in *Pride and Prejudice* in different ways. When I read Austen's comments, in her letters and as narrator, I am reminded of how she loves to tease. Like Hilary Mantel, I agree that Austen's novels and those of the mid-twentieth-century novelist Elizabeth Jane Howard share a tendency to be far less 'cosy' than an initial read would suggest, with an undercurrent of anxiety beneath the surface.

In my early readings I found it possible to read Austen's fiction closely and still to be comforted; to choose not to go, with Mantel, to the darker recesses of female constraints. The best writers allow us to choose where we put our attention at the time of reading, and they allow us to change our minds when we re-read. I think of the soldiers in the First World War who were given copies of *Pride and Prejudice* to read in the trenches, and those who received their copies after they had been broken by their war service and institutionalised for recuperation. They responded to the light, bright and glittering aspects of the novel, the dances and excursions, and no doubt found alleviation from the anguish of the moment. For them, the light and bright tones of the novel were salutary.

Austen's fiction has a history of being approached in this way, according to the needs of the reader. An early reader of that complicated novel *Mansfield Park* recommended it for its dancing and picnics. She, like many other committed Austen readers, preferred to ignore the turbulent emotional undercurrents that flow from the abuses, rivalries and threats to the high moral ground of Mansfield Park itself. Mantel points out the options. Austen's fictional endings that occur at the church door with a wedding might beguile readers into unquestioning contemplation of what is in store for the happy couples. Others might choose a less complacent contemplation.

When I first read about the Bennet family I was a novice reader of what we call literary fiction. I had neither the literary discernment nor the biographical knowledge to make inferences from contexts outside the novel, and I had not yet learned what reading 'closely' entailed. What I did have at that stage were needs, including a need to know that other girls who, like me, were less popular than they wished, also resorted to books for comfort. Perhaps it was this need that accounted for my strange and unexpected affinity with Mary Bennet, who for some readers is the least appealing and the most comic of the sisters. I felt an empathy that Austen does not offer but that later readers have shared and demonstrated.

Re-reading the novels in the twenty-first century has become a different experience, as I found when I returned to them in later life. Screen translations had by then taken root in my mind and imposed themselves on Austen's plots and characters. And then there is the fanfic. Mary Bennet has been a prime beneficiary here. Among the myriad prequels and sequels to *Pride and Prejudice*, a small collection of revisionist fictions have reimagined Mary as the swan who emerges from the ugly duckling of Longbourn. Writers with an inkling of Michel Foucault's ideas about the marginalisation of individuals in our institutionalised society use their power as novelists to bring characters in from the cold corners of a patriarchal society and keep them warm at the centre of a fictional universe. Thus Austen's heroines are transformed from victimhood to agents of their own lives.

This was what Austen had done in her own time, with Elizabeth Bennet and Emma Woodhouse. Latter-day writers have done it for Mary, liberating her from corners of the plot where she hovered with her less-than-pretty face buried in a book. Subsequently, she has been treated as an independent woman, as a romantically desirable heroine and as the forgotten sister who discovers that she has an identity. Looking back, I can find traces of all those versions of Mary in reflections on my later life.

In my adolescence, however, Elizabeth Bennet's parents were almost as significant as the heroine herself. In my first reading of the novel, the humour of their relationship was paramount. I didn't register that by the end of the first chapter the humour has turned a little sour. Mr Bennet's abundance of wit, some of which had obviously been passed on to his favourite daughter, serves as camouflage for his malice, which Elizabeth in no way shares. I read the human drama that was acted out in the Bennet household as pure human comedy because I needed to. Cracks in the family mirror might distort the relationships between characters, but I experienced only amusement as the absurd images played out in my imagination.

I recognised a mother who took refuge from family responsibilities in her 'poor nerves' and who required regular placating from her daughters. It was good to laugh about situations that were troubling in real life. I was also sufficiently autonomous in my reading to recognise that my own mother did not share Mrs Bennet's meanness of mind and paucity of information. I recognised a father who was also 'so odd a mixture of quick parts', some of which were eccentric and a source of enduring delight, others more puzzling and better ignored as, for the most part, Elizabeth was able to do. At the same time, I knew that my father was not reserved or, like Mr Bennet, capricious. I selected my points of connection unconsciously – the nervous vapours of the heroine's mother and the 'quick parts' and 'sarcastic humour' of her father – and I took from the novel for my immediate comfort a first glimpse of the commonalities that underline human experience.

* * *

As a girl who read girls' books compulsively, I was intrigued by the idea of a heroine. In real life I had discovered how important heroines were to my imagination on a blazingly hot, dry, dusty, typical summer day in my town. It was the sort of day that made me long for the evening, when I would sit with my mother on the broad steps of the portico to our house. We would wait for a cool change – even, if we were lucky, a downpour of sweet-smelling rain to settle the dust. The day I remember was in 1944, at the end of January, one of the hottest of the summer months and the beginning of my first year in secondary school.

I was sitting with about twenty-five other girls and boys in a prefabricated classroom. We would not be promoted to the main red-brick school building until we had served our time, two years, in the temporary accommodation, hot in summer and cold in winter, which housed a growing school population. My group of pupils had provisionally been assigned to an A class, and we were waiting for our English teacher to appear.

Mr B. arrived. He dropped the book he was carrying onto the table with an ominous thud before gesturing for silence. He was a wiry man with thinning hair and thick spectacles, and must have been at least middle-aged, as all our male teachers were at that time. The younger men were away doing war service. In December 1941 Japan had bombed Pearl Harbor, and our part of the world was now in conflict, with a war zone much closer to home than Europe.

The seemingly stern man called the roll and wrote his name on the board. Under his name he wrote a list of books. I can't recall all the titles, but I do remember that *The Last of the Mohicans* was among them, because the word 'Mohicans' was familiar from the cowboy and Indian pictures I had seen with my brother at the Saturday afternoon matinee in the Lyceum. I had also noticed some of the titles among my brother's books but, except for *Oliver Twist*, whose surname intrigued me, I had not been curious enough to open any of them: not *Treasure Island*, *David Copperfield* or *Flynn of the Inland*. There were about ten titles on the board, and Mr B. informed us that if we had not read at least half of them we could not expect to remain in an A class. I was mortified.

But even more than mortification and the fear that I might be demoted to a lower class was a sense of outrage. These books, I realised as the plots were briefly outlined, all had boys as the main protagonists. I looked around the room. The boys sat at desks on one side of the room, but we girls took up the other half. Where, then, were the heroines who interested so many girls? Where were Alice, Anne and Norah, each of whom had taken me to a place outside the dusty town where I was born and which I only occasionally left: to Alice's fantasy wonderland and her topsy-turvy adventures with weird and wonderful friends; to Anne's lush and fertile Prince Edward Island with its magical sunsets and her quirky way of describing people and her insistence that her name be spelled with an 'e'; to the world of Norah Linton, a truly adventurous tomboy who climbed trees with the boys on the Australian cattle station and had knockabout adventures with horses and cattle. I had longed to follow in the footsteps of these girls and find other worlds and other possibilities for a future life.

It would be years before I registered that 'girlie' stereotypes were not absent from the books about girls I liked, and that any insight into the violation of Indigenous people and their culture in their own country was absent from the Billabong books where

I met Norah. At that time, however, I was relieved that I was not demoted from the A class. And I was even more pleased that, when the final timetable was drawn up, it turned out that Mr B. was not to be our English teacher. When the door opened the following day, we were greeted by Mrs Eason's smiling face and the announcement that she was our English teacher for the year. In time, she would introduce me to the sort of heroine I most needed to meet.

Pride and Prejudice offers a superb template for the way heroines come to stand for something larger than themselves. It is partly, as I discovered, a matter of moral seriousness, even though the tone is light and bright. Compared with other characters, and in conversation with them, Elizabeth Bennet develops in moral stature. Whether her spirits are high or low, the choices she makes have implications for broader concerns than her circumscribed circumstances might suggest. In fact, those circumstances throw into relief the ambiguities that go hand-in-hand with reading Austen's fiction.

The two silly and shallow sisters, Lydia and Kitty, and the maligned Mary, who takes refuge from her plain looks in affectations of learning, highlight the appeal of the two older sisters. Surprisingly, the lovely and gentle Jane, who would make a perfect heroine in any one of the sentimental novels of the time, also forms a contrast by means of which Elizabeth shines more brightly. She is a great deal too apt, Elizabeth tells her, to like people in general, never seeing a fault in anybody. 'All the world are good and agreeable in your eyes.' Here is a characteristic Austen conundrum. Is the narrator unreserved in praise of Jane, or does Elizabeth provide the moral compass by which readers can navigate their way through the plot?

On my first reading, I took Elizabeth's commentary on her sister's conduct as sheer praise of Jane's virtue. 'With your good sense,' Elizabeth exclaims to her sister, 'to be so honestly blind to the follies and nonsense of others! Affectation of candour is common enough – one meets with it everywhere. But . . . to take the good of every body's character and make it still better, and say nothing of the bad – belongs to you alone.' As I became more familiar with the realisation of Austen's characters, though, I saw a pattern that undermines the idea of complete approval.

In *Emma*, the heroine, despite her many blunders, is on the same page as the author when she notes that Mr Weston, although kindly, compromises his values when he displays uncritical regard for almost everyone, including someone like the obnoxious Mrs Elton. And in the last completed novel, *Persuasion*, Anne Elliot values sincerity above all qualities; her suitor, Mr William Elliot, is 'too generally agreeable', apt to extend his friendship too liberally. In time, I learned to take Austen's counsel to heart, to place discernment above pretence, and to own my occasional dislike of people as a matter of preference rather than of malice.

Growing up in the 1940s, I wrestled with such dilemmas. I started to compare myself with the larger and more diverse population of girls who filed into the classroom. Entering secondary school, I sensed that I was approaching a new phase of development as far as relationships were concerned. There were more options in a larger school population. What were the rules? I had not yet met Jane Austen's heroines, but I was outgrowing the less complex girls created by L.M. Montgomery. For all their vivacity and energy, Anne of Green Gables and Jane of Lantern Hill did not struggle with those sometimes bewildering questions of discernment and discrimination. The childhood crushes and silly squabbles of their world were acted out in a way that simplified them. Mother Nature was often the most benign influence in their personal development. And an omniscient narrator usually settled everything, once and for all.

I can attribute my obsession with one of my fellow students to the many ways in which she differed from me and the other girls I knew. I pounced on her as a real-life heroine almost as soon as we settled into our first year of high school. Isabel, as I have already called her, lived on an outlying farm attached to a hamlet some miles out of town. She was among the pupils who now left their feeder schools and joined town children like me for their secondary education. But Isabel was one of a kind. I suppose her family came as close to the idea of 'county' as was possible in rural Australia. Her father was away at the war, a high-ranking officer in the armed forces. She and her older sister lived with their mother and a maiden aunt who, it was rumoured, was dedicated to supervising their homework and ensuring that both girls never looked less than immaculate and always came top of the class. Everything about Isabel spoke to me of something different but also infinitely desirable: privilege and success. Her sister was the school captain, in her final year when the younger girl arrived. They were both attractive: tall, slender, with long silky plaits finished with a flourish of wide ribbon tied into perfect bows. Their blouses were snow white, their uniforms without creases or stains. On rainy days when sport was cancelled and we gathered in the assembly hall for an impromptu concert that showcased students' talents, the sisters played piano duets by Mozart and Schubert. And they both excelled academically.

Even after all these years, it is easy to recall the mixture of adulation and yearning that overwhelmed me. I was middle class, and privileged, even with my Jewish background, but I sensed that I was not privileged in the same way as Isabel. I observed her from afar, never one of the group of friends who surrounded her. I saw that she was treated as someone special, even by teachers. And in many ways, she was. Even her pen was different. Many of us still dipped our steel nibs into inkwells that were set into our desks and filled with ink poured each morning from a large urn by a class monitor. My heroine had a handsome fountain pen and wrote in a well-formed hand. I noticed such things: her clothes and her possessions as well as her talent for drawing people to her.

Then, and I am not sure exactly when, I began to ponder as well as to observe. Like Emma, I gradually started to question my assumptions. I started to discriminate as well as admire, to notice details of behaviour, to ask 'what if' instead of taking the idea of perfection for granted. Did my reading of my real-life heroine make her, or my version of her, too good to be true? Was having such a thought a reflection of envy on my own part? I had no way of knowing the answers to these questions, and no way of understanding that I – like Elizabeth Bennet, who was yet to become a point of reference – was floundering in the mysteries of the human condition.

Harking back to these adolescent wisps of moral inquiry, I see that I was edging closer to the state of mind of an Austen heroine. I was no longer at home in or satisfied with the girls' books I had devoured until then. My head was churning with personal and ethical questions that have, over many decades, bewildered and fascinated me. And something changed. My heroine worship, dogged by feelings of my own inferiority and something that I suspected (and still suspect) was envy, was transformed into something quite different, something dynamic. Perhaps it was the ambition to be someone in my own eyes that changed my direction and helped to prepare me for the future at this stage of my growing up. Perhaps this was the intent that acted, like Macbeth's ambition, as a spur to action.

A dose of reality helped, too. I could look to my heroine for qualities that were both desirable and attainable, but changes to my appearance and my personality lay, I thought, outside the realm of possibility. There was no way of growing tall and slender, or of taming my unruly hair into glossy locks. I had never found it easy to make and keep close friends. But I could model myself on her in another way. I could refine my mind, immerse myself in my lessons and perform well at school. That seemed to be within the realm of the possible.

Until then I had been a mediocre student. My brother always managed to come top of his class with little or no effort. With similarly little effort, I managed to stay afloat about ten or twelve students from the top. I had never expected more of myself and nor, I think, had my parents. But now all the longings and wishes that had driven my heroine worship sprang into action on my own behalf. I kept my daydreaming for bedtime and listened attentively to what went on in class. I did my homework and more.

It almost worked. At the end-of-year examinations, I gave my erstwhile heroine a moment of concern. The final scores were so close that Mrs Eason, who was then our form teacher and possibly sensed that I was rising to a challenge, commented on the race to the top of the class with some interest. Isabel was once again the class dux. I had come second, although only a few marks behind, and the rivalry ended there. The following year Isabel left to attend a girls' boarding school in the city, and I continued to study assiduously and perform well.

In all the theories I have read about learning, I am not sure that I have found an explanation for what happened to me, that sudden surge of energy and immersion that transformed me within a few months from a non-performer to a serious contender for top place in the class. But that's what did happen. And there was an unexpected bonus: I had become a lover of learning. So perhaps the reason for my academic transformation is not to be found in theories about learning and cognitive development, but rather in a small story about wanting to count in the larger story of a life.

My relationship with the fictional heroine Elizabeth Bennet was as real and as connected to my own development as my relationship with Isabel had been. When I first read *Pride and Prejudice*, I recalled Mrs Eason, who rescued us from Mr B.'s male-oriented book list. By then, she and her husband had moved on from Griffith. Bill Eason was also among the breed of teachers who touch young people's lives and make a difference. He had transformed our school as master of the English department; eventually, many years later, he realised more fully his transforming educational theories, based on the thinking of the Indian poet and philosopher Rabindranath Tagore, by establishing his own independent school. As students, we had already profited from the bigger picture in his mind, encouraged by him to talk as well as to read, write and listen.

Mrs Eason was more of a classroom mentor. She was given to sharing with us her own encounters with literature and her love of drama. Having played the role of Rosalind in *As You Like It* while at university, she outlined the plot and elaborated on the qualities of Shakespeare's heroine. With the customary insecurities of a girl entering her teens, I admired a girl with such confidence, wit and spirit. I tried to imagine what it would be like to be the daughter of the banished duke, instead of the daughter of a country doctor. I equated the false accusations faced by the duke with slurs cast on my father's character in the anti-Semitic climate of the period. I had not yet studied Shakespearean set pieces with Miss Brain – which I would do as I became more seriously involved in the study of elocution and prepared for the exams held annually by the Trinity College of London – so, Mrs Eason's recitation of a passage was my initiation into the rhythm of iambic pentameter versification:

> So was I when your Highness took his dukedom;
> So was I when your Highness banish'd him:
> Treason is not inherited, my lord;
> Or, if we did derive it from our friends,
> What's that to me? My father was no traitor!
> Then, good my liege, mistake me not so much
> To think my poverty is treacherous.

Would I have the courage, the audacity, to defend *my* father if required? I thrilled to the force of the words. In them I found a freedom of the mind that Virginia Woolf, as I read later in life, put above even the power of the pen, a topic that I had heard debated by senior students at a lunchtime meeting of the Speakers' Club initiated by Mr Eason. 'Lock up your libraries if you like,' Woolf wrote, 'but there is no gate, no lock, no bolt that you can set upon the freedom of the mind.'

The Shakespeare passage laid a foundation for my first reading of *Pride and Prejudice* and prepared me for an introduction to the themes of the novel. Elizabeth's spirited defiance in her exchange with Mr Darcy's aunt exposes both the pride and prejudice of a formidable opponent. Lady Catherine takes pride in her inherited position in life and does nothing to restrain her prejudices against those of inferior rank. She believes that Elizabeth, in her right senses, would not wish to leave the sphere in which she had been brought up. But Elizabeth will have none of it. 'In marrying your nephew,' she parries, 'I should not consider myself as quitting that sphere. He is a gentleman; I am a gentleman's daughter; so far we are equal.' The wider classist assumptions implicit in Elizabeth's response are grist for contemporary literary and cultural discourses, but these were not my concerns as I dared hope that someday I might assert myself on my father's behalf with similar panache.

When I first read the climactic exchange between Elizabeth and Lady Catherine, it did occur to me that Shakespeare's Rosalind might be whispering the words in the ear of Austen's Lizzy Bennet. One of the joys of eventually becoming a 'serious' Austen reader has been the discovery of a long list of scholarly readers who have spoken Austen's name alongside that of Shakespeare. In Tennyson's judgement, Jane Austen and William Shakespeare both understood the smallness of life 'to perfection'. In the grander design, I have taken the connections between the dramatist and the novelist as evidence of the intricate relations between different works of the imagination and between works of the imagination and life itself. In this case, the connections have played a part in making me, if not altogether who I am, at least in part who I have always wanted to be: someone whose command of language is equal to the emotional and ethical demands of the occasion. Shakespeare is uncontestably the global model of choice.

You can find Austen's personal familiarity with Shakespeare's dialogue all over her novels; she recognised that every educated English person of her time had internalised Shakespearean language. In *Mansfield Park*, Henry Crawford tells Edmund Bertram that Shakespeare is part of an 'Englishman's constitution', familiar almost by instinct. Edmund agrees that the celebrated passages are widely known and quoted. 'We all talk Shakespeare,' he tells Henry. It is just possible, although unlikely, that Austen herself was unconscious of the echoes of Mercutio's 'Nay, gentle Romeo, we must have you dance' (*Romeo and Juliet*, Act 1, Scene 4), in the first words we hear from Mr Bingley in *Pride and Prejudice*: 'Come, Darcy, I must have you dance.' In contemporary terms, it is the 'weaponisation' of language as an instrument of power that Shakespeare and Austen share.

As a re-reader of Austen's novels, I can't compete with the intimate acquaintance claimed by A.C. Grayling, a polymath who has always loved Jane Austen's novels. When he was a student, he remembers, he used to 'go to bed with Jane Austen' every Easter holiday. But I have come to the same conclusion as he that Austen sets the example of how to do what great literature should do: reveal 'something about the human condition'. For Grayling, as for me, *Pride and Prejudice* is the ultimate exemplar as Elizabeth and Darcy come to a better understanding of themselves and each other. Grayling concludes that the novel is about how we learn to know what we know from an ethical perspective. Because he is a philosopher, he calls it moral epistemology.

There are many ways to tell the story of Elizabeth and Darcy, and although Grayling thinks as a philosopher, he doesn't always write like one. In simple, everyday words he enables Elizabeth and Darcy to spring into life. The concrete details, the vulgarity Darcy finds in Elizabeth and the snobbery Elizabeth loathes in him, grab readers with their immediacy and hold their attention. Grayling shows us what the literary critic George Lewes meant when he praised Jane Austen for the economy of means by which she made her characters ambiguous and complex. His basic way of telling the story of the novel makes me understand exactly why Lewes took George Eliot, who was his common-law wife as well as his literary protégée, out of London to read Austen's six novels as a preparation for her own career as a dedicated fiction writer.

I can imagine them in a cottage somewhere in the countryside, maybe a sanctuary like Wordsworth's Dove Cottage in the Lake District. I see them there, wrapped in woollen rugs and sitting close to the hearth as they read aloud, taking turns to do the different voices, and pausing frequently to discuss exactly how 'she', Jane Austen, does it. Lewes might have marked out the passages he wanted Eliot to notice, to demonstrate what he meant by 'the most perfect mastery over the means to her end'; how Mr Darcy's pride and Elizabeth Bennet's prejudice are not just words: they are attributes that shape the personalities of the two protagonists. Lewes would have wanted Eliot to catch sight of Darcy's weakness early in the novel, in an exchange that pits his self-confidence against the serpentine manoeuvres of Elizabeth's witty mind:

'[I]t has been the study of my life to avoid those weaknesses which often expose a strong understanding to ridicule.'

'Such as vanity and pride.'

'Yes, vanity is a weakness indeed. But pride – where there is a real superiority of mind, pride will be always under good regulation.'

Elizabeth turned away to hide a smile.

'Your examination of Mr Darcy is over, I presume,' said Miss Bingley; 'and pray what is the result?'

'I am perfectly convinced by it that Mr Darcy has no defect. He owns it himself without disguise.'

The aspiring novelist and the critic would probably have discussed how Darcy is totally undone by the combination of Elizabeth's wit as well as her charm. Because this is the sort of detail that counts in provoking the curiosity of readers, they would have noted the retrospective power of Darcy's intuitive recognition of the 'danger of paying Elizabeth too much attention'.

It would have been Eliot, I think, with her novelistic genius for planting ideas in readers' minds, who noticed that Darcy's fascination with Elizbeth's eyes develops into a fascination with her mind and her personality; and how, in admiring her, he discovers unknown parts of himself. Lewes, the critic, might have been more attuned to the way in which Elizabeth, too, is undone, by her premature judgements. Critical thinking informs her examination of who she is. She gathers and marshals the available evidence, subjects it to scrutiny, and draws a conclusion accordingly. She expresses her self-disgust when she, too, discovers parts of herself that she has failed to recognise. I think they would agree, Lewes and Eliot, that Elizabeth emerges as an intellectually virtuous heroine from her virtuoso Socratic performance of self-examination. Her words, 'till this moment, I never knew myself', might be spoken, in a different fictional universe, by Dorothea, Eliot's own short-sighted heroine in *Middlemarch*.

In reaching into the recesses of my mind to discover and shore up fragments that coalesce around a tale of my own growing up, I find that the words 'pride' and 'prejudice' are as relevant to my life as they are to Austen's novel, but on different terms. In reflecting on how my own life weaves together light and shade, I have borrowed the terms 'pride' and 'prejudice' from Austen, and I have coupled them as she did. But I have taken an alternative view of what those words can connote. I have used the words in a different sense to frame my formative childhood experiences as a narrative that, for me, rings just as true.

The notion of pride, in my story, is different from the solipsistic character trait depicted in Austen's novel. This, as Darcy discovers, limits him to seeing the world centrally and exclusively from his own point of view, and therefore requires recalibration. I understood pride in a more positive way, and that was because my father represented it to me as a human emotion that is positive and self-affirming. The pride my father felt in being both Jewish and Australian was a stabilising and enriching factor that I internalised without realising it.

As for prejudice, Elizabeth Bennet's tendency to make judgements before she considers the circumstances is one way to understand how prejudice functions. But for me, the news of the day when I was growing up, especially as it related to the precarious fate of the Jewish people, projected a view of prejudice that was like a rip-tide in which we managed to stay afloat as the years passed, and from which we hoped to emerge and recover our breath as the acrid smoke haze of the death camps settled. In reimagining my life as a child and adolescent, pride and prejudice were woven together as intricately as light and shade engage with each other in Austen's novel.

My father took pride in identities that were entwined, so he thought of himself as a Jewish Australian. We had read stories written by one of his favourite writers, Israel Zangwill. The characters who populate the short stories in *Dreamers of the Ghetto* act out the dilemmas of a people without a home of their own. We returned many times to the story of the poet Heinrich Heine, who lamented that he had a soul wider than the ghetto he was born into. I think my father's sense of celebration came from the fact that his children had not been born into such a confined space, that Dorothea Mackellar's sunburnt country of sweeping plains was a birthplace in which his children's souls would be free to roam.

An episode from my brief period at the convent illustrates how a blend of pride and prejudice provided the fabric from which a memorable childhood experience was fashioned. As I was only four years old when I was accepted as a pupil, it had been arranged that a slightly older boy who lived in our street would walk me home at the end of the school day. I had been there for about a week and happily settled when the nun, my class teacher, started the day by asking those children who had not said an early-morning prayer to 'stand up'. Thinking that this was an invitation, that the teacher wanted to tell us something of special interest about a prayer, I quickly stood to attention by the desk. Instead of receiving some new piece of information, however, I received a stinging slap on my leg. I was confused. If

I had been older, I might have wondered about the usefulness of telling the truth; at the time, I was overwhelmed by the thought that the teacher no longer liked me.

I managed to hold back my tears, but I seized the opportunity to reinstate myself when we were taken outside into the sunshine to hear our story for the day. We gathered around the nun to hear the story of Jesus. It was obvious to me that this person of whom I had never heard was a favourite, unlike me. Then, to my relief, I heard that he was Jewish. Something clicked.

Impatient to ingratiate myself again for not saying a morning prayer, I could hardly wait for the end of the story and the opportunity to let the teacher and the other children know that, like the hero of the story we had just listened to, I, too, was Jewish. I have no memory of what happened then, or whether there was any response from the nun, but that afternoon the older boy refused to walk with me. Instead, he told me to go ahead while he and a friend followed behind, throwing the odd pebble at my heels and calling me the odd name. What surprises me about this memory is that it is not associated with any sense of shame, fear or even being wronged. I recall only a sense of bewilderment that the boys did not understand how good it felt to be Jewish.

The story tells me two things about where I was at that moment of development. First, I had already at the age of four formed a disposition that could not tolerate disapproval. And second, at least one part of my identity was already firmly established: somehow my pride in being the person I was gave me some notion of entitlement as a human being that has helped me weather the racial prejudices that have assailed me from time to time. Somehow, my pride and the prejudices that I have encountered have not collided.

Whether this is a false or even defensive memory I have no way of knowing. My brother had a very different experience. Perhaps because he was a boy, prejudice took a more physical form, and he, being tough, never shirked the fisticuffs that ensued. I am not sure what I would have done in similar circumstances, but the convent narrative remains in my memory; my father's modelling of pride as self-affirmation seems to have served me emotionally and psychologically.

The same could be said for my father's pride in being Australian and, strange as it may sound in this post-colonial world, a British subject. This may have been, in Marxist terms, a sense of false consciousness, an unconscious capitulation to the dominant ideology, but in this spirit, he often took my brother and me into his study to celebrate the security of living in one of the extensive pink areas on the large globe that he would spin before our eyes.

Pride of this sort accompanied my lessons. When we read and recited poems, I identified imaginatively and equally with William Wordsworth's English daffodils and Henry Kendall's Australian bellbirds. My third-class teacher, Miss Currie, seized every opportunity to draw her Scottish heritage into the classroom. She taught us about Bonnie Prince Charlie and led us in a spirited rendition of 'The Bluebells of Scotland'. At Christmastime, she placed a chocolate Santa Claus on every pupil's desk. My Jewish heritage didn't make me feel like an outsider to Scottish history or to expressions of patriotism; nor did it lessen my delight in receiving a treat, although I had been told by my parents that Santa Claus was a fantasy figure who did not belong in my world.

There is something intoxicating in a surrender to early memories. Still, I am mindful that we have come a long way since pride in the British empire or any form of colonialism could be accepted with composure. So, I am aware that pride is a two-headed entity, just as I am aware of the scepticism of postmodern theory and of the failure of my generation's educators to speak truth to power in the classroom. The pride my father took in being received into and accepted by a host country is essentially different from the celebration of contemporary multiculturalism, which has its own contradictions and complications. But I cannot allow later sensibilities to dim the ways in which pride in being human, the enchantment of the imagination and a thirst for knowledge flourished despite the scourge of prejudiced minds. It strikes me that there is a core of communal humanity that sometimes wins out over prejudice, even in the worst of times.

Three examples from among the families who found refuge in my town come to my mind. The first were German-Polish refugees who had lived in the contentious Danzig Corridor. The daughter, Fanny, delighted her peers and teachers with her formal European courtesies. She became so proficient in English that, in her matriculation examination, she was at the top of the English Honours list in the company of Coral Lansbury, who went on to carve out a prestigious international academic career. A second family came from Vienna, where Mr F. had been a clockmaker. He adjusted to raising calves and poultry as well as delivering milk from the cans in his horse and sulky in the early hours of the morning. His wife, like my mother, suffered from nervous headaches, but she was more resilient and often provided continental pastries that were new to my palate; they tasted and smelled quite delicious. A third family, also from Austria, had a different story. Dr N. was accepted to set up a laboratory for the Leeton canning factory. Mrs N. – or Frau Doctor, as she had been known in Vienna – was Jewish by birth, although converted to Catholicism. She was a literary scholar. Whenever we met, I experienced the richness of European cultural conversation. They were interested in everything I was reading for my English Honours course, asked me questions, and stimulated me to engage with what I was reading with curiosity as well as pleasure.

On our walks through the town we talked about Tolstoy and Chekov, both of whom were new to me. Dr and Mrs N. were especially interested in theatre and obviously missed it in their new environment. I introduced them to J. M. Barrie, whose novels and plays I had encountered with Miss Brain. I remember a wonderfully enlightening discussion about the themes of *The Admirable Crichton*, the accidents and implications of birth and inheritance, and the restricted possibilities for acquiring rank and status. These conversations were exhilarating. They alerted me to the way shared reading could be a source of light in a dark world, forging friendships and creating like-minded communities.

Sometime between my childhood and my late teens, reading came to dominate my life. I relied on books as a way of understanding human relationships. And I noticed how life in novels was rarely all good or all bad; rather, it was a mixture of both. It was no accident that I entered Austen's fictional universe so easily. I had read Lewis Carroll's *Alice in Wonderland* when I was seven; the experience launched me into a world beyond the one I already knew. It accustomed me to straying from my own world into what the contemporary author, Niall Williams, in his novel *This is Happiness*, calls 'an elsewhere'; another universe from which I returned to the real world with new ways of navigating my pathway through life.

When I removed *Pride and Prejudice* from the library shelf, I must have been in the state of readiness, primed for the connection between myself an the book as described by the writer Vivian Gornick in her reading memoir *Unfinished Business: Notes of a chronic re-reader*.

I was ready, at that adolescent moment, to enter a world in which I experienced both sunshine and shadow, blended as inextricably as they are in real life. It was a fictional world, created not by a divinity, but by a writer who brought sound, personality and ideas into a coherent set of patterns that embraced a vision of life beyond the marriage plot. I was in this way initiated into a lifetime of reading about fictional experiences that eventually shed light on periods of darkness in my own life.

Chapter Four

Northanger Abbey:
Fiction and Friendship

There is nothing I would not do for those who are really my friends. I have no notion of loving people by halves, it is not my nature.

JANE AUSTEN, *NORTHANGER ABBEY*

When I settled down to re-read Austen's six novels in my Southern Highlands retreat, I found to my surprise that the novel I wanted to read first, because I remembered it least, was missing. *Northanger Abbey* was not only missing from my bookshelves, it was almost completely missing from my memory as well. I could recall a rough outline of the story so perhaps I had decided that I wouldn't want to read it again. I was impatient to make a start, so I walked briskly down the hill towards the village shops, noticing but not stopping to enjoy the flowering crabapples on the verge, and bought the only copy of the novel on the shelves of the Brown Bookshop. I chatted briefly with Nancy, the proprietor, and a customer who told me that she was a teacher and was planning to read the very same novel with her class in the next term. We made a date to have coffee one day soon and within the hour I was back in my reading room ready to embark on my reading remedy.

Every now and then readers know that they have struck literary gold. Five chapters into the novel I paused to re-read a paragraph. Here was Jane Austen, uncannily blending the skills of an early nineteenth-century novelist with what we now call literary theory. Except that she doesn't write like a theorist. As a fiction writer she avoids the sort of cant that was repugnant to her literary model, Dr Samuel Johnson. She manages to defend fiction within her own fiction without sounding like a theorist or even a teacher: '"Oh! It is only a novel!" replies the young lady . . . or, in short, only some work in which the greatest powers of the mind are displayed, in which the most thorough knowledge of human nature, the happiest delineation of its varieties, the liveliest effusions of wit and humour, are conveyed to the world in the best-chosen language.'

It is Austen alchemy. Who is the young lady? How did she get into the story? And how brilliantly she saves the author or the narrator from turning her fiction into a polemic. Sometimes Austen's literary imagination leads her into territory where less able writers tread too heavily. In one sentence, with all the irony at her disposal, she defends the novel against those moralists and critics of her time who would condemn fiction as trash, unfit for the education of respectable females. The unnamed young lady spells out exactly what readers get from novels. Here it is, she says, the essence of how fiction works, fiction that can be wonderfully comic while sending messages that are profoundly serious. And that is what you are about to read, she declares: a story that carries powerful ideas, understanding of the human condition and lively characterisations, written with wit, humour and mastery of language. She speaks the truth. These are the qualities I found as I turned the pages of *Northanger Abbey* as a mature reader.

Austen's early readers were not necessarily concerned about her powerful mind. By and large they didn't expect women novelists to have much of a mind at all. A woman was not thought to have the big ideas that accompany powerful minds. Both those phenomena were regarded as almost exclusively male. Even the brilliant Brontë sisters and the intellectually heroic George Eliot found it more prudent, as women, to use masculine pseudonyms. In Austen's lifetime, the perceived limitations of her life as a domesticated spinster were mapped onto the qualities of her mind, even though her special talent was recognised by no less important a critic than the successful novelist Sir Walter Scott: 'We therefore bestow no mean compliment upon the author of *Emma*, when we say that, keeping close to common incidents, and to such characters as occupy the ordinary walk of life, she has produced sketches of such spirit and originality, that we never miss the excitation which depends upon a narrative of uncommon events, arising from the consideration of minds, manners, and sentiments, greatly above our own.'

There is some genuine affection in Scott's tone, and I appreciate that he alerted the reading public to something extraordinary in this new writer; but he is almost as condescending about Austen's mind as Henry James would be almost a century later.

The explosion of feminist and post-colonial interest in Austen's novels in the latter part of the twentieth century mercifully said farewell to all that. This is when readers began to notice that women's business has never been the same since

Austen put her heroines on the page. Her fiction has become a benchmark for exploring a plethora of ideas about power relations in general and gender power relations in particular, in the western world and beyond.

I am addicted to the art of conversation. On re-reading *Northanger Abbey* I recognised for the first time the subtle contrast between Catherine's conversations with Isabella Thorpe and those with Eleanor and Henry Tilney. A discussion between Catherine and her genuine friends segues into my own interest in historical fiction, and the ways in which it has changed since the days of Sir Walter Scott, whom Austen admired, and envied in a playful way. He had no business to write good novels, she wrote to her sister with tongue in cheek; 'he has fame and profit enough as a poet'. When I compare the conversations in Scott's novels with the sparkling dialogue Austen scatters through her pages I wish she could have known how history would compare the quality of their novels in the twentieth century.

My interest in the novel genre and the way it treats history has grown exponentially as the years have piled up and confronted me with the challenges of the remembered past. Now I myself am becoming a creature of historical interest. It is appealing to explore, therefore, how novels reframe the present in the past and instructive to discover, in fiction, fresh perspectives on the business of living. History, Catherine complains, tells her nothing that does not 'either vex or weary' her. Miss Tilney turns the subject to the people who write history. Historians, she says, as she engages with her friend's observation, 'are not happy in their flights of fancy. They display imagination without raising interest'. The ensuing conversation is full of twists and turns that mirror the qualities of the girls' minds.

In the novel *Persuasion*, we read that clever, well-informed people who have a great deal of conversation are the very best company. The conversation between these two friends shows us why. It is clear that Eleanor Tilney is the 'best' company for Catherine while Isabella Thorpe is not, despite the premature avowals of friendship she offers in the words quoted in the epigraph. Their conversation is an exemplar for claims made in the manifesto delivered by the 'young lady'. The powers of Austen's mind are both concealed and revealed: concealed by Catherine's simple formulation of the problem, and revealed when we pay readerly attention to the dialogical nature of the conversation. The older girl is the better educated and more knowledgeable of the two, but it is Catherine's unsophisticated approach to the subject that makes the exchange provocative and relevant for contemporary writers, especially those who have chosen to channel the powers of their minds into historical fiction.

I am thinking of how Richard Flanagan takes historical figures and reimagines them. In his novel *Wanting*, he tells a compellingly insightful story that features the widow of Sir John Franklin, one-time Lieutenant-General of Van Diemen's Land, an official Protector of an Indigenous community, and the nineteenth-century novelist Charles Dickens. Flanagan also gives a voice to an Indigenous child, Mathinna, a girl of significance in her culture, who is reduced to a commodity by her false protectors.

What an overdue response this novel is to the stories that were fed to children of my generation at school. Mrs Aeneas Gunn is a writer with the best intentions, but the entitlement of white privilege corrupted her intention to learn from the Indigenous people who lived in the remote part of the Northern Territory to which her husband was sent by the government.

She wrote about her experiences in books that were childhood perennials for children of my era: *The Little Black Princess* and *We of the Never-Never*. She appropriated aspects of Aboriginal life as she perceived it; she told her stories in ways that ignored the realities of the relationship between Indigenous and non-Indigenous people.

Richard Flanagan raises these issues a century later, but unlike Miss Tilney's historians, he raises interest by allowing the resources of fiction to bear on historical characters; bio fiction, as it is sometimes called, tweaks history to reveal something about both past and present. His novel sends his 'flights of fancy' soaring above the boundaries of mere fact. He understands the distinctions and nuances of literary style. He puts into the mouth of Charles Dickens a dismissive comment on Jane Austen:

> 'I read one of Jane Austen's once, I think,' Dickens ruminated. 'Who these days would read more?'
> 'Macaulay,' said Jerrold.
> 'Precisely,' said Dickens. 'Unlike you, Douglas, she does not understand that what pulses hard and fast must be there in every sentence. That is why, since her death, she has suffered ever greater obscurity rather than growing popularity . . .'

The irony of Dickens's presumption speaks for itself. But why, I wonder, does Flanagan situate Charles Dickens in Austen's fictional territory? I have searched in vain for evidence that he had read her novels. However, Flanagan's invention does fit happily with what we might expect if Dickens had been familiar with her literary style. It also fits with the commonly held view that sales of

Austen's books were dwindling until the publication of the family memoir revived interest in her novels from a Victorian perspective; but not so comfortably with the discovery by Austen scholar Janine Barchas, of an almost unbroken production line of cheap editions of Austen's novels during the period in which Charles Dickens was a leading literary figure. However, the comment tells us something new and interesting about Dickens as both man and writer, and it also fits with evidence that we do have – such as, for example, Macaulay's passion for Jane Austen. It *is* a happy flight of fancy. And it allows Flanagan to penetrate Dickens's creative mind if not Austen's.

Catherine Morland describes herself as vexed and wearied by history. I was neither vexed nor wearied by Hilary Mantel's trilogy that follows the rise and fall of Thomas Cromwell, Chief Minister to Henry VIII. Historical fiction doesn't get any better, in my opinion. Mantel's prose explodes with the sort of energy that Dickens, as imagined by Flanagan, misses in Jane Austen's prose. I have been wary of aphrodisiacs since reading *A Midsummer Night's Dream*, but I can accept a literary aphrodisiac, and that's how Mantel's fiction seduces me. The shock of the new dazzles readers on every page.

I have recently been listening to Kate Grenville in radio interviews about her reimagination of Australian history. She, too, writes bio fiction. She reflects on how the present can be captured in and illuminated by stories set in the past. Her novel *A Room Made of Leaves* tells the story of Elizabeth Macarthur in letters, the epistolary form of novel with which Jane Austen experimented in her early writing. Grenville is also an innovator, and she cleverly transforms the epistolary novel into a memoir that challenges historical assumptions. Catherine Morland would have been neither vexed nor wearied by the result, and Eleanor Tilney would have found enough imagination to make any reader happy.

When I was a schoolgirl, we learned that Australia rode to prosperity on the sheep's back. For this blessing, we were told, we should thank John Macarthur of Camden Park. He had a wife, Elizabeth, and she was acknowledged merely as his helpmate, an appendage. She appeared in tandem with her husband, as if they spent all their lives together. But this alleged truth was, in fact, a fiction. John Macarthur was as much absent as present in their sheep-breeding lives.

We sat in our classrooms, girls on one side of the room, boys on the other, and listened to this story. And we assimilated gender models that have stayed with us for decades. We girls needed to hear Grenville's account, but the time was not yet ripe. Her story is timely; it sets us in Elizabeth Macarthur's past and retells that story as her achievement. It is framed by a claim to authenticity that is reminiscent of Daniel Defoe's introduction to *Robinson Crusoe*, an early novel in which fiction masquerades as non-fiction. Mrs Macarthur's fictional memoir sets free a voice that was silenced by history itself. The novel challenges the self-serving stories that nations tell themselves and challenges specifically dominant historical accounts of Australian progress.

The fictional memoir also reminds us that fiction, certainly since Jane Austen, has been about powerful feminist ideas. Grenville uses the past to remind readers of the continuing silencing and bullying of women, in the same way that Elizabeth Macarthur was bullied and oppressed by her husband. It has been almost beyond belief in recent times to learn from the Me Too movement that men, in personal and public relationships, continue to abuse women, despite the gains made in the intervening years. How can we reconcile the political gains made by women with abuses that have taken place and continue to take place in a series of public worlds – entertainment, retail and, astonishingly, political? This is not just a statistical problem. Because it belongs in the field of human relations, the problem invites paradoxical rather than mathematical reflection.

Present history shows that males continue to wield power, even within the Australian houses of government that purport to legislate for the good of the whole nation. I have found it confronting to watch episode after episode of a brilliant Australian ABC TV series called *Ms Represented*. There, in a public sphere that once banned but now in the twentieth century accepts them, women of power spoke out. Female members of parliament were invited by Annabel Crabb, a probing producer-presenter, to reveal how they are restrained still by traditional patriarchal assumptions that dismiss them as emotional and nurturing, weak and submissive. Men, on the other hand, project an image of themselves as rational, strong, protective, decisive. The series was all the more unusual in that the voices of presumably powerful women from both sides of the political divide were raised in unison to tell stories of male abuse. In each episode, woman after successful woman corroborated the old story, describing how their gift for expressing the dramas of the disadvantaged has been turned against them, sometimes patronisingly and sometimes aggressively, framed as typically female hysteria or typically female melodrama.

One day, when I was on school holidays, my mother was in conversation on our back veranda with Mrs H., whose sense of righteous indignation had nothing in common with the indignities of contemporary women. I was eavesdropping, a habit I cultivated both deliberately and diligently as a child. It was considered rude, but I had ways of burying my face in a book or staring into the distance to disguise my curiosity. (Perhaps because I was encouraged by the Old Testament and my father to believe in retribution, I wondered later whether the bout of deafness that hospitalised me for a short time as a schoolgirl was a just desert; and when deafness returned to put an end to the pleasurable habit in my adult years, the humour was not lost on me. It is the sort of humour, though, that is defined by the German writer Jenny Erpenbeck as what happens when you laugh anyway.) The conversation I overheard all those years ago makes me think of Jane Austen. It was insignificant in itself, and yet it sent a powerful message to me about human bigotry.

Mrs H., whose affectations of gentility would not have been out of place in an Austen novel, had dropped by our house to deliver a Christmas cake my mother had won in a raffle. Mrs H. was an acclaimed cook, and the fruitcake was made to the recipe with which she regularly won blue ribbons at our local Country Women's Association fetes. A few pleasantries were exchanged over the teacups, whereupon Mrs H. embarked hyperbolically on an account of her dislike of all things Catholic; everywhere in the world but especially in our town. She enumerated as examples the disproportionate extent of church property, its pre-eminent position in the town's topography, and her suspicions of some sort of relations between priest and nuns that I didn't understand but could tell were not regarded well.

I was bewildered because, apart from the morning prayer incident and its ramifications, memories of my time at the convent were pleasant enough. Father O'Dea often wandered into the playground and chatted with us. When my parents discussed the conversation with Mrs H. over our evening meal, they speculated that such animosity towards the Catholics might be a blessing, distracting people like Mrs H. from prejudices against the Jewish families in town.

It is a not-uncommon contemporary dilemma. What do you do when a friend expresses the sort of prejudice and ignorance that goes against the grain of everything you believe about human behaviour? Mrs H. reminds me that Jane Austen represented the Catholic–Protestant divide maliciously but deliciously, in a hilarious fight-to-the-death relationship between Mary Queen of Scots and Queen Elizabeth I. In the little volume titled *The History of England*, illustrated by her sister Cassandra, she positioned the Catholic–Protestant conflict at the heart of a historical parody.

It was years later that Mrs H.'s conversation drifted back into my mind. I was sitting in my reading sanctuary, immersing myself in one of Austen's ironical 'dialogues of civilities' in *Northanger Abbey*, allowing memory and imagination to fall where they would. I wondered whether my mother, like Catherine, was remiss in not challenging opinions that were mean-spirited, malicious and prejudiced. I thought about how both she and my father almost welcomed Mrs H.'s prejudices against Catholics as a preferable alternative to anti-Semitism. It did not occur to them then that the conversation was degraded; I wondered in hindsight if it were not also degrading to the interlocutor. I contrasted it with my memories of Dr and Mrs N., the Austrian couple with whom I had enjoyed uplifting conversations about human nature and an examination of the ideas to which it gives rise. There was nothing to compare. I recalled that the evil of prejudice was a motif that had run through my life.

When I retired from teaching English in the classroom I created a teaching resource called *Say NO to Prejudice*. I was continuing, I realise now, to spin a thread that has strengthened and unified different fragments of my life. The project was a natural extension of an oral-history experience that I had designed and coordinated to reinforce a Second World War history-curriculum unit in secondary-school classrooms. I enjoyed working with teenage students and child survivors of the Holocaust. I had returned to Sydney after a five-year period overseas. It was an inspiring distraction from the inner disquiet that I was experiencing on my return.

The project served my own needs at the time. And, as is often the case, those particular needs overlapped with an existing passion: my lifelong wish to challenge prejudice with more powerful stories and ideas. At the same time, it fulfilled a wish that had been expressed by many survivors: that their stories should be recorded and documented in a way that would encourage young people in all schools to think about what had happened to the survivors and their families in the middle of the twentieth century. They had their reasons: they wanted to encourage young people to understand the consequences of racial prejudice and to oppose them actively. It was also a way for most of the survivors to pay their own tributes to courageous strangers who had risked their own lives to help them survive.

If ever the quality we call empathy jumped out and stared me in the face, it was on the night that the students concluded the program with a formal presentation. Each group of student oral historians made an oral presentation to the living historian who had shared a story of survival. Leon was one of the child survivors. He had shared not only a story of what had happened to him, but also his beliefs about life and his optimism for the prospect of a better world. His group presented him with a square wooden box. Then one of the students addressed the following words to the audience of fellow students: 'This is a silk-lined box. It represents the smoothness of Leon's life at the end of a long, rough journey.'

Each student in turn took an object from the box and explained its significance: a pen that stood for the recording of Leon's story for future generations; a piece of barbed wire as a reminder of the sharpness of his memories and the untangling of his ties with the ghetto; a coin to represent the wealth of his memories; a single tissue to stand as truth that 'Leon's tears and ours are not wasted'; a peace sign to represent Leon's greatest hope for humanity; and, finally, a figurine of an angel to symbolise Leon's belief that he had been 'watched over'.

The last student closed the box and handed it to Leon, stooped, silver-haired, a smile on his face and eyes brimming with tears. 'The rest,' the student told his elder, 'is for you to add other cherished treasures and dreams.' This is not fiction; it happened before my eyes. But the words written by those students and delivered to Leon are literature, and they should be read as literature should be read. That, of course, raises another question: how *should* literature be read?

Jane Austen's manifesto for fiction in *Northanger Abbey* is one way of answering the question. Readers, the young lady implies, are confronted with ideas that drive characters to feel, think and behave as they do. They should also consider how the language of the novel influences and shapes their perceptions. And something else gradually dawned on me: after witnessing the power of the learning journey undertaken by the high-school students who developed relationships with Holocaust survivors, I gave empathy its name and acknowledged its value.

Although the word 'empathy' was not available to writers of Austen's generation, we glimpse its intent in Adam Smith's theory of moral sentiments and fellow-feeling that wove its way into the sentimental novel that Austen inherited and enriched. In recent years the significance of empathy has emerged in various disciplines including the field of literary studies. Here readers are framed in the act of thinking with or feeling with characters in a novel; or, alternatively, thinking about how characters in fiction think and feel with each other. The word empathy first appeared in the English language in the late nineteenth century as a translation of the German word *Einfühlung*, literally 'feeling oneself into' another phenomenon, perhaps a person, perhaps a work of art, perhaps a situation. It is related to notions about sympathy and identification, but not precisely the same as either. Sympathy is a little too close to pity, and identification suggests a loss of self. These were pitfalls that I had been determined to avoid in the way my students were encouraged to interact with their survivor interviewees.

What does it mean, I asked myself when re-reading *Northanger Abbey*, to read empathetically? Was my almost tender relationship with Jane Austen a sign of her empathy as a narrator, mine as a reader, or both? What do we learn about empathy when we engage with Mrs Morland, a busy but deeply engaged mother, her daughter Catherine, or Catherine's motherless friend, Eleanor Tilney? My thoughts turned to the possibility of learning to read empathetically. To help young people read in this way, I thought, would really be something.

Once my curiosity about empathy had been stirred, a strange thing happened. I found myself introducing the idea into my conversations and applying it to my increasingly frequent thoughts about learning and reading. I noticed the word cropping up in articles. One friend sent me an article that quoted the counsel offered by the eminent cosmologist Stephen Hawking to a young enquirer. The quality he would most like to magnify, he told her, is empathy, explaining that in his view 'it brings us together in a peaceful loving state'.

Elie Wiesel's novel *Night* is one of the earliest and most powerful testimonies to the enormous void in moral awareness in the absence of empathy. The Nobel prize-winning author reflected on why the heirs of Kant and Goethe, Germans who were among the best-educated people on earth, were not inhibited by their education from behaving as they did when they set out to exterminate whole human populations – not just Jews, but Romani, homosexuals, and people with intellectual or physical disabilities and mental illness. According to Wiesel, it was made possible by the fact that education – including education constructed around great literature – took the wrong direction. By emphasising theory and concepts and abstractions rather than values and consciousness and conscience, it subverted its own intentions. He was implying, I believe, that the factors contributing to the development of an empathetic consciousness were discouraged by the educational approach.

It's not hard to summon up historical examples to support Wiesel's passionate claim. It is, for example, instructive to think that the abstract exercise of working out how to use a railway system to carry as many people as possible to their deaths as efficiently as possible would take precedence over the fact that mass murder of human populations was the ultimate objective. Should we connect the ways in which reading at school has become an exercise in applying theories with the failure to find the usefulness and sweetness that Horace names as the essence of literature?

I had made extraordinary friends as a result of the oral-history project. Sabina was one of them. She had never revealed her Holocaust experiences, not even to her children. She agreed to participate in the project because she felt the time had come to share the historical events and moral challenges she had spent years trying to forget. We talked about that, and about Elie Wiesel's belief in the obligation of survivors to bear witness. Our friendship was cemented in conversations in which we talked about our mutual love of literature and ideas. I have no doubt that if she had lived in better times, a normal schooling would have led to an academic career. But from the age of twelve her schooling was disrupted as she moved stealthily from hiding place to hiding place.

Sabina, the adult, was an inveterate gift-giver. She gave me a copy of a volume of essays called *Ex Libris* by Anne Fadiman, not for any special occasion but because she wanted to share Fadiman's jewel-like meditations on what it means to love books. In turn, I contributed a paean to Sabina to a collection of older peoples' memories published by the local municipality where we both lived. It is not polished to perfection like Fadiman's beautiful writing, but it is a heartfelt account of the impact Sabina had made on my life. The piece was awarded another of the few small writing prizes that I have received.

Sabina's wartime experiences included the loss of mother, father and brother. Her life was spent in hiding, sometimes in homes with strangers, sometimes in underground hiding places. When the war was over she found herself sitting in a park, clutching a case with a few mementoes, and listening to tumultuous cries of victory. She did not remember how she got there. Later she noticed that the dress she was wearing had been lengthened with a mismatched piece of material. She had no idea how this had happened or who had lengthened her garment.

My essay contrasted Sabina's childhood struggle for survival in Poland with the innocence and trivial concerns of mine in Australia. I concluded that: 'Sabina is more blessed, if not more fortunate, than many of us whose memories are showered with a golden light. We have been spared her ordeal. But she has survived evil and renewed her life with the will to find meaning and peace . . . I have gained a new friend whose gentleness lights our future.'

Sabina attributed her moral survival to the common-sense virtues of decency and loyalty she learned from her mother. Her participation in the oral history project marked the beginning of a new phase in her life, her coming to terms with the past, because in that project she shared her experiences with the younger and cherished generation of her grandchildren. She became an accomplished speaker, generous with the time and memories that she shared with thousands of young people.

In 2005 Sabina appeared on the international stage. She was chosen to speak in Berlin on behalf of the six million dead at the opening of the Memorial to the Murdered Jews of Europe. She spoke not of regret or revenge but of the innocence of the children of the perpetrators; she urged all generations to move forward to a better, more enlightened and more moral world. Her own memoir and record of a life renewed and lived to the full is called *Destined to Live: One woman's war, life, loves remembered.* Reading the memoir is like reading Sabina herself, a lesson in love, courage, loyalty and empathy.

Sometimes I took my new copy of *Northanger Abbey* into the garden. I loved to sit in a small, paved courtyard when it was awash with afternoon sun. From my wicker chair I looked over a low hedge onto an expanse of lawn like the one described in the Austen family memoir, in which Austen's nephew re-created the rectory at Steventon where the Austen children were born and lived for many years. He imagined that Jane Austen might have rolled down the slope as a girl, as Catherine rolled down the lawn in front of the Morlands' fictional home when playing with her younger brothers and sisters. My lawn was as green as most well-tended lawns are in the garden-rich Southern Highlands, and it was flat, but I liked to imagine Catherine playing there as well, before she was old enough to accompany Mr and Mrs Allen on their excursion to Bath.

There is nothing like a girl's first venture from home. That great adventure is what gripped me as I re-read the novel and recaptured the excitement of being a young girl again. I was flooded with pleasurable imaginings of new horizons. With something of a surprise, I realised that, although older, I had now been offered a second turn in the whirligig of time. There might still be something to learn from Catherine's experiences.

After all, in real life we read both for pleasure and beyond pleasure. We read to pick up clues that help us to navigate our lives and relationships, and expand our understanding of ourselves and the world we live in. And on re-reading *Northanger Abbey* as I undertook my reading cure, I became convinced that this novel, like the others that Austen produced, was doing that for me, stimulating me to ruminate on fiction with a renewed awareness that what had been missed in the past might now be a guiding light for the future.

At school, teachers of Austen's novels sometimes forget or are encouraged to ignore what fiction is about. Their preoccupation with exams and marks and tertiary scores might trick them into reading for reasons that undermine the potential pleasure. This was my thought when I met the English teacher in the Brown Bookshop. A week or so later we continued the conversation at Palate Pleasure, a coffee shop that specialised in delectable cakes and mouth-watering pastries.

My new acquaintance talked about how she introduced her student readers to the novel. She needed to focus, she said, on the ways in which *Northanger Abbey* parodies the gothic novels that were popular in Austen's time so that they could relate to Catherine's fevered imagining when she arrives at the Tilneys' home. That was the thrust of the syllabus she told me; the lens, to use a fashionably theoretical term, through which students were encouraged to read the novel. It was not the way she had read the novel, but students were increasingly inclined, she had noticed, to pay almost as much attention to the syllabus narrative as to the story they were reading.

This seemed to be an extraordinary coincidence. The very aspect of the novel that had turned me off as a younger reader was now the focus of interest for student readers. The gothic imagination is important. I understand that. It has had its brief moment of dominion in the history of the novel. It helps to explain the strong emotional appeal of *Jane Eyre* and *Wuthering Heights*. It reaches an apotheosis in the science fiction of Mary Shelley's *Frankenstein*. It haunts Edgar Allan Poe's horror stories and those of other more contemporary American writers. And it has made a return as a dominant and recurring feature of popular culture, in which vampires abound. It has not disappeared from sight.

All the same, that does not strike me as the best focus for reading Jane Austen's fiction. I suspect that reading the novel imposes the present on the past, rather than allowing the past to illuminate present culture. It seems to me like a slippery slope down which readers slide to the simplest but not necessarily the richest level of pleasure. It recalls Elie Wiesel's warnings about theories and abstractions. If we want to use lenses, they might be more useful to focus the peripheral vision. The nature and authenticity of friendship and romantic intimacy are central ideas that shape the events of Catherine's holiday in Bath. They are more relevant to the lives of young people as they approach adulthood than a historical approach to literature, although Austen's parody is brilliant. Where is empathy in this approach? And how will the approach help young adults navigate their way in a complex and troubled modern world?

What is more important than having a friend? That question dominates the early part of *Northanger Abbey*. How happy Mrs Allen is when she spies her old friend, Mrs Thorpe. The search for friends – the relationships between Catherine and the Thorpe family on the one hand, and Catherine and the Tilneys on the other – is the hook that makes me want to know what is written on the next page. The novelist and literary scholar E.M. Forster was emphatic that the success of any novel is dependent on the interest it excites about what happens next. The conversation with my teacher acquaintance niggled me. I thought about Elie Wiesel again. My curiosity about reading at school was roused. For the first time in years, I felt the stirring of a new source of interest, something I hadn't noticed for a very long time. As yet, it had no clearly defined features. But being at peace in my cool-climate garden, I contemplated ideas about the pleasures of fiction, the qualities of friendship and lost opportunities to engage with stories.

Australian journalist Nikki Gemmell strikes a resounding chord in her regular column, when considering the significance of friendship. She is writing in a different time and from a different place, nevertheless her need to measure and distil her friendships at this Covid turning point in time harks back to ideas in *Northanger Abbey*, resonating with speculations about false friendship as we follow the progress of Catherine's relationship with Isabella. The pandemic has motivated the journalist to think about whether people 'rattle' her soul rather than nourish it. It is an illuminating distinction, and one that makes a telling point about friendship. Gemmell writes about conversations with friends in which signs of a narcissistic disposition preclude the possibility of authentic friendships. She prefers instead the sort of friendship in which minds meet and the sort of friend who helps her feel like a whole person, both recommended by Toni Morrison in her novel *Beloved*.

My brother was my first friend. The second was Connie.

I claim her as a friend of my heart and mind although she was a consequence of my invention. Marian Engel dedicated her novel *Lunatic Villas* to 'my mother, Mary Passmore, who once put four sticks in the flower bed and said, "Give them all names and you'll have someone to play with."' The name I gave my friend was Connie. It was chosen out of my affection for my parents' friend, Mrs Connie W. She and her husband were among the small number of people with whom my parents engaged socially when I was growing up.

My father had met the couple when he was still a bachelor, and they had formed an attachment through music. Mrs W. had been a concert pianist whose career was cut short by her deafness. Mr W. had been an amateur cellist. They hosted musical evenings in their farmhouse. Mrs W. was the accompanist and my father's pleasant tenor voice was a welcome addition in his bachelor days. His star acts were sentimental songs such as 'Trees' and 'The Indian Love Song', and he continued to sing them, to my delight, when we were on car trips. Perhaps those songs sowed the seeds of sentiment in my imagination. I don't know what Marianne Dashwood of *Sense and Sensibility*, stern judge that she was, would have thought of my literary and musical taste, but it may have its genesis in such musical experiences.

Ample without being stout, Mrs W. exuded an appealing warmth. Mr W. was different: large, intimidating and overbearing, with a booming voice. When the men went for a walk through the orchard to inspect the packing shed with its crates of citrus ready for sorting and dispatch, my mother and Mrs W. remained in the farmhouse parlour, discussing, comparing and recommending books that they owned or that they had borrowed from the town's private library. They were both fond of romantic dramas and, unlikely as it may seem, they, like many corseted ladies of their era, liked novels with an edge.

Some of the books my mother mentioned were on the shelves of a glass-fronted bookcase in my father's study. When I was older, I managed to find the key and dip into them. Among them, it is surprising to remember, was Radclyffe Hall's novel *The Well of Loneliness*, from which I gleaned a first inkling of what was then regarded as sexual transgression. My most treasured find, a book to which I often returned with wonder, was a novella by the Austrian author Arthur Schnitzler. I remember waiting for one of my mother's regular bridge afternoons, when her prolonged absence could be counted on, to read the novella *Fräulein Else* aloud, sinking into a young girl's stream-of-consciousness narrative of sexual stirrings, of depredation and of bourgeois family hypocrisy. I trembled my way into the young girl's consciousness and imagined that I was dying with her as she drifted into the last hours of her life.

Another book I devoured was Margaret Kennedy's 'bohemian' novel, *The Constant Nymph*. The characters are unexpectedly unconventional. Perhaps they offered readers like Mrs W. and my mother a view of other possibilities – not just the subversion of sexual taboos but a challenge to the very notion of respectability. The novel was a bestseller and was translated onto the screen three times. In a stage version, the leading role was played by Elisabeth Bergner, who fled the Nazi regime and had a second career in exile. Little did I dream that one day I would sit in the stalls and watch this actress bring *Fräulein Else* to life on stage at the Palace Theatre in Sydney, and that she would invite me to deliver a speech from Shakespeare in her dressing room after one of her performances. That, however, is a story for another chapter.

On the occasion I recall, the two ladies talked about matters other than books. Marina Warner is a writer who understands the enchantment of storytelling as well as, perhaps differently from, other writers on the subject. She reminds us that when we listen to the gossip of our parents or other adults we sometimes hear stories that make us think about a whole lot of new and strange things. Mrs W. opened up to my mother about life in the farmhouse with her bullying husband. The scene she described sounded horrific to me as I strained to catch the details from where I was supposed to be reading. Something that displeased her husband, she told my mother, resulted in punishment. Her husband locked her in a storeroom when he left for work in the orchard. She remained there until he returned and released her to prepare his lunch. My imagination lurched. When Mr W. had left the house with my father he was, in my eyes, not a particularly appealing man, but harmless enough. When he returned, still in the same gumboots and baggy sweater, he had been transformed into Bluebeard, and I turned away when he approached to kiss me goodbye.

The story troubled me, because by that time I had become very fond of Mrs W. On one of her visits to our house she had examined my favourite porcelain doll and subsequently presented me with a wardrobe of beautifully knitted and crocheted garments made to measure for Betty, whom I had named after my father's mother. It was natural that I would give Mrs W.'s name to the friend I invented to take my brother's place after he moved from our shared room and I found myself feeling lonely in bed at night. From then on, it was Connie who slept in the other bed. She was a wonderful listener, a friend to whom I told my secrets as Mrs W. had told her secrets to my mother. Sometimes that is just the sort of friend we need.

When I started school and gradually began to make friends of my own age, Connie's nightly visits came to an end. But for some reason my schoolfriends never really satisfied my desire for intimacy. Connie had given me a taste for a friend who would listen to my secrets, most of which were constituted of my parents' frequent arguments and my anxiety that one day they would not make up and our family would disintegrate.

I knew by instinct that it would be a betrayal to share my home life with strangers at school. My childhood friend Ruth and I grew apart once we were too old to talk about fairy tales. And Dianna, with whom I shared a love of literature in high school, seemed wary of getting too close. When we connected as adults she hesitated before telling me that she had been confused by my Jewishness. 'I wanted to invite you home,' she told me, 'but I wasn't sure what to give you to eat. And I thought you wouldn't want to come to my sixteenth birthday party because it was held in a church hall.' I remembered how I struggled to overcome my disappointment when I hadn't received an invitation; her explanation, years later, gave me a small and unexpected moment of happiness.

But again I was fortunate; during my final years at school I was so preoccupied with my studies that there was little time or space for friends. All my efforts went into my favourite subjects: English, history, Latin and French. I worked hard at maths and science, but I never grasped the fundamentals of either. It was a matter of sink or swim when examinations came around. Fortunately my marks in my 'good' subjects compensated for my weakness in what we now call STEM subjects, and because my aggregate was among the top 100 in the state, I was awarded an exhibition, or scholarship, to university.

It is unsettling even now to remember how anxious I was about the first day on campus. I worried about how I would get there, how I would find my way around the buildings, whether anyone would talk to me. The previous night I had dreamed about taking an unfamiliar journey, and I had woken to anxious premonitions of being lost. I wound my plaits around my head, hoping to make myself look less like a schoolgirl, and dressed in the sort of clothes I associated with teenage film idols such as Elizabeth Taylor: a flared corduroy skirt, ankle-strap sandals and a string of beads at my throat. I caught the bus and was lost in my own reverie when a girl about my age dropped heavily into the seat beside me and announced her presence with a breezy greeting.

'Is this your first day at university like me?' she asked, and when I nodded said, 'I'm Lillian – Lillian Roxon. I'm from Brisbane. I don't know anyone. Do you?'

I shook my head. We both expressed relief at having met each other. Immediately I relaxed. I registered that the girl next to me was plump, that her skin was lovely, deep cream in colour and the texture of velvet. Her face was round and pretty in a way that, as I remember it now, was both exotic and innocent. At once the floodgates of conversation opened as this extraordinary person, unlike anyone I had ever come across, poured out details of her life. She rarely stopped to draw breath, and her confidence took *my* breath away. She spoke; I listened. I thrilled to the thought that I had found my first new friend. And then she dropped a bombshell that reminds me now of my mother's favourite Yiddish idiom, which translates into English as 'it was meant', suggesting that the full force of destiny is working for you.

'I'm looking out for someone called Ruth,' she said. She didn't remember the last name but knew the person she was looking for came from the country. She thought she might not find her.

'You have!' I told her.

Our shrieks might have disturbed our fellow passengers, but I wasn't looking to check. We exclaimed at the coincidence and I deduced that the suggestion came from a mutual friend, an older Brisbane girl I had become friendly with the previous summer when we had both spent a holiday with a member of my extended family.

Lillian's enthusiasm was infectious. In no time, we were deeply engaged in a conversation that, like those between Catherine and Isabella, had little to do with the 'delicacy, discretion, originality of thought, and literary taste' mentioned in *Northanger Abbey*. I was soon contributing my share of intimacies in a conversation that my mother would have considered deeply shameful. And on a public bus! But I didn't care.

However, promising as our first conversation was, it transpired that there was no way I could keep up with Lillian, either in the way we used words or in the dramas of our home lives. By comparison, my family life was a dull and drab thing. I fell silent as scenes from her life, acted out with the sort of gusto recommended by William Hazlitt in a celebrated essay, filled with expression and passion. I was travelling on the 360 bus from Dover Heights to Central Station, but I might have been in the Theatre Royal watching a performance of an Ibsen drama as she introduced a parade of characters: a tyrannical father who, inflamed by his daughter's tendency to plumpness, threw out her breakfast of scrambled eggs, declaring, 'Eggs make fat'; a mother, meek and docile, flurried, doing nothing, unable to protect her children from their father's irrational rage; a younger brother who needed her protection, which she regretted she was no longer there to give. Never mind, she told me and herself; now she was excited to be joining her brilliant older brother, a philosophy student who had urged her to get away from the stifling atmosphere at home and start to live a 'real life'.

Disappointing though it was at the time, it was predictable that Lillian and I were not, in fact, meant to become close friends. It took only a few weeks to realise that my hopes for an intimate relationship would not come to fruition. My attitude to life, although hopeful and even confident, had about it a natural sense of restraint. I lacked Lillian's intensity, her zest, her energetic impulses to turn life into an adventure. Besides, her confidence was warranted; her writing had been published in magazines since she was fourteen, so she knew she had the talent to be the successful journalist she was destined to become. Even as we wandered together down Science Road on the first day, two novice students in search of our grown-up identities, it became obvious that our tastes and dispositions were fundamentally different.

I lingered over tables that displayed notices about drama societies while Lillian engaged, spontaneously and wittily, in conversation with strangers at almost every stop we made. She was totally inclusive, sharing her opinions with everyone she spoke to. Like Mr Weston in *Emma*, she was both generous and indiscriminate with her intimacy, a tendency I noted although I had not yet read the novel. I was fortunate, though, that it saved me on that fraught day. Within a few weeks we merely greeted each other in passing.

As the year progressed, I was vaguely aware of Lillian's progression: from an ingenue, wide-eyed with wonder at new possibilities, to a female follower of the Push, a band of radical male philosophers, scholarly, amateur and, it seems to me now, wannabe adversaries of middle-class values. Robert Milliken, who published a biography of Lillian in 2002, described the Push as the successors to the Freethought Society, which was founded at The University of Sydney in the 1930s, and whose members were opposed to all forms of authoritarianism.

The Push admitted women to their ranks on strictly masculine terms. Some seventy years later, the Push females seem less like intellectuals than hangers-on, although I doubt that could ever be said of Germaine Greer who arrived on the scene a few years later.

Milliken's biography follows Lillian's trajectory from a 'reluctant virgin' in the early 1950s to a successful international journalist by the end of the decade, and then a key figure among New York's celebrities in the 1960s, participating in the cultural, artistic and especially musical revolutions.

In another strange but insignificant intersection of Lillian's life and mine, it was in the Philosophy Room that I attended the first meeting of a new drama group called the Sydney University Players. By the end of our first year, Lillian had become a campus identity, widely dispersing her provocative witticisms; when our paths crossed, usually in Fisher Library, I noted that her conversation always played with sexual innuendo. In my own way I had become an identity, too, having been cast in leading female roles by both the blossoming Sydney University Players and the already blooming Sydney University Dramatic Society. That was something Lillian never mentioned when we encountered each other, but perhaps members of the Push had better things to do than attend university productions.

How to account for the failure of a friendship to materialise from our chance meeting? It may not be as puzzling as the relationship riddles and blunders that readers encounter in Jane Austen's novel *Emma*. I could not match the rock-and-roll energy that was Lillian's signature characteristic, but I also think that I was impatient with the naivety that, it appeared to me, made her vulnerable to male exploitation. With hindsight, I remember that the circles of people with whom Lillian chose to identify were a little like novels with which I simply did not engage.

Milliken writes that the three graduates of Sydney's most prominent selective girls' high school who became Lillian's lifelong friends were at home in the socially, intellectually and sexually adventurous atmosphere of what would come to be known as the Push. I was not by nature either socially or sexually adventurous. I was curious about sex, but I had not yet decided exactly what I wanted to do with my body. I certainly did not want to trade it for acceptance of any kind.

This, right or wrong, was the way I read the social interactions among men and women on the one occasion that I was invited by the Push leader to join their regular table at Manning House. I had achieved some prominence as an actor, and I think I might have been invited for that reason. It might have been some sort of trial. If so, I am sure that I did not pass muster. It must have been obvious to everyone around the table that I was conversationally out of my depth, as my lack of social currency in subjects of interest to the assembled group effectively rendered me silent.

On the other hand, already influenced by Jane Austen's novels, I sensed the ambiguity in the relationship between males and females at that table. There seemed to me to be nothing either distinctive or distinguished about conversations that swirled around academic personalities and sex. If the Push were put under a feminist microscope today, it would, I believe, carry the DNA of attitudes targeted by the Me Too movement. I have a clear recollection of how entertaining Lillian made her story about a lovers' tiff that had resulted in her black eye. I wondered then whether something darker might be buried beneath her endless flow of witticisms, the mirthful delight she took in embarrassing others and the unfailing appearance of joie de vivre.

And yet, a sense of sadness and loss tinges my memories of Lillian Roxon, who was crowned unofficially as the Queen of Rock and author of the first encyclopaedia of rock music, and who tragically died from an asthma attack in the early 1970s. I regret that, in her regard, I did not qualify for her friendship, although I think I might understand why. I wonder if in Lillian's eyes I was, as Jane Austen was described by her cousin Philadelphia, 'a little prim'. If so, she was not the first nor the last to detect a strain of primness in my disposition. In one of many therapy sessions later in life, my analyst suggested that Bizet's Carmen might lurk beneath my public persona. I played with the idea but could never engage with it seriously. Whether repressed, suppressed or simply non-existent, Carmen's blood type seems not to course through my veins. On reflection, however – and thus swings the thought pendulum – perhaps a little of Carmen's passion, or a dose of Lillian's zest, would have filtered out some of the melancholy that overtook me as the light in my marriage grew dimmer.

I met with Lillian only once after we both graduated. I was aware in a vague sort of way of her successful transposition to New York, but I had no idea how large a figure she had become. I heard of her from time to time because for Australians who had known her at university, visiting Lillian in New York was an obligatory stop on the tourist itinerary. One of her visitors was my friend Robert, on his way home from Canada, where he had completed his training as a psychiatrist. It is interesting that he had reservations about whether Lillian's celebrity had brought her satisfaction. He thought she was troubled rather than jubilant.

My final sighting of Lillian was in the early 1970s, when she was visiting Sydney. I ran into her in Double Bay, at a popular restaurant called the Cosmopolitan. It was famous for its jazz piano and its European menu, which included Vienna schnitzel and Hungarian crepes with hazelnut filling. The outing must have been a birthday treat for one of my four children because we were all there: mother and daughters in our Double Bay best and father and son in suits and ties. Lillian, who was part of a lively group, spotted us across the room.

She waved and came over to say hello to me and meet the children, then we moved aside to exchange a few private words. I doubt that she was thinking, as I was, of our long-ago rollicking bus ride to a brand-new life. To my surprise, her beautiful light-grey eyes clouded, and she wondered aloud whether she hadn't missed out on something in her life, seeing, she said, my perfect family. She would not have guessed my thoughts. My family life was already strained, while she, I reflected, had the world at her feet. But I did not share my thoughts with her as I enquired about her future plans. If we had forged a real friendship in the past, we might each have helped the other to see alternative truths in our lives.

These are the sorts of ruminations that transformed my re-reading of *Northanger Abbey* into a meditation on friendship. One of the pleasures of life in the Southern Highlands was my weekly bushwalk with new friends, a remedy for one of the less-attractive aspects of living in the Southern Highlands. Property owners who made weekend visits to Bowral to join the local 'A-listers' put me in mind of the city–country divide dramatised in *Mansfield Park*. Bushwalking, on the other hand, was exactly what I needed, in the sort of company prescribed in the novel *Persuasion*: clever well-informed people with plenty of good conversation. We met once a week in the car park attached to the community swimming pool and close by a cherry walk. In springtime the cascades of pink and white blossoms were floral reminders of why we had chosen to live in this area of incomparable horticultural delight.

So once a week I left my tranquil house and garden to walk through the surrounding bush in the best possible company. As we hiked along bush tracks that took us up narrow and sometimes steeply pitched inclines, we mixed and matched conversationally. We shared knowledge about plants and birds as well as opinions about films, books and plays. Most of us made frequent excursions to Canberra and Sydney to keep up with art exhibitions and theatre, so we had much of interest to talk about.

The only couple in the group – I'll call them Doug and Lily – had backgrounds in finance, so our conversations touched on economics as well as the arts. They had moved from the eastern suburbs of Sydney, where they had been neighbours of my friend Sabina and her gracious and generous partner, originally from Denmark. The introduction was one among Sabina's many gifts to me. Their friendship added lustre to my life in the Southern Highlands. They both loved gardening, Lily was an inspired chef, and the house, garden and cuisine reflected the ambience of their favourite travel destination, Provence.

Among our band of walkers, a few members of the Jane Austen Society contributed to the conversation with talks about the author, and we shared stories about ways in which her fiction had become important in our lives. One of my bushwalking friends had an amazing memory for Austen's quotes – those sentences that, taken out of context, can put new life into everyday conversations.

Northanger Abbey is studded with throwaway lines that reveal something about the potential of the heroine, Catherine. Her quip 'I cannot speak well enough to make myself unintelligible' is among Austen's wittiest quotations. I returned to it often, as my reading rehabilitation led me to explore the ways in which the novels were described and analysed by more academic readers. That was when I started to compare the convoluted discussions and specialist language of some contemporary theories about how fiction works with the simple approach to what matters in fiction articulated by 'the young lady' of *Northanger Abbey*.

In my re-reading of the novel I savoured Catherine's conversational ventures into friendship as she settled into her temporary surroundings at Bath. A meeting with Isabella Thorpe, in which her new acquaintance vows eternal friendship on the spot, is a triumph of Austen's artistic mastery over Isabella's shallow nature. The conversation between the two girls, we are told, 'turned upon those subjects, of which the free discussion has generally much to do in perfecting a sudden intimacy between two young ladies; such as dress, balls, flirtations, and quizzes'. What Jane Austen can do with anticlimax is sometimes a pathway to everyday wisdom.

In my riper years I was puzzled by my initial lack of interest in this novel. I wondered whether the plot twist that draws Catherine and her unregulated imagination into the special effects of the Tilney home and its unfulfilled promise of a dreadful mystery might have accounted for my earlier lack of interest. Now I was better informed about the theory and history of fiction. I had known nothing then about the birth of the novel as a form of literature, and the legacy that Austen had inherited from sentimental conduct novels and escapist gothic novels. I had no idea that Austen parodied both genres in the novel that she wrote when she was in her early twenties, but which was not published until after her premature death.

I had shared part of the publication history of *Northanger Abbey* with my accidental friends outside Barclays bank in London, but more details are needed to complete the story. A novel about a heroine called Susan was written 'about the years [17]98 and 99', according to Cassandra Austen's recollections. The author, as I explained to my new acquaintance in the queue, was paid ten pounds for the manuscript but, when it had not been published after six years, she requested that her manuscript be returned (signing her letter *Mrs Ashton Dennis*, signalling by way of the initials that she was angry), and let her publisher know that she intended to publish independently. She also wrote a preface to explain that the chronology was by now some years out of date. However, it was not until 1817, following her death, that the ten pounds required by the original publishers was paid by Henry Austen so that the novel and its updated preface might be included in the posthumous volumes of her work.

I had decided to start on my re-reading journey by taking the road least travelled, which is why I began with the novel least read, the one written early but published late. Because *Northanger Abbey* had suffered the fate of other books that we think we will never read again, I had made that early visit to the Brown Bookshop and quickly formed a bond with the owner.

My relationship with Nancy was propitious. She had a love of books that reminded me of the enthusiasm of Penelope Fitzgerald's heroine in the novel *The Bookshop*. Unlike the fictional Florence, whose success in establishing a good bookshop for her village neighbours foundered on their Austenian vanities and rivalries, this owner was universally acknowledged as a gift to the community. She had earned accolades for her lengthy career as a specialist bookseller and the care with which she served her book-loving customers. She persuaded me to develop a relationship with the local Friends of the Library, following a format that I had tried out previously for a women's organisation in Sydney.

With her backing, we promoted the program as Conversations about Books. For the inaugural event, I presented the background to Tracy Chevalier's novel *Girl with a Pearl Earring* as a prelude to commentaries that focused on core aspects of the novel. A local artist talked about Vermeer's painting techniques and the relationship between Vermeer and the Golden Age of Dutch painting; a psychotherapist analysed the nature of the fictional relationship between the artist and his sitter. We concluded our conversation about powerful ideas, painting and light, and characters who turn their heads away from the light, with a glass of chardonnay in the local vineyard that hosted the event and as many Dutch cookies as our readers could eat; Jane Austen might have enjoyed the company.

Nancy also helped to promote a book I had recently edited: *A Big Ask: Interviews with interviewers*. For some reason, during the 1990s radio and television interviews had taken centre stage as forms of entertainment as well as sources of information. Interviews and interviewers, their skills, their techniques and the quality of their voices, had become a hot topic of conversation at social gatherings as well. I found myself involved in heated and often fascinating conversations about the relative strengths and weaknesses of interviewers whom we all called by their first names. 'Why did so-and-so let a shonky politician get the better of her?' we would ask, or, 'How does so-and-so manage to engage interviewees in intellectually stimulating conversation?'

My interest in broadcasting had a whimsical beginning. I had been inspired way back in time by the mother of one of my schoolfriends. She was the only working mother I knew; perhaps her example explains how her daughter May developed her own independence, leaving school after the Intermediate Certificate and learning to fly a single-engine plane. I addressed May's mother as Mrs R. when I visited their house, which was a few streets away from where I lived, closer than my own home to the foot of Scenic Hill. But when I sat on the carpet alongside the wireless in our dining room to listen to 2RG, the local wireless station, she was Carol, who chatted with local identities about everything that went on in the district.

When I was about nine years old, I spent a prolonged period in hospital, recovering from a bout of deafness. (I don't know why I was confined to bed, but in those days bed rest seemed to be prescribed for all maladies.) My father visited me on his hospital rounds each day to insert plugs of cotton wool soaked in an acrid-smelling liquid into my nostrils before training a lamp of some sort, ultraviolet or infrared, on the central part of my face. Apparently it was a technique he had learned at the Mayo

Clinic during his study trip. When the timer rang, a nurse would remove the plugs and wash away the remaining traces of the black liquid that smudged my face. My mother visited me later in the morning to damp down my thick hair and tame it into plaits. For the rest of the day I read, did puzzles and, best of all, pretended to be Carol, the broadcaster. I suppose the nurses were amused when they heard me practising my broadcasting skills, standing on the bed and holding the reverse side of my large Mason Pearson hairbrush a few inches from my mouth, as if it were a microphone. I hijacked any of them who were willing to play along, answering my inquisitive questions and talking about themselves into a pretend microphone.

Eventually I left hospital with my hearing intact and my curiosity about people's lives firmly entrenched. Curiosity has remained an enduringly present itch in my disposition. It ignited my urge to read and kept my passion burning with an intensity that drove me to re-read the fiction that captured my imagination. At times, curiosity is part of the remedy taking my mind off the pain of an experience and focusing it elsewhere, such as on trying to fathom the circumstances that surround it.

Curiosity prompted my continuing fascination with interviews as, in my adult life, I mulled over why this way of communicating had become so prevalent in popular culture. My curiosity gave me the daring – my grandfather would have congratulated me on my chutzpah – to approach some of the giants of public broadcasting in the late 1990s and solicit their views on what an interview is: a structured series of questions, a meeting of two minds, a conversation or even an art form? Among the fifteen public broadcasters whose cooperation enabled me to develop a hypothesis and make a distinction between public interviews and those conducted privately by doctors, lawyers, recruiting agents and others, Robert Dessaix came closest to marrying the art of the public interview, directed at an audience, to the art of fiction.

I asked Dessaix, whose daily radio sessions on books and writing were essential listening in my daily routine, whether he thought that interviews had become the most popular means of receiving and sending ideas. His answer could apply equally well to a question about why people read fiction:

> As to why people are reading, watching or listening to these interviews, I'm not so sure. Partly there's a voyeuristic interest I suppose (the pleasure of eavesdropping), and they are partly interested in what for example Dennis Altman [an Australian academic and pioneering gay-rights activist] might have to say because he's been observing a certain kind of cultural development of a marginalised group over many years and they're eager for insights. But what they really want to do, I believe, is *re-read their own lives* [emphasis added]. In seminars for emerging writers I used to tell them, 'No one's interested in whether *you* loved your mother or not, they couldn't care less, but they're very interested in whether *they* loved their mother or not . . . they want to have light thrown on their own lives and the interview is a wonderful way of letting this happen.

Reading this again twenty years later, I think of the advice given by Jane Austen to a novel-writing niece: 'You are now collecting your People delightfully . . . 3 or 4 families in a Country Village is the very thing to work on – & I hope you will do a great deal more, & make full use of them while they are so very favourably arranged.'

Austen's is not precisely the advice that Dessaix offers, but it is similarly succinct – a confident message about how best to wrap social relationships in stories about people – and it is offered by a master craftsperson.

My interview with Phillip Adams took place in his large townhouse, surrounded by an impressive collection of archaeological artefacts. The broadcaster's greeting was warm and welcoming. A celebrity presenter, Adams referred to himself as 'a dilettante' who embarks nightly on prolonged conversations with high-profile subjects about their ideas. Re-reading his answers to my questions, I notice that what he thinks matters about an interview often matches with what I have thought matters about Jane Austen. He speaks of the importance of voice, the spoken voice that I regard as a key to entering Austen's fictional world. He emphasises the importance of tone, the warp and weft of playfulness and intimacy that create a special bond between interviewer and interviewee, as they do between writer and reader. He discards the possibility of authority and courts irreverence. 'I regard it as a great success if I can get people with whom I'm discussing something of immense seriousness to laugh. It doesn't diminish the seriousness of the discussion, but it makes it more human, more accessible.' Jane Austen would probably agree; Elizabeth Bennet certainly would.

In her interview for my book, Jana Wendt spoke about 'ordinary' conversations that precede the 'extraordinary' conversations that take place on air. She was then a current affairs interviewer and presenter who moved for reasons of principle from her high-status position as a commercial star interviewer to a smaller space in public broadcasting. She expressed the view that the conversations are best when they combine emotional relaxation with intellectual stimulation. Here, Wendt connects with Jane Austen. She draws together two contradictory notions, relaxation and stimulation, in her interview conversation, and for me that's as good a way as any to describe the mood and tone in which the heroine of *Northanger Abbey* walks and talks with her new-found friends.

My book was published to some acclaim. It was featured in colour on the front page of the Media Supplement of *The Australian* newspaper and a double spread of excerpts from the book appeared inside. Such is the uncertainty of publishing that the initial flurry of interest was not reflected in the sales. To my mortification, I saw several copies remaindered for two dollars in a less-prestigious Bowral bookshop than Nancy's just two years after it was published.

When I was sixteen, the same age as Catherine Morland, I lived in and for the present. But like other girls of her age, I had great expectations for the future. When I re-read *Northanger Abbey* I was approaching eighty. The joy of re-reading is the chance that it offers to read differently. Now I have only to think of Catherine Morland's progression from a girl who 'had by nature nothing heroic about her' to a girl 'in training for a heroine' to catch hold of a state of mind that fits my own as I look back on the experience of friendships in my own life. I think about how eagerly Catherine connected with Isabella, and how reluctant she was to let go of the connection even when doubts about her behaviour could not be avoided.

The idea of connections has played itself into my life. I cannot explain why I connected with the Sydney Harbour Bridge simply because I was born in the year it was opened. The year 1932 is a tenuous enough connection between a life and a bridge, but often the image of the coathanger structure as well as of my birth flash in and, as quickly, out of my mind when the date crops up in conversation. My first schoolfriend Ruth and I connected over our love of fairy tales, and each of us flourished in the friendship. My first viewing of *Pride and Prejudice* is memorable today for the connections I made between Elizabeth Bennet's parents and mine, between myself and Mary Bennet as bookworms, and between Elizabeth and Jane Bennet and the girl I could only dream of being.

'Only connect,' the novelist E.M. Forster counsels both writers and readers. That is obviously what I failed to do when I first read *Northanger Abbey*. How reassuring it might have been then to follow her 'personal improvement' when I, like Catherine, was 'between fifteen and seventeen'. When I resolved to re-read the novels with a renewed spirit I was in my seventies but I connected with Catherine immediately. I also connected with the idea of the novel for what it suggested as well as what it showed me. It struck me that the young lady who raved about the novel was more than a figment of Austen's imagination. She was the embodiment of fiction in its many guises, including a philosophical exploration of how to live a good life.

I looked on my bookshelves for my copy of *Meditations* by Marcus Aurelius. The Stoic philosopher's advice suited my purpose. He tells us that the present is all we have, and at eighty years of age that strikes a true note. But then I recalled reading about the Lebanese-American poet, painter and philosopher Etel Adnan, who assures us that the condition of mortality pulls us just as inevitably towards the future. And that, for me, has proved to be just as apt.

So here I was in my eighties, indulging in dreams of the future. In the days when all girls kept autograph books, someone – I think it might have been Miss Brain – had written in mine that there is nothing wrong with building castles in the air; we just need to put foundations under them. After the quotation she wrote the name of the philosopher Thoreau. I was already living in my castle, and something told me that in the following decade I might manage the foundations as well. Already I was starting to feel that I was approaching again that most intoxicating state, the one we call falling in love – and this time it was with life.

My years at university had been a glorious present in many ways, one in which I began to make important decisions about friends and ideas. Some choices paid off; others were problematic. On re-reading *Northanger Abbey* at the tail end of a lifetime, I had the benefit of being in a new present, looking back on half a century of living from a new vantage point. And from this new present moment, the perspectives backwards and forwards didn't look so bad; the bounties I had so far received and taken for granted gave me sufficient hope to continue the journey, milestone by milestone, as advocated by Marcus Aurelius: to get out of bed in the morning, to remain sane, and to renew the taste for the cup of life, filled to the brim with fiction and friendship.

Chapter Five

Sense and Sensibility: On Balance ...

Know your own happiness. You want nothing but patience
— or give it a more fascinating name, call it hope.
JANE AUSTEN, *SENSE AND SENSIBILITY*

I was torn. But the die was cast. In 1974 we packed up
our household and contemplated life in another country.
We had decided to move to Israel for an indefinite period.
Re-reading the novel *Sense and Sensibility* in the Austen
marathon of my latter years, my thoughts turned to this
episode in my life. When Mr Dashwood's death deprived
his family of their beloved Norland Park home in Sussex,
they, too, contemplated a change. Theirs, unlike ours, was
a forced move, and they moved to another county, not to
another country.

Still, as the early chapters of the novel foretell, stories of
resettlement represent new chapters in hitherto well-ordered
lives. The Dashwood family is fortunate to be welcomed by
a new community of friends and neighbours. They can be a
little inquisitive, like Sir John Middleton and Mrs Jennings, but
Jane Austen forgives them, I think, because they are kind and
generous. The hopes of the two daughters rise and fall as new

experiences shape their thoughts, feelings and conduct.

Unlike the Dashwood family, my family was not, in any formal sense, dispossessed. But what we voluntarily left behind was precious. Our settled life on the north side of the Sydney Harbour Bridge had lasted for fourteen years. That's a whole childhood. A family of six, our ages ranged from eleven to forty-three years, and in many ways our lives were enviable.

But in the preceding years adolescent relationships had proved to be challenging for my older children. My son's moods were less sunny and more confrontational than they had been when he was younger. And my oldest daughter was in perpetual and dramatic conflict over her friendships and panic over her schoolwork. No longer was she a recipient of gold stars; instead, I became the recipient of phone calls from her school when she failed to turn up for classes. With my own parents and Mr and Mrs Bennet in mind, I tried to remain placid; but perhaps quietude faded into quiescence.

It had never occurred to me that I might one day regret the idea of marriage. But increasingly, my mood turned from disappointment to something more like melancholy. As I became lonelier in my marriage, I asked myself whether it might serve me and my children better to live independently. I felt that the traditional nuclear family was not working for me, but I was fearful of disrupting it; especially when my mother enumerated all the ways in which I would be worse off. Why had I not become more demanding myself? she asked. How could I tell her that her relationship with my father had made me dread discord?

I think of the story of Thomas Carlyle, nineteenth-century

historian and man of letters, and his turbulent marriage to Jane. Their quarrels were legendary, and their friends disagreed about who was at fault. Samuel Butler declined to pass an opinion. 'It was very good of God to let Carlyle and Mrs Carlyle marry one another,' he remarked, 'and so make only two people miserable and not four.'

In any case, I had decided to dismiss my mother's advice and try to find a better way of being together as a family.

The worst of the prospect of leaving was my own fear of failure. At times I reminded myself of Lady Macbeth's words, whose power I had felt when I played the part in a university production in what seemed a lifetime ago. 'But screw your courage to the sticking place,' she admonishes her faltering husband, 'and we'll not fail.' But it didn't work for me offstage – because, as I reminded myself, the Macbeths were planning a criminal action, not a marital separation. What if the children fell apart? Wouldn't that make me feel like a criminal? What if I fell apart myself? How would they live without me? The nuclear family at times seemed like something precious; why would I throw it away?

The idea of starting over again in another country seemed like a more creative way to seek new possibilities.

The decision to leave Australia was a shock to our parents and siblings, as well as to our friends. This new chapter in our lives started with my son's gap year. After passing his matriculation well enough to qualify for any faculty, he had no idea what he wanted to do. He would have liked to make a trip to Europe, but he settled for a suggestion to spend a year with a youth group in Israel. We farewelled him at the airport in July 1973, and in October the Yom Kippur War erupted. The experience was transforming. How could a young adult return to a life that, by contrast, seemed bland and uneventful? At the end of the year, when we travelled to Israel to see him again, we made a dramatic decision. Our son expressed a wish to enrol in a preparatory course to study architecture at the prestigious Technion, the Israel Institute of Technology, in Haifa; our oldest daughter made a case for remaining in Israel herself. Influenced, perhaps even carried away, by this expression of Jewish identity that we knew we had fostered, we put down a deposit on a townhouse north of Tel Aviv and returned to Sydney to organise the move.

Of course, this summary of events is just one way of telling the story of how we came to live in Israel for five years. It omits the nuances, doubts and uncertainties that pervaded our thoughts and conversations. There are other ways of explaining why we exchanged a secure and established existence in Australian for the unknown.

The opening sentence of Austen's novel *Sense and Sensibility* rumbled my composure as I sat at my breakfast table contemplating the loss of paradise for the Dashwood family. 'The family of Dashwood had been long settled in Sussex,' the narrator tells us. A little later, Marianne, the most highly wrought of the three Dashwood daughters, expresses her feelings: '"Dear, dear Norland!" said Marianne as she wandered before the house, on the last evening of their being there, "when shall I cease to regret you! – when learn to feel a home elsewhere!"'

The shift of focus in my mind from the Dashwoods to my

own family took me by surprise. It was many years since I had thought about the decision to start life again in a new country. I found myself reflecting that my children, too, left behind a home filled with childhood memories. I let my mind dwell on the fourteen years that they had enjoyed in our house and garden on Sydney's North Shore.

It was an autumn morning in the Southern Highlands, and the pages of the book were bathed in the soft eastern light pouring through the kitchen window. When I raised my head I caught sight of tiny crimson-and-emerald rosellas as they darted through the bronze foliage of the maple tree that I could see through the large pane of glass. I closed my eyes and visualised a different scene. I saw a low white bungalow with dark red shutters, a soft green lawn stretching out to a high photinia hedge, and a port wine magnolia tree flowering in a corner. We had bought the house from an elderly couple for whom the garden was like their child. They had nursed the back and front lawns to perfection, and terraced extensive areas with beautifully tended garden beds. Roses bloomed and heliotrope tumbled down the stone borders.

My older children came to the house as toddlers. Everything about it, especially the garden with its secret nooks and hidden crannies, took possession of their hearts. A lane between our house and the next one was a perfect track for the billycarts that my son and his friend Richard, who lived in the street behind ours, built and raced together. Our oldest daughter was thrilled with her bedroom, the frilled organza curtains, and a glimpse of the Harbour Bridge from the window. The two younger girls came home from hospital to the nursery. It was the only home they had known. As they grew older, their bedrooms were furnished to their tastes, filled with their dolls and toys and books. On the other side of the lane, a large friendly household of parents and daughters welcomed any of the children at whatever hour they chose to wander to the back door and knock.

The first chapter of *Sense and Sensibility*, like all Austen's first chapters, shows us what is at stake when lives are unsettled. It is another example of Austen's economy of means. She interweaves language, information and narrative to enrich the imaginative possibilities of the story that is about to unfold. For that and other reasons, the novel warrants more than the mild appreciation extended to it in the Austen family memoir. The themes are more complex and more carefully embedded in the novel than early readers imagined. One of these, the theme of resettlement, had escaped me, too, in earlier readings. But it touched a minor chord at this later stage of my life, given the strong memory of our sojourn in Israel.

Likewise, the story of the two older sisters hit a nerve. Their reactions to leaving one home and settling in another play into Austen's literary imagination. They serve to dramatise two contradictory modes of behaviour. Elinor's exercise of self-command requires her to hide her natural feelings from others. Her imperative is to avoid expression of feelings, but not necessarily to deny that she has them – not to herself, anyway. Her challenge is to keep the stereotypical British stiff upper lip. She succeeds superbly, if to her own cost.

Marianne's sensibility reverses the process. She wears her heart on her sleeve. There is 'no moderation' to the unrestrained expression of her emotions. This is not sensibility as we use the term in the twenty-first century, to suggest a form of sensitivity and, increasingly, a source of empathy. The development of empathetic intelligence involves a way of connecting with people and nature without losing hold of our own identity. Yes, we wonder about others and we try to imagine what it is like to walk in their shoes, but we keep our feet in our own. An eighteenth-century sensibility is something else. In the act of sympathy, Marianne loses her sense of self and surrenders to both private expression and public displays of her emotions.

I recognised these two extremes in the novel. They are rendered as suppression and expression, and I could see how I also alternated between these two states: on the one hand a determination to keep my feelings hidden in public; on the other a violent expression of feelings in private. Swinging from one extreme to the other depleted me emotionally, robbed me of my energy. It also reduced my capacity to make good decisions. That, I think, is the message Austen delivers in her fiction when she shows how mistaken Elinor and Marianne are in the presumptions that influence their decisions.

By the time I had reached the end of the first chapter of the novel, I had sorted out the complicated family history. I had familiarised myself again with the circumstances that had brought Mr and Mrs Dashwood and their family to reside on the Norland estate, and those that required them to move into Barton Cottage, now that Mr Dashwood had died. I paused. The Dashwood family's transition from their settled existence in Sussex was not a matter of choice. I, however, was implicated in the decision to disrupt my family. I needed to accept my share of responsibility. This was a case, perhaps an exceptional one, when if either of us, as adult parents, had objected strongly to the move, it would not have taken place. So there were questions to answer.

Had I capitalised on the enthusiasms of my older children as we travelled around the country, making friends and meeting members of my mother's family? If I had, I think the process was partly unconscious. It was rationalised at one level by revived memories of my father, who had died suddenly and unexpectedly at the age of sixty-five. I felt a renewed sense of his pride in the family's roots in the land of his birth and of the Bible that we had read so often together. The emotions and thoughts that enveloped me at night excited me. The idea that had been floated tentatively grew apace and coalesced into the possibility that a change of home and country might be a solution to a raft of family issues.

In an unexpected way, my night-time meanderings resonate with a technique that Jane Austen, it is postulated, pioneered; there can be no doubt that she developed it to perfection. Free indirect discourse, as it is called, blurs the boundary between narrator and character. Subtle grammatical tensions in pronouns and tenses and the removal of quotation marks work together to expose the interior working of the subject's mind. This is how Elinor Dashwood decides on the reasons for changes in her suitor's conduct towards her:

> His want of spirits, of openness, and of consistency, was most usually attributed to his want of independence, and his better knowledge of [his mother] Mrs Ferrars's dispositions and designs. The shortness of his visit, the steadiness of his purpose in leaving them, originated in

the same fettered inclination, the same inevitable necessity of temporising with his mother. The old, well-established grievance of duty against will, parent against child, was the cause of all. She would have been glad to know when these difficulties were to cease, this opposition was to yield, – when Mrs Ferrars would be reformed, and her son be at liberty to be happy.

In this dramatisation of Elinor's mind, Austen's readers are invited to witness her elaborate introspection and to share her deluded perception. We learn, as Elinor does in a later chapter, that Mrs Ferrars, although unpleasant, is not the real culprit. The reason for Edward's duplicitous behaviour lies elsewhere.

If I were writing an autobiographical novel in the third person rather than a memoir, I might use that technique to represent my own solitary nocturnal deliberations:

In her mind, Ruth tossed her feelings from moment to moment during the long night and turned her thoughts into reasons for migrating to Israel. Why shouldn't she encourage the idea? The older children were already there in their minds and hearts. And the younger girls would soon adjust. For her part, she wasn't happy anyway; and for his, an adventure with his family might make him more available for her.

Reading this paragraph, I feel that I am reading myself with new insights. I follow my mind as it looks for a way to avoid a breakdown of family life. Emulating the stylistic signature of Austen's fiction in the passage, I expose my own interiority.

I think of Shakespeare and the soliloquies that reveal and conceal hidden desires and motives.

It is this sort of inwardness that is lacking from the sparse sequence of events I described above as the reasons for leaving Australia and setting up home elsewhere. My willing participation in such a life-changing decision reflects, I think, the state of my mind as I, like Elinor, rationalised to myself the ways in which each member of my family would benefit from the disruption. I am not sure that I understood then the extent to which my decision to act was governed by my loss of confidence in the current state of my family's welfare, and my desire for some sort of transformation. The underlying state of my mind was as troubled as Elinor's. It reflected the liminal space that I had been inhabiting, shifting moment by moment from feelings of helplessness to intimations of hope.

Reading *Sense and Sensibility* again in the comfort of my rural retreat, I imagined how Austen's novel might help me understand what I had really hoped to gain from the family resettlement. I felt some affinity with both sisters as their intimate relationships disappoint their expectations and test their dispositions. Their temperaments sit at opposite poles of the spectrum: Elinor's conduct is governed by reason, Marianne's by emotion. Jane Austen called these dispositions 'sense' and 'sensibility'. And, because I sometimes notice the finer points of grammar, I see that she pulls them together with what I recognise from Mrs Eason's grammar lessons in high school as a coordinating conjunction.

I think grammar serves a useful purpose. The generation

of educators that followed my own managed to undermine confidence in the use of syntax. They forgot, or perhaps they didn't know, that an understanding of how grammar works allows us to use language in ways that make subtle distinctions and project nuanced meanings. To make the point, Flaubert, so it was reported, would spend the morning placing a comma and the afternoon removing it. It is strange that the generation that fostered the groundbreaking idea of multiple meanings in life and literature rejected as useless and boring those finer points of grammar that allow us to express more precisely what we want to convey.

I think that Jane Austen knew what she wanted to say and used her knowledge of language to help her say it as precisely as she could. So there is no way that sense is being compared with sensibility; rather, the two states of being are seen as complementary. And who can account for the specific nature of any individual reader's curiosity? I, for example, am interested in questions raised about what the terms sense and sensibility mean in eighteenth-century philosophical thought. They help me think about my own life, as I reflect on what happens when the goodness, honour and prudence for which Elinor strives is confronted by Marianne's more complicated emotional responses.

In my reading retreat I decided to explore the grammar of Jane Austen's mind. I gave in to my grammatical instincts. I decided to ponder the difference between the 'and' of Austen's title, and the 'or' that she doesn't use but that some readers have chosen as the implied meaning. I opened my old and battered copy of Otto Jespersen's essential rules for English grammar, found the small section on conjunctions, but nothing there enlightened me. The distinction between coordinating and subordinating conjunctions has no bearing on the title.

Ms Google came to my rescue, pointing out that coordinating conjunctions join two elements of *equal* grammatic rank and importance. Aha! My instinct is confirmed; it is not a matter of choice. That light-bulb moment puts Søren Kierkegaard's existential and poetic expression of the self in the picture. The Swedish philosopher asks for clear moral choices at all times. But Austen is not asking for a choice; she is suggesting that the human imagination is bigger than either sense or sensibility. It embraces both and is improved and amplified as a result.

The worst thing about memory is its unreliability. I warm to Paul Fussell's ideas about what he calls a 'modern memory' in his book about the Great War as a way of enlisting personal memories to understand cultural and historical changes. In my memory, the 1950s and the 1960s have merged into one long continuum. When I revisited Jane Austen's fiction at my leisure half a century later, I turned to the memories they evoked to look more closely at how my thoughts and my emotions meshed. I discovered while making this account of my life that profit and loss were distributed throughout those years.

Between 1955 and 1963 I had four babies: a boy and a girl born two years apart then, after a break of three years, two girls, again two years apart. That was my fairy-tale experience, if ever I had one. To my surprise, I felt great joy in being a mother-in-waiting each time. But it doesn't surprise me that my family life consumed my physical and my psychic energies to the exclusion of my wider cultural and historical consciousness.

During my reading rehabilitation I had an opportunity to calculate the losses, and in some small way make amends to myself by trying to catch up with times gone by. I felt deep regret for missing the music revolution, because that, I think now, was a moment in time when I lost touch with my older children. I am not sure how I managed to ignore what was taking place all around me, as I continued to listen exclusively to the hits of the 1950s: love songs crooned by Frank Sinatra, Bing Crosby and Mel Tormé, and the soft, slow, seductive jazz and lyrics of Nat King Cole. My two older children, on the other hand, responded enthusiastically to the music of their age. Eventually they brought the outer world into my circumscribed vision, but I didn't try hard enough to understand its relevance to their lives. I had tried hard but never succeeded in converting them to the love for fiction that had transformed my own childhood. They did not come to it naturally as I had done, although they were proficient readers and we sometimes enjoyed reading and talking about books together. But I failed to register that they found *their* meanings in music. I recognise now that the connection with music of their time, together with their own musical gifts, facilitated their reflections and satisfied their emotional needs as fiction had, at their age, satisfied mine.

My son was an enthusiastic trumpeter. I was sorry when he gave up the piano, but it proved to be the right choice and the new instrument brought him years of immense enjoyment. He played in the high-school orchestra as well as a local brass band. His practice sessions in our music-cum-rumpus room introduced me to the sound of the Tijuana Brass. The blast of fanfares stirred up my musical imagination when he practised

Herb Alpert's 'A Taste of Honey' followed by different versions of the Trumpet Voluntary.

My oldest daughter's talent was different. Her extraordinary memory for lyrics, as well as her talent for harmonising, filled our house and car with echoes of protest movements, their targets, and the drug culture. I scoffed when she insisted that 'Puff, the Magic Dragon', a song the younger daughters had brought home from their infant classes, was really about drugs. It threatened the fairy-tale vision of my children's life to which I was, by then, seriously addicted. I refused to believe that such a message would be delivered by the wholesome-seeming Peter, Paul and Mary. I listened happily to the records of Joan Baez and Bob Dylan without realising that their songs were taking young people into a world of new ideas. My children were way ahead of me. They had already grasped how radically culture was changing. The music they heard was a reflection of a generation that questioned authority, that was rebellious, that took drugs to relieve their pain and that rejected the civilities with which I defended the status quo. I didn't pay attention to the words in the same way that I did when I read books. Maybe it was different with The Beatles. It was hard to ignore such a global phenomenon, but I never warmed to anything about them. In their case, I think that I did get the message, loud and clear, and I spontaneously rejected it. The four young men represented a generational gap that frightened me because it was so confronting. Their music put me out of touch with my children. I refused either to budge or to use the music to build a bridge of understanding between us. The Beatles represented danger. They were openly, successfully and defiantly alienating my children from core values that had been forged when I was their age. In different times, as the war came to an end, the threat of anarchy had been replaced by the restoration of an established order that had made me feel safe again.

Later I realised how much I blundered, rather like Emma in Austen's novel. It was the mood of the time that I rejected. I wasn't receptive to where my children were in their adolescent lives, to what it was that made The Beatles so important to them. I missed the appeal of a musical message that resonated with their adolescent fears and longings. They were living in the moment of their rebellion, when young people recognise that they don't necessarily want to be their parents all over again. The Beatles symbolised all that. The agency they proffered was not only in the lyrics; it was in the music, in the innovations they brought to sound and rhythm. Their way of combining words and music was different and irresistible.

I might have been a better friend to my children in their need if I had recognised that my own project in life, the creation and protection of a happy family, was just a different version of the same impulse. I, too, was driven by my determination not to be like my own parents. This was a subject for conversation and sharing, an opportunity lost. If I had talked to my children about The Beatles I might have remembered the moment at which I saw Mrs Bennet in my mother and Mr Bennet in my father and made a pledge that one day I would do parenting differently.

Hidden anxieties about the state of my mind and a stubborn attachment to the dream of happy families may explain why I fell for the music and lyrics of Richard Rodgers and Oscar Hammerstein II. The story of the von Trapp family mirrored my female fantasy: a male parent's recognition that, by fulfilling

173

the needs of a family, especially a delightfully talented family, he could fulfil his own needs as well. We listened to the songs from *The Sound of Music* so often that all the children knew them by heart. On occasion, all four, musical beyond the reasonable expectation of a parent who loved music but couldn't produce a tuneful note, could be persuaded to sing one or other of the songs. Each time they performed my favourite – 'So Long, Farewell' – all my doubts about whether it was worthwhile striving for the preservation of the family unit fell apart under the weight of my sentiment and pride. These were my wish-fulfilment moments, traps of a different kind for the perplexed among women of my generation.

Even so, I remain ambivalent about the sort of love preached in the music of the sixties. Joan Didion, the American writer who caught the essence of the moment in her articles and essays, found music people such as Janis Joplin 'confusing'. Her realisation that something important but misunderstood was happening to a whole generation infuses her 1968 essay 'Slouching Toward Bethlehem'. After observing firsthand what was happening in the Haight-Ashbury area of San Francisco, she gave a report that was also a diagnosis. It was not about hippies at all, she concluded; it was about disaffected children. In her view, the hippie era ended with the Manson murders in 1969: a drug-induced massacre, with sexual inflections, of beautiful young people. Her essay was a piece of social criticism that, regrettably, I did not read until it was all over. By then it was far too late to make the essay a topic of conversation with my teenage children.

Two o'clock and time for lunch. Life in Israel brought children and parents together for the main meal of the day.

School was done and a break, lunch and siesta preceded the afternoon's activities: breadwinner back to work and children to a combination of homework and leisure. Usually I took the opportunity to read with the younger daughters before their tutor arrived to help them with their Hebrew. They were proving to be better linguists than their mother, chattering away with friends who dropped in to see the strange new Australian family that had moved into the street. I caught only a word here and there, but there was more giggling than conversation. Early signs of my children's good spirits lifted mine and persuaded me that the resettlement was going well.

One day, my older daughter was home from her boarding school in the north of the country, so we varied our after-lunch program and, instead of joining the rabbits in *Watership Down*, the allegorical novel by Richard Adams, we gathered around the record player. Of all the songs I heard that day, the one I remember most clearly is 'American Pie'. And of all the culturally significant music that I recall from that period, Don McLean's song is the one that I now wish I had taken more seriously.

After hearing it for the first time, I played it for myself many times. I think McLean's voice and words roused again those parts of me that were needy: feelings that were masked by the surge of energy brought on by the efforts we were all making for a successful resettlement for the family. I continued to sense that something was missing from my life, but it had become easier to bear. Perhaps it was because I had been thinking about art as allegory in the story we had been reading about animal displacement that the loss of the American dream touched me so deeply.

McLean takes the structure of folk music, verse-verse-chorus, repeats it six times, and turns it into an anthem for the disillusioned Vietnam generation. Deceptively simple, the lyrics are compressed as the best poetry often is. He uses every technical device that good writers use. In *When I Was a Child I Read Books*, her beautiful meditation on her life and her writing, Marilynne Robinson shares her thoughts about fiction. Narrators, she tells us, call on every resource they have to try to make the world comprehensible. That's precisely what McLean does. The references in 'American Pie' were appropriated to speculate on the compromised soul of middle America. For my children's generation, the American dream was over.

Musical, historical, political and broad cultural allusions delivered a message that I missed, because I wasn't familiar with the sources. I had been buried in domesticity for too long, and I had forgotten how to read attentively. I was asleep to signs of a more widespread breakdown of religious belief: the church bells are broken and the Father, Son and the Holy Ghost have decamped to the American coast. I had read *The Great Gatsby*, so I should have known what that means. International politics are there as well: the space race and nuclear tensions betray the promise of the past and seem to be the work of Satan. McLean is a brilliant narrator, and in this song he speaks for a generation without hope. It was a powerful message.

I re-read the novel *Sense and Sensibility* as one of a succession of chapters in my life. In this one, I, like Elinor and Marianne, had experimented with a new way of finding a balanced life. I took time to reflect on how the elemental aspects of human experience – love and loss, grief and joy, confidence and uncertainty – had played out, and I felt that, on balance, I had arrived at a better place in my life, at least for the time being.

Sitting in the calm of my Southern Highlands home, I could not have been further from the rapid pulse of my life in Israel. But I was able to recapture a sense of my own grim determination not to lose hope: not for me, for my family or, more ambitiously, for my generation of women. I recalled that not everything worked as I would have wished. It was a mixed bag. My husband was enjoying his professional life but working within a bureaucratic system had its problems. After three years, my son had left Israel with his partner and they both continued their architectural studies in London. That was an irony. But my oldest daughter was thriving as an air force officer and my middle daughter was full of enthusiasm for school and life in general. My youngest daughter was not as fortunate; her initial enthusiasm for a different lifestyle and a new language faded, and it was not until she transferred to a school with an English curriculum that she regained a modicum of her good spirits.

As for me, my life had changed, and much for the better. I had made some good friends. Miri, my neighbour, was a Professor of History at Tel Aviv University. She watched over me carefully, noticed when I showed signs of anxiety, and navigated me into the university system. She arranged an appointment with the American head of the English faculty, and I enrolled in a master's degree in English literature. I felt like one of the Canterbury pilgrims. April had arrived and the drought was broken.

Out of the blue, a second friend pulled off a coup on my behalf. Adele and her husband were passionate Zionists who had emigrated many years previously from South Africa. Adele's husband had already done us a great service when he recommended just the right boarding school for our oldest daughter. Their own children had been born in Israel. Adele sometimes confided that because she and her children did not share the same mother tongue it was not always easy to communicate at the deepest emotional level. Some people pay a high price for their passions. Adele acknowledged to me that her passion to live in Israel and raise her children in her second language interfered with the bonding she hoped for.

However, she was grateful to have secured a tenured position at the American International School, where teaching positions were highly sought after, and she passed her benefits on to me. Early one morning, I received a call from Adele. 'Can you be here by midday and give a lesson on *Antony and Cleopatra* to a senior class?' she asked. Their English teacher had been called up unexpectedly for military duty and left no notes. I gulped, said yes, and spent an hour highlighting the passages I would read aloud. I planned to invite the students to compare the love themes in the play with those in any book they had read or with love scenes in any film they had seen.

The students enjoyed the lesson, and within a few months I was invited to take up a part-time position that fitted with my university timetable. I had every reason to be as hopeful as Elinor tried to be in her new life at Barton Park, and more reason than Marianne to be fulfilled emotionally by the events that were unfolding. I found myself renewing my interest in literature and life, and as a result my thinking and my feeling lives seemed to be integrating in an unexpectedly pleasant way. When we decided to return to take responsibility for our ageing parents in Sydney following their decline in health, I was approaching the age of fifty and hoping for a happy landing when I returned home. Sadly the subsequent decade during which I established my public persona as a community identity and educator was also a time of increasing personal perplexity. So my retreat to the country cottage when I was approaching my seventies was a long overdue opportunity to find the remedy I craved.

Chapter Six

Mansfield Park: Remembering and Forgetting

If any one faculty of our nature may be called more wonderful than the rest, I do think it is memory. There seems something more speakingly incomprehensible in the powers, the failures, the inequalities of memory, than in any other of our intelligences.

JANE AUSTEN, *MANSFIELD PARK*

Regular visits to a tiny village in the Southern Highlands nurtured a sense of wellbeing as I adapted to an independent life at Lantern Hill. From the windows in my reading room I looked onto the slopes of Oxley Hill. At least once a week my little car all but drove itself up Oxleys Hill Road and turned left. To the south lies the historic township of Berrima, with its beautifully preserved Georgian and vernacular architecture, and its rows of charming little shops and eating places. I usually headed for a complex of sandstone buildings that includes the Surveyor General Inn, built in 1834, where patrons can select their steaks and throw them on the barbecue, as well as a nursery of cool-climate plants and shrubs, a rustic cafe and an emporium.

The emporium was an Aladdin's cave, a hodgepodge of small studios on different levels where a variety of merchandise was displayed: down one flight of steps for soft cashmere and alpaca sweaters for ladies; down another for gentlemen's riding gear that might have been sourced from Savile Row; another for antique bric-a-brac and trinkets; and my favourite space, where I could lose myself in nostalgia among cascades of fine Liberty lawn that reminded me of the dresses worn by Alice in my illustrated copy of *Alice in Wonderland*, and by my three daughters when they were Alice's age.

At some time during my re-reading of *Mansfield Park*, I adopted the habit of drawing on my memory, remembering episodes from my life, no doubt at times in one of the ways that Fanny Price enumerates. . I waited to release my memories until I had done my browsing and, when unable to resist, my shopping. Then I sat down to indulge in them, along with freshly baked scones and tea served in a pretty china teapot, at one of the mismatched tables in the Magpie Cafe.

I had never thought of memory as an intelligence until I read Fanny's words. Until then it had seemed more like a box that holds representations from the past. But as I read and re-read what Fanny meant by memory, I began to think of it as 'a dynamic faculty' – as scholar Sue Campbell labels it in her book *Relational Remembering* – that springs into action, sometimes as an agent acting autonomously, forming attitudes and directing behaviour. And wise little Fanny alerted me to the possibility that memory might have a mind of its own; it can be powerful, it can be unbalanced, and it can also fail.

As a re-reader of the story about a ten-year-old child who was transported from her messy overcrowded home in Portsmouth to her aloof relatives and the order and space of their home in Northampton, I noticed that Fanny took with her only the good memories. She pined for her brother William, but memories of their good times together kept love alive in her heart. And when her older cousin Edmund treats her with brotherly affection, she is better able to bear her present difficulties.

Fanny's story prompted me to wonder whether memory might have as much to do with being useful as being reliable. I had sometimes thought that other people conflate or edit their memories, without realising that this is the nature of the beast. When comparing memories with my brother about shared experiences and episodes, I realised that they often differed. When I retreated to my Southern Highlands cottage, I hoped that I might re-examine memories associated with a sense of loss and loneliness, and perhaps retrieve others that were more affirming and might, as Fanny found, redress the inequalities.

Visits to Berrima brought back many memories associated with my first job in the wider world. After graduating, I had applied for a position in a girls' boarding school in the small Southern Highlands township of Moss Vale, not too far from where, many years later, I would live in my yellow cottage. But it was not the landscape that attracted me in the first instance. It was partly the desire to leave my parents' home, which was now in Sydney. I craved independence, and the feeling that teaching might be a rewarding career inspired me to look for a resident position in a boarding school.

The school principal was a classics scholar, the youngest woman to be appointed head of a prestigious private girls' school in New South Wales. At the interview, I was impressed by Miss

G. I had been nervous about my lack of a teaching qualification; however, she acknowledged the value of a major in education in my bachelor's degree and was pleased when I offered to add speech training, for which I did have a teaching qualification from the Trinity College of London, to the subjects of English and history. I was charmed by her gracious manner, accepted her offer of the position, and agreed to take up residence, with duties, in one of the dormitory blocks.

Neither the rapport nor the rapture lasted. The principal's offer to mentor me in the art of timetabling, of which I had no experience, did not eventuate; she was always too busy. However, I soon adjusted to my senior classes, and loved reading speeches from *Macbeth* to them, and *Pride and Prejudice* with them. But I found the junior classes challenging. One girl in particular, Caroline, was more than challenging; her disruptive behaviour moved me to raise my voice. Projection, a gift on the stage, was not so welcome in the corridors of a school. Miss G. heard my voice from her office and rescued me; later, she reprimanded me, explaining that the girl, who had been sent to boarding school as she was adjusting to a new stepmother, needed more gentle handling.

Miss G. also corrected my English grammar. I was always nervous when speaking with her, and one day explained to her over morning tea that the speech-training sessions I spent with the girls were not 'that' different from the elocution lessons I had received in my youth. Using a demonstrative adjective instead of an adverb! Mrs Eason would no doubt have been disappointed, and I was mortified by my lapse.

But worse was to come. Teachers were rostered for activities after church attendance on Sundays. In my turn, I was rostered to take a group of girls for a walk across the fields to Berrima. Without map, compass or indeed an adequate sense of direction, I managed to get us there and took pleasure in my first glimpse of the tiny hamlet. The way home was a different story. We wandered around until it was dark, and a convoy of cars came out to take us back to school for a late supper. Miss G. was not pleased.

Then I blotted my copybook yet again. If not rostered for weekend duty, I returned to Sydney every Friday. I was met at Central Station by my hero, to whom I was by then engaged. The first train for Sydney left at four o'clock, and I finished teaching for the week at noon, so I hit on the idea of hitchhiking. By catching a ride to Liverpool, from where frequent and regular trains ran into the city, I could be in my hero's arms at Central Station before the country train had even left Moss Vale.

I did not think of this as flouting convention, but when Miss G. caught wind of my routine, she changed my timetable so that I had afternoon classes every Friday. A few weeks later I handed in my notice. It was accepted without demur. In that moment, I felt the weight of disapproval with which Lizzy Bennet was greeted by the Bingley sisters when she strode across the muddy fields to visit her sister at Netherfield. I felt no more shamed than Jane Austen's heroine had, and I returned to live in Sydney feeling as though I had gained in independence and would be able to hold my own in my parents' house.

A small second-hand volume of *Jane Austen's Letters, 1796–1817*, selected and edited by R.W. Chapman in 1955, lay open on the window seat in my bedroom, where I settled myself to re-read, and remember past readings of, *Mansfield Park*. I had picked it up during a browse at the popular paradise for book lovers located over the hill that I could see from my reading room.

I was already habituated to driving up and over Oxleys Hill Road, especially in autumn, when the beauty of rolling green expanses and spectacular displays of golden, scarlet and bronze foliage transformed it into a breathtaking landscape. Descending the hill from its peak, I turned right whenever I wanted to spend a few hours among the endless rows of new and old books in Berkelouw's Book Barn. Over the years I found copies of many novels written by Charles Dickens, a few of the Brontë novels, and treasured copies of *Pride and Prejudice* and *Mansfield Park*.

The barn – which has since been made over to incorporate a fine-dining venue – has a history that is also a story; aptly because both 'story' and 'history' are related to the Greek word for learning by enquiry. A proper enquiry into the property that became the Book Barn uncovers a long history of First Nations homelands and the presence of a number of clan and language groups. In a startling coincidence, given its later usage, the site has been a traditional teaching place for educating children in Dreamtime stories. Two centuries ago, a parcel of land in an area with the Aboriginal name of Bullio was granted to a private citizen by Governor Lachlan Macquarie. In 1977 a Dutch family of antiquarian booksellers who had survived the Holocaust acquired the estate and transformed it into a repository for their huge collection of rare and second-hand books, a mecca for book lovers from all over the state.

I drank many cups of excellent coffee in the cafe while poring over my purchases of second-hand classics. I don't have the mind of a collector; my criteria were dictated by my preference for books I have already read, in embodiments that will sit comfortably in my hand or find easy lodging in a medium-size handbag. R.W.

Chapman's *Letters*, for example, measures fifteen by nine and a half centimetres; it is one centimetre thick. I favour leather or board covers, fine paper and clearly defined fonts.

As Chapman's small volume was at hand, I thought I might as well begin my re-reading of *Mansfield Park* with Jane Austen's letters to her sister. In this way I could pay homage to another of my favourite novelists. E.M. Forster also wrote a novel about a place that is occupied by a family with conflicting moral positions and challenged by changing times. The edifices, Howards End and Mansfield Park, are not particularly distinguished by their architecture, although they are both pleasant enough. But each offers a moral challenge to the people who reside there.

Forster opens *Howards End* with three letters from Helene Schlegel to her sister Meg. It is an inspired jump into the narrative. I want to pay him a tribute, because he was among the first to distinguish the pretensions of some of Austen's admiring readers from the novels she wrote. He praised her own leap of literary faith, from the flat characters in the entertaining novels that she borrowed from the circulating library to the rounded, complex and finely layered heroines who have inspired readers, filmmakers and other storytellers as well.

I applied Forster's sentence quite literally, flipping through the letters in Chapman's collection and pausing when my eyes rested on an appealing word. 'Your Lilacs are in leaf, ours are in bloom,' the writer informed her sister, her 'dearest Cassandra', in spring of the year 1811. I paused to look across a rose bed and a stretch of green lawn to a herbaceous border and my very own lilac tree in full bloom. Lilac, often taken to symbolise love, was one of Austen's favourite trees. After comparing the state of the lilac with that on her brother's estate in Kent, she continues. The horse chestnuts, she informs Cassandra, are 'quite out', and the elms 'almost'. I was thrilled by the coincidence. I had recently removed an overgrown elm from my own garden, but I had replaced it with a horse chestnut.

These connections between the letters, the novels and personal memories are reading moments to be treasured. Like many of Austen's readers, I have wished at times that Cassandra had not destroyed some of the letters and censored others with her scissors. She must, however, be forgiven. She may have wanted to save embarrassment to family and friends; her sister had a gift for the comic but scathing comment. Or perhaps, like the heroine Elinor Dashwood, she considered the observation of privacy in the case of personal letters to be a moral imperative. So I put aside the precious collection and turned to the first of the novels published in Jane Austen's Chawton years.

Following Mr Austen's retirement and the passing of the rectory at Steventon to the eldest son, James, in 1801, the family rented accommodation in Bath or took breaks to visit relatives. After Mr Austen's death in 1805, the women were joined by their friend Martha Lloyd, and spent four years wandering around the southern parts of England. They lived in rented properties, spent time with relatives and finally shared a house in Southampton with the family of Frank, the sailor brother who was born between Cassandra and Jane and who eventually rose to be Sir Francis Austen, an Admiral of the Fleet. The arrangement saved money and also meant that Frank's wife and children had company while he was at sea. But it must have been a relief when Mrs Austen and her daughters were offered permanent accommodation.

It was in a renovated bailiff's cottage on Edward's estate

at Chawton in Hampshire that the three women together with Martha settled at last. Why it took Edward so long to accommodate the female members of the family is a question often asked. It is speculated that the death of his wife, Elizabeth, following the birth of her eleventh child enabled Edward to make the offer. Although Cassandra and Jane often stayed with Edward's family at Godmersham Park in Kent, their role was as much that of family help as family visitor. The aunts developed loving relationships with their nieces and nephews, but it appears that Jane was not especially popular with her sister-in-law.

Perhaps Elizabeth passed on some of her distaste to her oldest daughter, Fanny, although aunt and niece had always been exceptionally close. I shuddered a little when I read a letter in which Fanny, late in life, assured a younger sister that, without the assistance of Mrs Knight who had adopted Edward, both Jane Austen and her sister, Cassandra, 'would have been, tho' not less clever and agreeable, in themselves, very much below par as to good Society and its ways'. Had Fanny, the favoured niece, understood anything about her aunt's social criticism? How was it possible that she signed off the letter with a reluctant endorsement of society's opinion rather than a disclaimer of its manners? I do not expect the perspicacity of Virginia Woolf, who wrote: 'Never did any novelist make more use of an impeccable sense of human values. It is against the disc of an unerring heart, an unfailing good taste, an almost stern morality, that she shows up those deviations from human kindness, truth and sincerity which are among the most delightful things in English literature.' But the fact that Fanny was a woman of her time does not excuse her snobbery, given the hours she spent in conversation with her brilliant and adoring aunt. That bond, it seems, was superseded by matters of class, even though Fanny's father was also her aunt's brother.

I read *Mansfield Park* for the first time, I remember, during the long summer break between the first and second years of my arts degree. I had read *Pride and Prejudice* at school and *Emma* for Miss Herring's course. I don't recall much of the critical commentary; only the famous passage in which Walter Scott compares Austen's exquisite delicacy to his own 'bow-wow' style of writing has secured itself in my memory. I don't remember either why I chose to read the fourth published novel at that stage, rather than either *Northanger Abbey* or *Sense and Sensibility*. They might have been more logical choices, but *Mansfield Park* was, unbeknown to me at the time, a more auspicious one.

There are three volumes to *Mansfield Park*, in the style of the conventional three-decker novel of Austen's time, each with its own centre of narrative gravity. In the first volume, the heroine is introduced as a child. We skim through her first five years in Northampton in two chapters. After all, as Austen informed Anna, another favoured niece, one does not care for girls until they are grown up. By the time she turns fifteen at the beginning of the third chapter, Fanny is established at Mansfield Park. Aunt Norris's behaviour towards Fanny is abhorrent; she torments and exploits her, mentally and physically. Some readers compare Lady Bertram's treatment of Fanny to her husband's exploitation of slave labour. But the sort of 'serious noticing' recommended by James Wood in his book of the same name is a corrective to this charge; the nature of Sir Thomas's investments in Antigua is not specified in the novel. Austen's point about life at Mansfield Park can be made closer to home. Under Edmund's tutelage, Fanny gradually becomes educated, through reading and conversation, in ways that put to shame the Bertram girls' traditional education, which emphasises rote learning and the primacy of facts.

Sir Thomas, Fanny's patron, displays an odd mixture of compassion and reserve in the farewell he makes to her as he departs England to oversee his investments in Antigua. After delighting her with an invitation to her brother to visit Mansfield Park, he adds: 'If William does come to Mansfield, I hope you may be able to convince him that the many years which have passed since you parted, have not been spent on your side entirely without improvement – though I fear he must find his sister at sixteen in some respects too much like his sister at ten.'

I was once told by mother that I was too short and too plump. She equated my appearance with my chances of finding a husband when the time came. That is what I think of when I read Sir Thomas's words, and I understand why Fanny's eyes were red; not, as her female cousins declared, because she shed crocodile's tears at her uncle's departure, but because she felt that she was deeply disappointing to someone whose approval she craved.

I think she was wrong, and perhaps I was wrong about my mother, too. Later in life, I realised how deeply my mother was entrenched culturally in ideas about female appearance and the marriage imperative. So perhaps was Sir Thomas when he referred to the fact that Fanny's slight sixteen-year-old body was not so different from the way it was when William made his first visit. His expression of surprised delight when he returns a year later to find her more robust seems to endorse my surmise.

Of course, it is what happens in the year of his absence that changes Fanny, physically and psychologically. She becomes more engaged in the social activities of the household as Sir Thomas's authoritarian presence fades and the family relaxes. Life is enlivened and complicated by the arrival in the neighbourhood of Mary and Henry Crawford. The sister and brother offer more sophisticated and worldly companionship and unexpected romantic possibilities to which the Bertram siblings readily capitulate. The visitors are catalysts for moral predicaments that only Fanny and Edmund recognise. And Edmund is so smitten by Mary, and Fanny so disorientated by her increasing romantic attachment to Edmund, that the points of their moral compasses start to spin.

Much narrative energy is invested in putting on a play once Sir Thomas is out of the way. When Fanny's cousins and their new friends decide to rehearse and perform for their own entertainment, as the Austen family did while Jane was growing up, it may well be that the author was drawing on past experiences to test her more mature moral position. Austen family memories offer a record of high jinks in the barn as James and Henry, the oldest brothers, recruited members of the family, including their vivacious and sophisticated cousin Eliza de Feuillide, to take on the roles. I can see Jane Austen looking on in high glee at the flirtatious rivalry of the two brothers for Eliza's favours, whether unmarried, married or widowed as she was after her French husband was guillotined. Even then Jane's imagination must have been stirring, and it is not hard to see vestiges of Eliza in the irresistible Mary Crawford.

It takes time to see through the charm and allure of Mary Crawford in the novel, as William Deresiewicz explains in *A Jane Austen Education*, his account of how he was challenged by Jane Austen. His perceptions changed as he started to notice things in the seductively glamorous crowd he was mixing with in his non-fictional life. I, too, observed things about the social set with whom I consorted when I was a young wife. In some ways, the bonds of friendship were strong; we collaborated in picking up children from school and delivered meals to other mothers when they were sick. But when it came to flirtations the rules changed. There were rules, if not moral standards. One of our male friends declared sententiously that making a play for your best friend's wife was off limits.

No one was off limits for either Henry or Mary Crawford. However, many readers find the fictional Crawford brother and sister irresistible, despite continuing evidence in the novel that pursuit of their own happiness inflicts pain on those they called their friends. By comparison, Fanny Price is considered 'dull and dreary' – even, according to Kingsley Amis, one of her harshest critics, 'a killjoy, a blighter of ceremonies and divider of families'. In his earliest of many readings of the novel, Deresiewicz describes Fanny as passive aggressive and Mary and Henry as free and charming, glittering spirits who bring light and energy into the sober world of Mansfield Park.

Later readings changed Deresiewicz's mind. His views of Henry and Mary shifted as he had more varied encounters with people who led a glamorous life. He calls it a process of mutual illumination. *Mansfield Park*, in fact, taught him something about those experiences, which in turn showed him something about *Mansfield Park*. In the end, he notices different things about Fanny: her strength of character as well as her capacity for 'learning'. I hoped that my own re-reading journey would serve me in the same way – that I would notice aspects of the novel that I might have missed in the past, or notice them differently because of the changes in my own life; and perhaps find in them insights to make my own future brighter and more affirmative.

Deresiewicz confesses that he never did grow to like Fanny and never disliked the Crawfords as much as he knew he should. In admitting how they continue to fascinate him, he reveals something about himself and, more significantly, something about what it is to read in the context of our own individuality and our unique life patterns. Freedom of mind is the prerogative of both reader and writer. As individuals we decide whom we like and whom we forgive. In his final reading for his book, he finds Fanny admirable but dull. I wonder if his view will change as life brings him additional encounters with his peers.

Memory connects me with Mansfield Park – the place – in a way that I discovered only when I re-read the novel later in life. I read again about 'the little girl [who] performed her long journey in safety', from Portsmouth, where she lived in poverty with a large unruly family, an incompetent mother and a feckless father, to a new and much grander home, where she had been taken in by relatives as an act of charity.

The circumstances and details are different, but the idea of a small child and a relocation to a strange house transported me to a long-forgotten memory of my own. It was a soft summer's evening on the beach. My parents, my brother and I were having a farewell picnic the night before we children were to spend some months in a nearby house. We were playing happily near the water, country children for whom the sea was a novelty. My brother pointed out the imprints of crab claws in the damp sand. They went sideways. We traced them with delighted curiosity.

Quest Haven was a spacious house not far from the beach where we had our picnic of fish and chips. It was a place where children could be left temporarily for 'quality care', and we were to stay there while our parents were abroad. The connections between Fanny, Quest Haven and Mansfield Park are slight, but that's the way memory and fiction were beginning to work for me. So in re-reading *Mansfield Park* I relived my time at Quest Haven.

I was younger than Fanny, and I was not expected to work for my keep, but I, like her, had to learn to live in a hierarchical household, separated from a beloved brother by barriers imposed by our age difference. In the sprawling house there were rooms set aside for circumscribed age groups: 'little' children like myself, 'middle' children of my brother's age and 'big' children whom I don't remember seeing at all. Each age group occupied a space that was out of bounds to the others, at least as I remember it.

Reading again about young Fanny, I empathised, perhaps even identified, with the emotional deprivation she suffered at the hands of relatives. I empathised even more deeply with her longing for her brother William, who had remained at home in Portsmouth; that was more personally relevant. Moments together with my brother, unless stolen, were few and far between. I felt lonely, lost and confused, and longed for his company. I remembered the timidity with which I crept to the door that separated us. When Tom Bertram, the oldest sibling at Mansfield Park, called Fanny Price a creep mouse, I wanted to shake him.

My heart engaged with the heroine who was called, to my consternation, 'a female prig-pharisee' by one of Austen's greatest admirers. What could Reginald Farrer, the writer and botanist, know, I asked myself, of the impact of homesickness on a child who feels abandoned and powerless? How did he, who memorialised Jane Austen with an abundance of praise on the centenary of her death, miss the truthfulness of Austen's depiction of a forlorn child who succeeds finally in discovering and safeguarding her own moral compass?

It is all about how we read and especially when we read, I suppose. Farrer has proved to be, in many ways, an inspired and influential reader of Austen's fiction. He wears a virtual milliner's shop of hats: first and foremost as a perspicacious reader, but also as public servant, playwright, novelist, botanist, flower painter and traveller. His tribute to the power of Austen's fiction to sustain multiple readings is rapturous: 'Thus it is that, while twelve readings of "*Pride and Prejudice*" give you twelve periods of pleasure repeated, as many readings of "*Emma*" give you that pleasure, not repeated only but squared and squared again with each perusal, till at every fresh reading you feel anew that you never understood anything like the widening sum of its delights.'

My understanding of and delight in the novels has been amplified by Farrer's readings, but in the case of *Mansfield Park* I suspect that he does not have in his memory reservoir, as I do, the lived experience of a bereft child.

I had discussed my experience of Quest Haven with a psychoanalyst when I was at a low ebb during my forties. We considered how those months might have shaped my disposition, my personality and my relationship with my brother, to whom I clung ferociously in my heart. We even paid lip service to the concept of childhood abandonment. But nothing about the way I felt actually changed. It was only when I surrendered myself to re-reading *Mansfield Park* with an open mind and engaged with Fanny's resistance to male authority that I felt as though a remedy might already be at work, dissolving the source of pain, freeing me to learn from Fanny's example when she rejected Henry Crawford's suit, that audacity of mind might be masked by diffidence of expression:

> 'I *should* have thought,' said Fanny, after a pause of recollection and exertion, 'that every woman must have felt the possibility of a man's not being approved, not being loved by some one of her sex, at least, let him be ever so generally agreeable. Let him have all the perfections in the world, I think it ought not to be set down as certain, that a man must be acceptable to every woman he might happen to like himself.'

The boldness of Fanny's claim struck me as extraordinary. Despite its linguistic indeterminacy, Fanny's thought propelled me right into the present moment and the many ways a man assumes, as Hedda Gabler noted in Ibsen's play, that he is the cock in the yard.

Then I remembered the mothers. Miri, my neighbour in Israel, for example, was outspokenly proud of the virility of her handsome sons. It was the 1970s. Germaine had already spoken. But my kind friend, with her PhD in history and a budding interest in psychology that led to her subsequent training as a Lacanian therapist, unaccountably took pride in her sons' sexual conquests and the number of women who found them irresistible. This does not diminish Miri in my eyes, but it opens them to the complicity and collusion of generations of women in producing sons who take their entitlements – emotional, sexual and personal – for granted.

* * *

The theatrical elements of *Mansfield Park* connected with where I was in my life when, in the summer vacation of 1949, I first read the novel. I had spent many months of that year deeply immersed in rehearsals and performances. Furthermore, I had just recently emerged somewhat bruised from an episode in which my judgement and my sense of principle had been tested. So matters of conscience and the development of moral fibre in Fanny Price spoke immediately to my own state of mind.

The background to this life-changing episode returns me to the university quadrangle and places me at the noticeboard close by the Philosophy Room, a landmark for my almost-friend Lillian. A new dramatic society, the Sydney University Players, had been formed and the initiators were calling on students to bypass the established Sydney University Dramatic Society (SUDS), with its limited opportunities for newcomers. I joined a handful of students to attend an inaugural meeting the following week.

Two extremely handsome first-year students who had been involved in theatricals at the prestigious boys' school from which they had matriculated the previous year chaired the meeting. David, who went on to become a celebrated and often controversial Queen's Counsel, was clearly in charge. He had a flair for rhetoric and a cultivated radio voice: rich, deep and beautifully modulated. He explained why he believed that we, as newcomers, would never be cast in SUDS productions, given its established clique of actors.

The second-in-command was more theatrical. Robert's blond hair was swept back from his broad forehead, and he approached the lectern carrying *Acting: A Handbook of the Stanislavski Method*, from which he read with histrionic panache, assuring us 'there is another kind of theatre. You come in and take a seat as one of the audience. Without your being aware of it, the director transports you from the world of the audience to that of the stage where you become a participant in the life being depicted in the play. Something has happened to you. You no longer feel like one of the audience.'

Elaborating on the text, Robert displayed his skill as a communicator; he would go on to a career as a psychiatrist. His advocacy for Stanislavski inspired me. In my mind, I put aside everything I had always admired and hoped to emulate in an actress like Sarah Bernhardt. Her genius for imposing her charismatic self on dramatic characters was no longer my goal. I wanted to act in the Stanislavski way: to disappear into the character and the drama, so that the audience would think of no one but the character I was playing.

Within weeks the new society was functioning. A small group of politically minded students – from a less socially but more academically elite boys' school than David and Robert – attempted a coup. A couple of them came from prominent Labor families and pushed for a selection of plays that carried social messages. But they drifted away after failing to find the large cast required to produce *Strife*, John Galsworthy's play about a confrontation between miners and mine owners. I was disappointed. When we auditioned, I had been cast, to my surprise, as Madge, a sexy working-class girl. It was unlike any role I had imagined playing, but it gave rise to a new view of who I might become on stage.

I absorbed myself in this drama of intrigue within the Players. It gave me a sense of living on the edge of what mattered in life. Once the takeover had been quelled, David came into his own as an autocratic but highly effective leader. Without further consultation, he decided that we would prepare a production of

Ibsen's play *Ghosts*; and without auditions he posted a cast list, a rehearsal schedule and a performance date in June. I found myself in the lead female role of an emotionally distraught mother. David cast himself as the doomed son, Oswald, and appointed himself producer as well.

Imagining Ibsen on one side and Stanislavski on the other, I stepped into the role of Mrs Alving, determined to bring her to life using the vocal strategies and techniques that I had practised in Miss Brain's sitting room. The production was performed in the Union Theatre, where a barber shop by day became a dressing room by night. David proved to be a producer/actor extraordinaire. He organised the hire of sets and costumes; rallied a team of stagehands and lighting technicians from among students in the schools of architecture and engineering; and, at the age of seventeen, he directed novices like me and the rest of the cast with superlative aplomb.

Our performances as anguished mother and despairing son received ovations on the night and good notices in *The Sydney Morning Herald*. Lindsay Brown, a drama critic who was not renowned for being charitable, wrote of Mrs Alving – more or less, according to memory – that the actress moved through the labyrinth of fate with grace and dignity. It wasn't a lot, but it served my ego well.

I was enormously excited when I attended the first-night party hosted by the Norwegian ambassador. This was another of David's triumphs, this time wearing his promoter's hat. The room thronged with a more sophisticated crowd than I was used to, drawn from embassy staff, higher echelons of university faculty and some of David's more patrician social circle. When I saw the elegant women in attendance I wished my mother had allowed me to buy the sleek velvet dress I coveted when we went shopping in the David Jones department store. But it was expensive. So we walked across Castlereagh Street to the popular boutique called Coral Lea and walked out with a shiny green taffeta dress, frilled at the hem.

Perhaps my youthful appearance accounts for the surprise and also the extravagant praise with which I was greeted on arriving at the party. The transformation from middle-aged Mrs Alving on stage to a sixteen-year-old girl dressed in green taffeta might have been slightly baffling. But wasn't that exactly what I had aimed for, when Robert had read to us from the Stanislavski handbook? And my brother's comment, when I arrived home to tell everyone about the party, pleased me more than any other: 'A few minutes after you came on stage,' he said, 'I forgot you were my sister.'

Ibsen's *Ghosts* has risqué sexual content, like *Lovers' Vows* in *Mansfield Park*, and was also bound to cause consternation in some quarters. Again, David's political instincts came to the fore; he consulted Clive Evatt MP, who was assistant treasurer in the Labor state government and had been an active member of SUDS in the 1920s, about censorship issues. Receiving an assurance of support in the event of any difficulties, the canny producer invited Evatt and his family to the first-night performance and party. On a more personal level, Dr and Mrs N. from Leeton, who now lived in Sydney and were excited that I was to perform, had asked my mother whether she was aware and perhaps alarmed that the play was 'about syphilis'. My mother answered no to both questions, and to her credit, she was not in the least perturbed. On the night, my dear friends sent me a huge bouquet of flowers and were among the first to come backstage and say how much they had enjoyed the production.

I had not been in the least agitated by the sexual elements of the play. Nor was I surprised by the possibility of censorship. I was learning about sexuality in books, if not in practice. During the previous year, while preparing for the English Honours examination, I had read *The Picture of Dorian Gray* and everything I could find about Oscar Wilde. I had also discovered George Bernard Shaw. On Speech Night I had been presented with two volumes of his plays inscribed in my Latin teacher's elegant handwriting to the 'Dux of Fourth Year'. Shaw distinguishes between his 'pleasant' and 'unpleasant' plays. In his preface to *Mrs Warren's Profession*, one of the 'unpleasant' plays, he wrote that he had written it to draw attention to the true social and economic causes of prostitution, and continued: 'I could not have done anything more injurious to my prospects at the outset of my career. My play was immediately stigmatised by the Lord Chamberlain, who by Act of Parliament has despotic and even supermonarchial power over our theatres, as "immoral and otherwise improper for the stage".'

Reading Shaw's plays and his prefaces taught me to regard literature as a way of thinking about the ethics of behaviour. I invested all my beliefs about human conduct in trying to understand Mrs Alving's dilemma as she decides whether or not she should assist her doomed son to take his life.

When I read *Mansfield Park* for the first time, at the end of the year in which I played the role of Mrs Alving, I connected both the novel and the drama with ethical ideas about virtue and moral significance. This was not just because Fanny and Mrs Alving are shown to be wrestling with crises of conscience. Fanny must decide whether she can refuse to take part in the theatrical on principle in the face of social disapproval; Mrs Alving's is a starker dilemma. But questions about virtue and moral salience were more personal as well.

Not long after the successful production of *Ghosts*, I had received a summons. I could not believe that I was making my way through the once-unfamiliar quadrangle and a small walled courtyard to have afternoon tea in the office of the vice-chancellor, whose wife had issued the invitation. She spoke to me as the patron of SUDS. She had been in the first-night audience, and I now recognised that she had been among the guests I had met at the embassy party. She complimented me on my performance and wondered if I would be willing to audition for the role of Lady Macbeth in an upcoming SUDS production.

This was an unusual twist to the story of exclusivity that had attracted me to my own drama group. Usually, casting for the major SUDS production of the year, the Shakespeare text that had been prescribed for school leavers, was preordained, and came from within the ranks of the society. This year, it appeared, none of the regulars was thought suitable to play the role of Lady Macbeth, and so their patron had offered to approach the person who played Mrs Alving. Me? It seemed like a dream come true.

Of course I was flattered. And I was tempted. But it also meant breaking ranks with my Players comrades, who were, by now, my best friends. Questions of rivalry, loyalty and principle were involved. Discussing the offer with them, I sensed ambivalence, but no one advised me against accepting the role. I agreed to meet the more glamorous set who ran the established society and was seduced by their charm. Reading *Mansfield Park* so shortly after the event, I recognised that I was not immune to the allure of the Crawfords. I succumbed.

I turned up for weeks of rehearsal in a small city hotel with a theatrette on the top floor. It was a dark musty space that smelled of greasepaint and perspiration, but it was adequate for performing one-act plays. Other venues were found for major productions. After the first enthusiastic greeting, the core SUDS membership more or less ignored me. I learned a lot about voice production and stagecraft from the director, who started each session with exercises in voice projection that amplified what I had already learned in Miss Brain's sitting room. But Sam, the director, was a testy man, and on one occasion he threatened to replace me with George, a young male actor, so that the production would be true to Shakespeare's time. In another quirky coincidence, the same young man was the member of the Push who became, according to Milliken's biography, Lillian Roxon's first lover.

I relished the role, but my relationships with my original friends among the Players never recovered, and taking a bow at the end of each performance, the thrill of applause and recognition was diminished by my moral compromise.

Still, I continued to act, for both SUDS and the Players, and there were highlights in my theatrical career that were life-enhancing. I was able to emulate, to applause, Dame Edith Evans's famous delivery of 'the handbag' line, as Lady Bracknell. The production of *The Importance of Being Earnest* took place in the Wallace Theatre, where I had listened to Miss Herring and met Emma Woodhouse. The Players took a production of Jean Cocteau's *The Eagle Has Two Heads* to an intervarsity drama festival in Hobart. We played there in the beautiful small Theatre Royal, which had been renovated for the visit of Sir Laurence and Lady Olivier only a few years previously. Allan B., who joined ABC TV a few years later as executive producer, was a dream director. His civility and courtesy were unparalleled as well as being sincere. When he used his habitual address, 'dear heart', I really felt that it was for me alone. And he gave me my head, encouraging me, in my role as a reclusive queen, to bring an element of melodrama to the twenty-minute monologue that dominates the first act of the play – less Stanislavski and more the Grand Guignol of Sarah Bernhardt. Our production was received as one of the two outstanding entries of the year.

I believed my acting days were long behind me when I had one last hurrah on stage. My friend Allan K. was the instigator. I had met him in the crowded Wallace Theatre back in the days of undergraduate lectures, but it is not lecture halls that I associate with this good friend. That was where we went to listen to lectures. My memories of Allan are memories of talking: wonderful conversations about our futures as we wandered around the quadrangle, sat on the lawn in front of the Great Hall, or drank bitter black coffee at a Manning House table. On Friday evenings we dressed up and met for a gin and tonic in the Palm Court of the Australia Hotel, talking above the musical ensemble, as likely as not about our introduction to T.S. Eliot's fears for western society, a wasteland that we were not above celebrating as we tinkled our spoons in our cocktail glasses. We were young and optimistic; we talked loudly and laughed a lot.

A somewhat indolent student but an outstanding tennis player, Allan moved among the university academic and sporting elite with grace and wit. He also excelled at friendship. After taking as long as possible to complete his bachelor's degree, he surprised us all by pursuing a successful career in radio and television. (As the inaugural producer of *Play School*, he was named as one of the most influential Australians in *The Bulletin* magazine in 2006.) In the late 1960s he gathered the stalwarts from our university days and established the Sydney University Graduate Theatre. It was a realisation of a dream as he chose and directed plays in the company of his friends. Casting for his production never seemed to be a problem for Allan. Arthur Dignam, Terence Clarke, Henri Szeps, Leo Schofield and his then wife Anne, all of whom became identities in Sydney's arts world, rallied to Allan's call.

At first I resisted the suggestion that I should act again, on the grounds that I had four young children, it had been a long time, and I had lost my nerve. But Allan knew the difficulties I was experiencing around my identity and encouraged me to believe that I had a gift worth preserving and a reputation worth reviving. He asked me to read Christopher Fry's verse drama *The Firstborn* and offered me the role of the Egyptian princess, Anath.

The play dramatises the story of the Jews' exodus from Egypt, but, unusually, the emphasis falls on the death threat to the firstborn son of the Egyptian pharaoh. The drama reaches its climax when Anath pleads with her brother to let the Jews leave Egypt in order to save the life of his son, a role played by a young, nervous and inexperienced Henri Szeps many years before his rise to fame.

My friend probably guessed before he asked me that victory was assured. I knew it would be difficult to make arrangements for rehearsals and performances, but as soon as I read Fry's poetic lines I ached to deliver them in a theatre, almost more than I had wanted anything in my married years. I dropped the children at my parents' apartment while I rehearsed on weekends. I remember registering that my father looked pale and unlike himself when he returned the children to the rehearsal venue a week before the play was due to open. A few days later he had a massive heart attack, but then appeared to recover. Disappointed to miss the opening night, he was interested in every detail when I sat by his bed and described the stage setting and the audience reaction to the high drama in which death is an invisible presence.

On the second weekend of our scheduled performances we had a Saturday afternoon rehearsal followed by an evening performance, and this one did for me something that method actors dream of: it generated an atmosphere that transcended words and actions so that, as a performer, I lost all sense of personal identity. Following our final curtain call I whispered to Allan, 'I felt death take my hand tonight'. He put his arm around me and led me offstage to where my husband was waiting to tell me that my father had died during the afternoon.

Re-reading *Mansfield Park* sixty years after my first reading, I had connected my malaise with the sense of loss I experienced at Quest Haven. But I found my centre of interest shifting with the times in different ways. In my earlier reading the first volume was especially relevant to my lived experience. Questions of performance and moral choice in the novel had taken centre stage as a framework for thinking about my involvement in theatre and its impact on my friendships and my conscience. When I turned to the novel in the twenty-first century, I could not ignore the fact that I was living in a different historical world. In a post-colonial age, attention must be paid to questions raised by Edward Said's analysis of *Mansfield Park*. He read the novel as emblematic of a cultural tradition that is inextricably bound up with European colonialism. That does not mean Said has the last word when he places Jane Austen first among the suspects in the literary canon. Recent scholarship suggests that he neglected to probe sufficiently the politics of Jane Austen's family. Nevertheless, as a contemporary reader I can't afford to ignore Said's criticism of Jane Austen for reasons, he claims, associated with the upholding of ideals about the British empire. I can, however, pay greater attention to the text than he does, even though my reading, too, reflects my past and present experiences, memories and beliefs.

Sir Thomas has returned from overseeing his investments in Antigua that support the lifestyle of Mansfield Park. He comments on the improvement in Fanny Price, 'a fine blush having succeeded the previous paleness of her face'. Although the nights are no longer as merry as they were in his absence, Fanny seems to enjoy the quietness along with her uncle. And she loves to hear him talk of the West Indies. She assures Edmund that she talks to her uncle more than she used to:

'. . . Did not you hear me ask him about the slave-trade last night?'

'I did – and was in hopes the question would be followed up by others. It would have pleased your uncle to be inquired of farther.'

'And I longed to do it – but there was such a dead silence!'

This direct reference to the slave trade has become the catalyst for a whole new area of Austen debate. In my reading of the novel I have found it less fruitful to explore the pros and cons of Austen's complicity in imperialism than to reflect on the changing nature of the youthful Fanny's moral awareness as she raises a lone and unanswered voice within the walls of Mansfield Park. The dead silence belongs to the Bertram family, not to Fanny Price – and certainly not to Jane Austen, because the words are there in the text.

Within the comforting walls of my reading refuge, I reconsidered what I had learned from re-reading *Mansfield Park*. There is something about stories that helps us to understand our lives. I already knew that. Whether myths, legends, fairy tales or fictions in their varied forms, fantastical stories attract human beings at the deepest level of feeling. Marina Warner, who has dedicated her work to understanding why we love stories, believes that the world inside the head is as important as the world outside, and that the difference between the world we experience and the world that is imagined – she uses the word 'conjured', which suggests to me a sort of magic or spell – starts to play a significant role early in our childhood. She draws attention to the *Arabian Nights*, those extravagant imaginations that my father gifted to my brother and me as bedtime stories. The exotic tales offered us imagined 'others' from whom we each learned something, possibly something different, about ourselves. Maybe they made my brother into an adventurer, a successful risk-taker like Sinbad, for that's what he proved to be in his adult life. I, on the other hand, more akin to the hero of Stefan Zweig's *Beware of Pity*, seemed to lack the strength required to shrug off a burden that was perhaps of my own making.

My friend Betty, whom I met when I first arrived in the Southern Highlands, had given me Zweig's novel to read and insisted that I keep it for future reference. I was beating my breast about what I might have done to the stability of my family when I decided on a separation. She insisted that I should read Zweig's story of a man whose good nature prompts him to accept a heavy burden: marriage to a girl with a physical disability because she is the daughter of a valued friend. There are, of course, other considerations; the girl is sweet and rich. But the increasingly unwelcome prospect of continuing in the marriage merges into an exploration of pity in its diverse forms ranging from 'weak and sentimental' to 'creative' kinds of pity.

Reading about Fanny and thinking about the negative ways in which her diffident nature has been understood, I started to consider a third perspective and wonder whether I had fallen into an unacknowledged state of self-pity.

In her book *Once Upon a Time*, Marina Warner identifies the defining characteristics of fairy tales. The stories they tell, she says, are short, they are familiar, they mix the familiar with the unfamiliar, they are imbued with accumulated wisdom, and they are linguistic entities. Such stories are consoling, Warner tells us, leading listeners and readers into more optimistic mental and emotional landscapes.

Putting down my copy of *Mansfield Park*, I surveyed the lovely landscape through my window; the tranquillity, warmth and brilliance that Emma had experienced after a storm were now much closer to my inner feelings. In the landscape of Jane Austen's imagination, I had followed the deepening tensions between Fanny and Mrs Norris as the latter resents Fanny's enhanced status within the family. I had considered how Fanny's future role at Mansfield Park seemed more assured as questions of justice around the management of the Bertram estate highlight the struggle to identify and preserve a personal set of values. My re-reading of the novel raised some of the issues that I had encountered during my earlier reading and reaffirmed, in the light of Fanny Price's brave stand against male coercion, my determination to act according to my values but in my own interests.

I reminded myself of Austen's genius for representing the warp and weft of light and shade in her fictional universe. It comes back to Miss Brain's ideas about modulation, the transfer of aesthetic concepts to the real world, and the imaginative union of memory and text. My recent re-readings had added new dimensions and new memories to my own imaginative resources. More specifically, some of the shadows cast by experiences in Quest Haven and later moral dilemmas, those lost and those survived, had been dispersed by the sunshine of remembered pleasures in the domain of the theatre. The magic of reading felt like a remedy for my once ailing soul.

Chapter Seven

Emma: A Critique of Love

Never, never could I expect to be so truly beloved and
important; so always first and always right in any man's eyes
as I am in my father's.

JANE AUSTEN, *EMMA*

Pride and Prejudice, *Mansfield Park* and *Emma* were the novels I
had re-read most frequently in the years before I undertook my
reading remedy. I had returned, too, to *Persuasion* and *Sense and
Sensibility* from time to time, but I cannot claim, as many Austen
readers do, to have re-read each of the novels every year. I was not
quite as assiduous as Catherine Helen Spence, an Australian writer
and social activist born in Scotland in 1825. (Like Jane Austen more
than a hundred years later, she appeared on a national banknote;
in Spence's case it was the Australian five-dollar note issued for the
centenary of Federation.) She wrote that 'so great a charm have
Jane Austen's novels had for me that I have made a practice of
reading through them regularly once a year'. She applauds Austen
for her 'exquisite miniatures', but her praise suggests that she read
the novels for the same pleasure and in the same way each time. If
so, she would have lost the most valuable advantage of re-reading.

I am pleased that I have learned to read in a different way, rising with each reading to a greater understanding of Austen's fictional domain, placed by every reading in a different stage of my life and finding a different significance in each novel. When I thought about these shifts before reading *Emma* one more time, I recollected that from my very first reading of the novel I had turned to ideas about love when thinking about the heroine. I had framed my first perspective of Emma in her motherless state. Because Thelma Herring introduced her students to Emma as a motherless girl, I wondered what it might mean to Emma to have lost her mother before she could even remember her. In subsequent readings, I reflected that a form of self-love, encouraged by an indulgent governess and companion, might have put Emma's development at risk and threatened the natural progression towards emotional maturity. I thought about how the requirement to love our friends and neighbours tests our judgement and our emotional resources and, finally, how we fix our minds on what we want from ourselves and from romantic love. As I approached the novel again, I formed these perspectives into a constellation of ideas about love itself that I would apply to whatever imaginations about my own life might be stimulated by the narrative.

If, as Reginald Farrer, whose essay I often re-read, proclaimed with gusto, the pleasures of the novel *Emma* are inexhaustible, then so, too, is its investigation of love in Emma's life: filial love, neighbourly love, romantic love, love of others, self-love and love of self. Emma's loving relationship with her father is tested on the wedding day of her governess, Miss Taylor. As Mr Woodhouse settles himself to sleep after the wedding, his daughter contemplates future evenings as an adult alone in his company. She resolves that nothing should change. That scene was enough to evoke an image of my own father. I put the book aside and stumbled into a light-bulb moment: a realisation that my relationship with my own father had, unlike Emma's, deteriorated as I formed independent ideas about my place in an adult world. He remained as permanent a presence as ever in my emotional landscape, but I found myself resisting him as our ideas diverged, rather than separating in a way that established my autonomy while retaining the intimacy and trust of our childhood relationship.

It had not occurred to me that my father would die young, as sixty-five surely was even in the 1960s. I was definitely not prepared for the shock. I was not prepared, either, for the intensity of my grief; a feeling that I had lost something as vital to my life force as a kidney or a lung. For months after my father's death I was haunted by the whiteness of his face when he had returned the children to me after my final rehearsal for *The Firstborn*. It had been a windy August afternoon, and he was wearing, as he usually did in the cold weather, a woollen scarf that he called a muffler wound around his neck. A soft felt hat was pulled over his forehead at an angle like the one actor Humphrey Bogart wears as he farewells Ingrid Bergman in the film *Casablanca*, and memory has conflated the melancholy mood of the film with the mood of that day.

My father adored his grandchildren, and they had hugged him as they said goodbye. I remember feeling a renewed rush of love as I saw how much pleasure they took in each other's company. My oldest daughter clung to him; she reminded him, he always told her, of his mother, the singer of his childhood

215

lullabies. She claimed a special place in her grandfather's heart, as he does in hers to this day. I felt a flood of gratitude, too, because he never refused to help me out when I needed a babysitter for weekend rehearsals. The memory of his face on that day recurred constantly as I adjusted to the pain of no longer having a father. I don't remember feeling guilt for the way we had grown apart, but certainly I felt regret.

The tenderness of Emma's love for her father and his for her evoked that memory as I continued my Austen odyssey. I had thought of Mr Woodhouse as a fussy but lovable old man who doted on both his daughters, but especially on Emma as his remaining companion. It doesn't take long to realise that he also has a tendency to put himself at the centre of the little world in which they live. The English poet Matthew Arnold, I had read with surprise, liked the nickname of 'Mr Woodhouse'; I wonder if he detected a note of familial subversion as well as devotion. I had noted Mr Woodhouse's fussiness around his daughter's health, and indeed his own, and thought of him as overprotective. On re-reading the scenes in which he imposes his wishes on Emma, I considered for the first time what their relationship conveys about the nature of a father–daughter love, and respected Emma as she remained calm and loving when dealing with 'habits of gentle selfishness'.

In my later re-reading I paid more attention to the language. I took account of Emma's 'gentle sorrow' on losing the presence of her beloved governess in her everyday life and recognised that there is no 'shape of any disagreeable consciousness' in her sorrow. Here, in the first chapter, we have a glimpse of an Emma whose feelings are at odds with the careless behaviour we witness later in the narrative. She resigns herself, we are informed, to a succession of evenings of 'intellectual solitude' in her father's company. As a reader, I found plenty of faults in Emma, but she treats her father, always and wholeheartedly, with both love and respect, even when it is not necessarily in her own interest. This, the educator Maxine Greene believes, is what empathetic love is all about. As I immersed myself in the novel, I noticed for the first time that Emma eventually learns to embrace others as well with the empathetic gentleness she has previously reserved for her father, her sister and her nieces and nephews.

At last I could see how Austen helps us to love Emma in spite of herself. 'I am going to take a heroine whom no one but myself will much like,' she warned, and I have always marvelled at the clever means by which the author ensures that her prediction does not come true. Somehow, Emma survives all her faults, and the novel becomes a testament to the nature of empathetic love, and to the reward of good and attentive reading. Austen enables us as readers to learn from experience as Emma does. She gives us, each time we see Emma with her father, an intimation of her potential for improvement, a goal for all Austen's heroines, and shows us that it stems from the nature of her unconditional affection for her father. The gradual way in which this dawned on me was accompanied by pauses to think more searchingly about my relationship with my own father.

Mr Woodhouse is fairly transparent. My father was a complicated man. He was more akin to Mr Bennet, whose selfishness was of a less gentle kind. Nevertheless, there is a common thread to the behaviour of all three. My own father, like both fictional fathers, was invariably successful in asserting his own will; recalling this, I went down a long-forgotten memory path to a period in my life when I had resisted my father's single-mindedness in the only way I had available. I had never thought about it consciously until that moment, but now I recalled how, as I grew older, I had refused my father's requests to recite for him as I had obediently done as a schoolgirl. Claiming that I had forgotten the words, I declined to give him the pleasure he asked for. Looking around me at my lovely reading space and out at the vision of trees and sky, I reminded myself that my present good fortune was funded by his bequest. In that moment, I realised I possessed a steely determination that I had not previously acknowledged.

I think that my refusal to recite was the only way I ever defied my father and, to be fair, he made few demands. But my resistance was the only way I knew to separate from him, emotionally as well as politically. These two elements became inextricably bound up in each other as I started to develop political orientations that differed from his own and our relationship grew less intimate. We continued to share our pleasure in stories and poems, sometimes in magic moments like those in Rome when we recited together by the River Tiber, but we were increasingly at odds about questions of justice and fair play.

I have no idea why or when my father developed an unswerving hatred of anything and everything associated with communism, but the mention of the word and the suggestion of the ideology roused him to a state of fury. The two volumes of plays by George Bernard Shaw that I received as a school prize were my initiation into ways of thinking that led me away from my father's black-and-white view of how the world works. Shaw's plays and his prefaces introduced me to ideas that confronted the concept of truth to which Jane Austen brings her own brand of subtle scepticism in the first sentence of *Pride and Prejudice*.

Having no Google at my disposal in those days, I had no easy access to information surrounding the issues, but by that time we had a public library in town, and I hunted down essays on socialism, Fabianism, and Beatrice and Sidney Webb in the pages of the *Encyclopaedia Britannica*.

If my father had read the sentence, 'it is a truth universally acknowledged that in our society men are born equal, and men and women are treated equally', he would have nodded his head in affirmation. Of that I feel as sure as it is possible to be without his say-so. As far as he was concerned it would be sinful to say otherwise; in Australia, he believed, we lived in a perfect society, one that had enabled him to escape religious persecutions and to rise in the world. The matter came to a political head between us when we went to see the film *Pygmalion* at the Lyceum Theatre. My father thought that Alfred Doolittle the dustman, father of Eliza the heroine, was hilarious. He laughed himself into a coughing fit as he mimicked his lines and his dialect on the way home in the car.

We had just crossed the railway line when I ventured the opinion that the character was more than comic; Alfred and Eliza were examples of the unfairness in the way the world works. Eliza shouldn't need to learn to speak differently, I argued.

My father pulled over the car and turned off the engine. He was angry in a way that I had rarely seen. He reminded me that he paid good money for me to learn how to speak in my elocution lessons, and I needed to think about where that money came from. If I didn't approve of money, I might want to stop my lessons.

The argument was no more rational or sophisticated than that, and I sensed my father's determination to control my thoughts.

That may have been another line we crossed at that moment. But when, years later, I saw how he doted on my children I warmed to him again. And six decades on I was reminded by Emma's empathy for her father that perhaps I could have done it differently, that the emptiness I had experienced deep-down when he died might have been a symptom of unfinished business. My sole consolation was the thought that I had recited my father's favourite psalm, the twenty-third, at his funeral memorial.

Emma, the 'Book of Books'. That is how it is described by Reginald Farrer in my favourite piece of Austen criticism. He has a vast reservoir of knowledge to feed his imagination, and he draws on this to capture the essence of each of the six novels. He is vehemently opposed to the idea that Austen was limited in her creation of fictional worlds. It stems, he says, from a view of Jane Austen as a person of absolute propriety. Too little is known about her to make claims about who she was or what she understood. All we really have to go on is the novels themselves. And I agree with Farrer: they show that she understood the world she lived in better than most of her contemporaries.

Farrer loves the novel *Emma* above all the others. It receives his most extravagant praise, for in that book, he proclaims, 'the whole thing is Emma'. His admiration for the creation of a perfect book with an imperfect heroine is shared widely by readers who are both devoted and well informed. Some share his praise for the creation of Emma as a character who represents the peak of English high comedy. And some, like me, come to love Emma over time and slowly, as we read and re-read. It took time for me to overcome my irritation with Emma's easy assumptions of entitlement, not only to her privileged life but also to knowledge itself: she is undoubtedly the proverbial know-all, and know-alls are rarely endearing.

If reading *Pride and Prejudice* was, for me, especially about learning to read, then re-reading *Emma* was more generally about acquiring a love of reading in the very act of reading. Reflecting back on how I have been affected by the novel over the years, I think that I began a journey towards empathetic engagement on my first reading of the novel at university. The concept of empathy and its implications for connecting with fictional characters was not then part of the critical vocabulary, however. I cannot remember thinking in those terms until a review of my Holocaust survivor teaching resource commended the oral-history project I had designed for appreciating the central role of empathy in teaching and learning history. I have come to understand that empathy is not the same as either mere sympathy for or total identification with something outside the self; its purpose is to encourage autonomy as well as imaginative engagement with whatever 'the other' happens to be: a person in real life, a fictional character, even 'just' a book.

Strangely it was a film version of *Emma*, rather than the novel, that awoke in me an awareness of the deeply hurtful consequences of the heroine's unempathetic behaviour. It was not the 1995 film *Clueless*, although its loose translation of the novel has been the most popular among younger Austen fans. That film made me wonder how anyone could get Emma so wrong. As Roslyn Arnold, master teacher, insisted when the film was coupled with the novel for study on the English syllabus, Emma is *not* clueless at all; rather, she follows carefully plotted clues until she reaches a better understanding of herself, her relationships and her place in her own small world. I have tried to relate to the popular culture of a group of Los Angeles teenagers in the mid-1990s, but every viewing has left me feeling cheated. I cannot find it in me to respond empathetically to characters who shriek and bicker their way through a seemingly meaningless succession of social encounters. I miss complexity in both the heroine and her cohort of idle friends. Yes, it could be argued that Emma's neighbours, although more subdued, engage in similarly trivial pursuits in the customs of their own time. But somehow the humour associated with charades and dancing and even hat-trimming has a sharp, pointed relevance to larger human concerns, while *Clueless* makes no such claims for the leisure activities of the American high-school students. They failed to show me anything I might have missed in reading *Emma*, the novel.

That is the point of making a film about a novel, surely: to illuminate or enrich or comment intelligently on the novel that is being glossed. The fundamentally faithful film version of 1996 achieved that for me. While nothing from *Clueless* has filtered back into my re-readings of the novel, my subsequent readings of *Emma* have been enriched by the reimagining of the more traditional film. It may be a little syrupy at times, and Harriet is seriously miscast, but Gwyneth Paltrow, the actor who plays Emma, registers powerfully, with both face and body, the appalling cruelty of her taunt to Miss Bates. One can see that she fully comprehends the failure of empathy that Mr Knightley explains in the novel: 'Were she a woman of fortune, I would leave her every harmless absurdity to take its chance, I would not quarrel with you for any liberties of manner. Were she your equal in situation – but, Emma, consider how far this is from being the case. She is poor . . .' I was shattered by Paltrow's performance, her Emma's spontaneous recoil from her own behaviour. That scene remains the most memorable to me of all attempts to translate Austen's fiction into film. Still, the stylish version released in 2020 has its wonderful moments as it exposes the flaws in Mr Woodhouse's disposition, perhaps to the point of caricature. The sense of class entitlement is sharply observed when even Mr Knightley, the finest of men, takes it for granted that his valet will pull up his socks.

In the garrulous but unfortunate Miss Bates, Austen, in the novel, creates a character who, true to life, rouses both irritation and pity. Who in life has not met someone similar to Miss Bates? Who has not been, like Emma, similarly unaware of the impact of ill-considered words? Who has not wondered whether, on occasion, their own behaviour has been as irritating as hers? In each case, a little reflection is called for, and self-reflection is the habit that Emma has not developed under the guidance of her indulgent father and her doting governess. It takes Mr Knightley to turn her in that direction.

Re-reading *Emma*, I lingered over the incident at Box Hill. I scanned my own hill and drifted into a reverie about what it means to be empathetic, as a reader and as a human being. I poured myself a glass of locally produced white wine from the vineyard on Centennial Road, and savoured the subtle flavours of herbs, lemongrass and chamomile. I pondered the discipline required to discriminate – not just between flavours, but between different aspects of the human disposition. On the one hand, Emma had been pitiless in taunting Miss Bates. But from another perspective, it is clear that the quality of Emma's pity is strained to the utmost by the duties she is expected to perform as first lady of the village.

Reimagining the scene with the film in mind, I wondered at the subtle means by which the novel *Emma* gives fresh meaning to the historically trivialised Golden Rule, 'love thy neighbour'. Here, as in *Pride and Prejudice*, we are confronted by questions about universal truths. Rules, which have the ring of universality about them, are put to the test in Austen's fictions. It is true, as Mr Knightley assures Emma, that absurd people put themselves at risk of ridicule. But Miss Bates is an exception to the rule; she is poor. *Were* she to be Emma's equal, he says, using the subjunctive mood, she would not be an exception. The quality of empathy that Knightley's rebuke stirs in Emma is the key to her change of both mind and heart as she considers the impact of her thoughtlessness on a powerless person. And it is more than that. The development of an empathetic disposition is what sets Emma on the path to her own selfhood. As I sipped my delicious wine, I thought that it was a lesson from which I, too, could learn.

On the opening page of my first copy of *Emma* I had circled the word 'seemed' in the first sentence: 'Emma Woodhouse, handsome, clever, and rich, with a comfortable home and a happy disposition, *seemed* (my emphasis) to unite some of the best blessings of existence; and had lived nearly twenty-one years in the world with very little to distress or vex her.'

In the margin I had written 'subjunctive/doubt?' I remember now that Miss Herring read the passage aloud twice: only the second time did she stress the word 'seemed'. That was to make us aware that good writers have subtle ways of using language to cast doubt on what seems to be a straightforward statement of fact.

The opening sentence of *Emma* has neither the elegant phrasing nor the philosophical reach of the famous sentence about universal truth in *Pride and Prejudice*. But in a more down-to-earth grammatical pattern, the sentence is imbued with Austen's gift for irony and for foreshadowing what is to come. She also demonstrates and optimises the subtleties of the subjunctive mood. She uses it to show readers that Emma's existence is not as blessed as it seems. Her irony is realised as Emma experiences, in scene after scene, the distress and vexation from which she had been shielded by her governess.

After Miss Taylor's wedding, Emma plunges into a succession of projects that backfire. Her projects follow, all in the subjunctive mood. It *seems* to Emma that her friend Harriet will be better off married to her putative suitor, Mr Elton, than to her existing suitor, Mr Martin. It *seems* to Emma that Frank Churchill must be in love with her. It *seems* to Emma that Jane Fairfax must be in love with her friend's husband. In fact, nothing is as it *seems* to Emma as a person or *Emma* as a novel on first reading. As readers we arrive at this understanding over time; as *a* reader, I wondered if I needed to learn this about my own life as well.

Perhaps I made the marginal note about the subjunctive mood to emphasise the syntactical condition of the word 'seems'. I had long been familiar with and interested in the grammatical term. I had enjoyed grammar in my English, Latin and French classes, but my special interest in the subjunctive is probably due to my mother. I was intrigued by the pride she took in using it, and in her ability to use it correctly. It was, for her, a sign of being educated. And as I read the novel over time, the circled word invariably prompted thoughts about the choice of what I named a subjunctive life, or a life valued for what it 'seemed' to be rather than what it actually was. I wondered whether this view of life might be a characteristic of my own maternal bloodline and even a source of intergenerational anxiety.

It probably starts with my grandmother Hannah, whom I never met. I felt that I knew her, though, from the photograph in which she sits, composed and gravely beautiful, among her seven daughters. They range in age from young adults to my mother who, resting against Hannah's knee, looks to be about four years old. They are a fine-looking lot of girls, dressed immaculately in white dresses without frills, except for one, apparently the best-looking and, my mother explained, Hannah's favourite; her dress has a flounce at the hem.

My grandfather is there, too, a religious man with a bushy beard and a black hat. Isaac's duties as a priestly Jew left him little time to work in the printing firm where he edited and copied sacred texts, so it was a blessing that Hannah's religious background enabled her to earn extra money as a teacher. They must both have cared about their reputation, how they 'seemed' to others. When the sixth daughter was born, the one before my mother, Isaac Cohen decided that the baby was to be named Ahuva, a Hebrew name that means 'beloved'. This was so that no one would think they were disappointed not to have had a male child. It is inconceivable to me, given the times and the circumstances, that Isaac was not disappointed. But perhaps I am mistaken. Perhaps it was his assurance to the deity to whom he prayed three times a day that he bore no ill will for the arrival of yet another female mouth for his wife to feed.

I was always fascinated by Hannah's story. When my mother shared her memories with me, I think she sometimes forgot that I was her daughter. I became the audience she needed to keep her family alive in her heart, and she spoke with an intensity that etched Hannah's story into my memory. Or maybe it is because my grandmother's story carries fairy-tale elements that it gave such a powerful stimulus to my young imagination.

Hannah's family came from Kobryn, in what is now Belarus. On a passport document issued in 1906, Hannah's father's occupation is listed as tradesman, but this may have been for practical reasons. According to family legend, he was a gifted religious teacher and astronomer, so perhaps my grandmother, like Jane Austen, received her education by listening to her father's lessons to the boys to whom he gave tuition in his own home.

The gradual transition of the family from Eastern Europe to Canada and then to America began with a son called Jacob in about 1889. He was next in age to my grandmother and, like Jane Austen and her brothers Francis and Charles, to whom she was close in age, they had a special childhood bond. But by the time Jacob prepared the way for his family to migrate to a land that offered the family both religious freedom and more opportunities to rise in the world, Hannah had long been settled in Palestine in the home of a childless aunt.

Hannah's experience has become the stuff of fairy tales in my imagination. The aunt may not have been a wicked stepmother, but she certainly played a key role in removing Hannah from her heartland as well as her homeland when she offered to relieve the overburdened family of one of the daughters when she migrated to Palestine with her rabbi husband. Hannah's older sister had been selected initially, but she had a boyfriend. On the day of departure she hid, so the younger girl was plucked up in her stead. A few years later, Hannah was married off by her aunt and uncle to a penniless and profoundly religious man whom she had never met. Hannah resented her husband from the start for his inability to provide the basic necessities. I gathered from my mother, who

227

spoke of her father as a kind, clever and good man, that Hannah never grew to love her husband, or to forgive him, either.

While I was deeply immersed in my re-reading of Jane Austen, I was contacted by a member of my mother's American family who was working on a family tree. The family in America had prospered; I could not help wondering if they had ever realised or acknowledged the straitened circumstances in which Hannah and her large family lived. If they had received the black-and-white photograph of the parents and their daughters, perhaps they had not guessed. Perhaps it *seemed* to Hannah's relatives that she and her daughters, like Emma, had very little to distress or vex them. I pondered whether Hannah experienced some degree of bitter disappointment in her own fate, and whether this had passed to my mother who, as the youngest daughter, might have been, like me, her own mother's special confidante. Intergenerational trauma on a small scale, perhaps? This was a possibility I had never considered, but it became part of my reflective process.

Hannah's story and her shaping influence on my mother's and, indirectly, my own sensibilities is not yet over. Her determination to dress and educate her daughters in ways that eschewed the label that poverty might have imposed on them led to an exceptional opportunity for my mother. How Hannah managed it I cannot imagine, but she seems to have been as determined as she was beautiful and succeeded in enrolling my mother in a prestigious school for girls. The school had been established in Jerusalem by a philanthropist from the English branch of the Rothschild family. It was meant to cater to the daughters of wealthy Jerusalem families, for whom an English curriculum might lead to higher education in England. A few poorer girls were eligible if they could manage to get an interview and pass a fiercely competitive selection process; somehow, Hannah pushed her youngest daughter over the line.

This time a fairy godmother appears by magic. Miss Annie Landau, the school principal, took a liking to the little girl wearing her one pair of shoes and her neatly mended hand-me-down clothes; she showered her with gifts: language, book loans and propriety in the English manner. It was as though the awe-inspiring woman who was known by the city's intelligentsia as the Queen of Jerusalem guessed that one day my mother would need to know about tea parties and calling cards and wearing hats and gloves in some faraway place. But neither she nor my mother could have guessed either the circumstances or the destination.

Hannah was as busy and determined as Mrs Bennet when it came to finding husbands for her daughters. With all but my mother, the youngest, married off she was optimistic when approached by a matchmaker in search of a bride for an Australian doctor. Six weeks later, my mother and my father were on honeymoon in Venice, posing among the pigeons in St Mark's Square. They both look trim and elegant in the photographs. My mother is wearing a fur coat that had been sent to her by her sister Ahuva, who had married an Argentinian furrier and was by then living in Buenos Aires. My father looks like the complete dandy, sporting a small moustache and wearing a three-piece suit.

Once settled in the dusty township that became her home, my mother must have thanked Miss Landau from the bottom of her heart. Her familiarity with the protocols and courtesies of English society must have smoothed the path as she settled into the incongruous formalities of a social life among the wives of doctors, dentists, bank managers and prosperous shop owners of what had only recently been called Bagtown.

The local people were charmed by my mother's 'beautiful English', and she herself vaunted her faultless use of the subjunctive mood whenever it came to what Miss Landau had taught her about 'iffing and wishing', as she called it.

To those conditions I added 'seeming' when I first read *Emma*. My later re-reading of the novel connected with my personal life in ways that I would not have imagined in earlier readings. This time I related to the notion of 'seeming' in a more personal mood. To observers, my mother must have 'seemed', like Emma, blessed: gifted, charming, pretty and prosperous. While it was Mrs Bennet with whom I originally connected her, I realised there might also be a drop of Emma's blood in her veins.

As a daughter, I had wanted to make a claim on my mother's heart, but I think I realised at an early age that she was depleted by her obsession with the family of parents and sisters she had left behind. Hannah might have been the same if not for a penurious husband and seven daughters whom she was determined to educate. She must have put thoughts of her birth family behind her as she became the rock upon whom her children depended. She also expected and probably deserved a return on her investment.

The only condition my mother made on accepting my father's proposal was that he would continue to support her parents as she had done since she left school and found employment in the public service of the British Mandate government. After her marriage, she worried every month until her parents died that my father would forget to send the bank draft or that it might not arrive in time to pay the house loan to which the married daughters continued to contribute. Every week she wrote letters to her parents and sisters, making everything about her life 'seem' perfect. And she often talked about them to me with what I understand now was a yearning in her heart. Recalling the tangled web of mother–daughter relationships that was as much my legacy as was my beloved Lantern Hill, I wondered how much more I might learn from Jane Austen's examination of the human heart.

The copy of *Emma* that sat alongside my notebook when I attended Thelma Herring's lectures, with the question about the subjunctive, is the one I continue to read for leisure and pleasure. It is not scholarly, it has no introduction, and I now have at least five other editions for reference, each with a thoughtful commentary by an Austen expert. My most recent acquisition, published by Cambridge University Press, has its own story: I won the beautifully produced set of nine volumes of Austen's work at a Jane Austen Society conference that I almost missed because of a traumatic family bereavement. Too tearful to remain for the afternoon session, I left my bundle of raffle tickets with a friend. When I returned in the evening, I was greeted with the news that I had won the first prize. My fellow Austen readers, knowing of the family bereavement, were happy for me; consolation from the universe, a friend remarked.

I go to the Cambridge volumes when I need them for reference. But they don't have the notations, some in pencil and some in ink, that greet me like old friends when I open my original copy of *Emma* with its faded pink hard covers and slightly frayed edges. I had received a fine-quality Parker fountain pen from my parents when I matriculated, so, with my copy of the novel and a thick exercise book, I was well equipped for note-taking when I attended the first lecture on the novel.

Our favourite topic in Miss Herring's tutorials had been, of course, Emma herself. It was refreshing to meet other people who cared as deeply and talked as freely about heroines as I did. Over a few sessions in our smaller tutorial group, there was a shift from the will to judge Emma to a willingness to understand the frustration of a talented young woman with limited choices in life. Discussions at school had been less stimulating, less open to debate. Having older males in our group charged the dynamic with a frisson I had not experienced before. Despite the age and gender differences, we became a sort of reading fellowship, drawn together by our interest in Emma the girl, in *Emma* the novel, and in each other.

I had never had older friends, but I came to know some of the mature men in the tutorials that were held in smaller rooms off the quadrangle. I found that age was no barrier to friendship, at least when sharing thoughts about fiction and fictional characters. I usually sat next to Arthur and Ray, who had served in New Guinea and were then in their late twenties; closer to my age than Mr Knightley was to Emma's. They had both joined the Sydney University Players, too, and we started to mix socially on weekends when we met in Hyde Park for our own version of picnics and parties. It all got a bit complicated when elements of romance crept in, something for which these new friends seemed to me to be too old. Advances were rejected, the message was received graciously, and no hearts were broken. But later, considering George Knightley's romantic reticence as I re-read the scene in which he tells Emma that if he loved her less he would have been able to talk more, I thought of how I had succumbed eventually to a youthful boyfriend for whom talking came almost too readily; and how I had extrapolated, as mistakenly as Emma, from our endless conversations that married life would continue in that vein.

Among the books on my shelves I found another precious reminder of Miss Herring's lectures. My better-preserved copy of *Aspects of the Novel* by E.M. Forster is slimmer than *Emma*, and the blue-green cloth cover is embossed with the author's entwined initials stamped in gold. First published in 1927, the volume contains a discursive introduction to a series of lectures on, yes, just what it says in the title, aspects of the novel: story, people, plot, fantasy, prophecy, pattern and rhythm. In his essays Forster uses Jane Austen as a benchmark for talking about everything that he considers significant for forming an opinion about what makes fiction work.

Forster's conclusion seemed incontrovertible when I read my 1949 pocket edition. He wrote that although the next 200 years would no doubt yield enormous changes in the subject matter of novels, human beings and what matters to them would remain unaltered. That sort of thinking was turned on its head by the European philosophers who emerged from the war years with theories that have changed the way we understand ourselves, culture and society. We can no longer count on certainty, they tell us. The golden days of 'theory' have come and gone, as the literary critic Terry Eagleton has noted. Eagleton is clear that things will never be the same again. The ideas of Foucault, Derrida and other such influential thinkers, with their subversive and original theories about what culture represents, are embedded in the public consciousness and also in prevailing assumptions about meaning and certainty. We are no longer the same people we were when Forster made his prediction. Many of us no longer think the same things, let alone say them. Culture changes with us and is changed by us. According to research, technological change of a kind and a degree that Forster could not have contemplated has physiologically affected the way the brain works in the generation that was born into the internet age. Who would have thought?

So Forster got it more wrong, in some ways, than the science-fiction serials such as *Flash Gordon* that my brother and I watched at the Lyceum on Saturday afternoons. As often happens, it is fiction that comes closer to the truth.

The idea of connection crops up incessantly in what I read and has become integral to the way I think. But as I connected the dots, as my mind wandered from *Emma* to Forster, sitting in my reading room so much later in life, I realised that connection was what I had lost as my life fell into separate fragments. Could reading novels, even Jane Austen's novels, put Humpty Dumpty together again? Because, it suddenly became clear, that was what my re-reading project was all about.

I came across the field of neuroscience and the knowledge it produces almost fifty years after I read what Forster had to say about fiction. Like Forster, neuroscientists sometimes use Jane Austen as a benchmark when trying to understand how fiction works in the brain. Austen's novels have the peculiar attribute of being both popular with readers in search of entertainment and endlessly interesting for those who turn to fiction as a source of illumination about literature and the human condition. I am always happy on Jane Austen's behalf when new ideas about fiction fit comfortably with the young lady's manifesto in *Northanger Abbey*. Even though this new knowledge has led to all sorts of theories about how the brain has adapted to reading, and how literature is an aesthetic experience that plays with the brain in specific ways, it has no argument with Austen's views that good novels transmit powerful ideas, successfully create characters who remind us of the people we know, and use all the resources of language to illuminate the complexities of the human condition.

Nothing as complicated as a meeting between fiction and neuroscience was in the air in 1949, when my fellow students and I met with our tutors to consider the language and the structure as well as the characters and the ideas in *Emma*. But I so enjoyed the experience of Miss Herring's lectures that I was prompted to think then, for the first time, that to be a mistress of literature in the classroom might really be, as Elizabeth Bennet said of being mistress of Pemberley, 'something'.

It was a new thought. My friends from school, Ruth and Dianna, had enrolled at the Sydney Teachers' College, but I was unsure what I wanted to do. I had in the past thought about law. I had been a successful debater at school, often leading my team to victory in interschool competitions. 'You should do law,' one of my teachers said. 'You would be a good barrister.' I canvassed the idea during an interview with the university student adviser, but she was not encouraging. 'There's no point unless you did Latin Honours at school,' she said. So when it happened that thinking about teaching a novel like *Emma* to a class brought on a little thrill of excitement, I was pleased that I might have stumbled on a potential vocation.

I changed my mind when I experienced the excitement of acting, and the satisfaction that came from assuming and stirring to life the persona of a stranger. I changed it once again as the prospect of marriage overtook my theatrical aspirations and I looked for an interim occupation; interim, that was, to the promise of domestic bliss. It was then that I recalled the tutorials on *Emma* that had transformed my idea of reading as a shared pleasure. The promise of repeating the pleasure with young readers in my own classroom had taken me to Moss Vale and introduced me to the natural landscapes and cultivated gardens of the Southern Highlands.

In 1996 Hermione Lee produced a new biography of Virginia Woolf who had been, in her lifetime, one of the most perceptive commentators on Jane Austen's characters, her heroines in particular. A remark that Woolf makes about herself catches my eye. 'How I interest myself,' the novelist wrote in her diary, conveying a strong sense of her own achievement. I can imagine Emma Woodhouse making the same comment, and I agree with Woolf's biographer that Jane Austen would have said the same of herself, but in a totally assured way and without a shred of Virginia Woolf's lingering emotional fragility.

I, too, have found myself interesting, and I can honestly say that even when I have felt sad I have never felt bored; there is always something to think about, something to fire my imagination. Early in my life I confided in Connie, the secret friend of my own invention. As I grew older Connie disappeared from her home under the bed, but conversations have continued in my head space as I played out the pros and cons of beliefs, opinions, attitudes and fundamental values rather like *Alice in Wonderland*. Re-reading *Emma*, I connected with the heroine and the way that loving one's self might be a recompense for what seems to be missing in reality. It occurred to me as I followed Emma's trajectory that she learns to discard the narcissistic elements of self-love that have put her at the centre of every relationship, while preserving a sense of self-worth and generating the resilience required to move forwards to an improved state of self-knowledge. This seemed to be a model worth considering.

Of course, I was more than sixty years older than Emma when I reached this understanding of her psyche, but it occurred to me as I returned to my reading that it was not too late for me, that there is no time limit on the human will to change. I like the idea of what the critic Lionel Trilling calls intelligent love, the state of mind and imagination that he discovers in Emma when she reaches a better understanding of herself and others. There is solace to be found in the idea of love, like memory, as a form of intelligence. And I marvelled at the endless opportunities provided by Austen's heroines to learn about love. It is a matter of reading again and again, and always attentively. She always 'holds up' to attentive reading, as her admirer Thornton Wilder wrote. And although Jane Austen's life might have been narrow in its range (including her presumed sexual inexperience), just as her novels might have been limited in their social scope, her observations and ideas grow in the rich and fertile soil of an imagination that inspired me to put other versions of love, the love of reading empathetically and love of self, at the centre of my life.

Chapter Eight

Persuasion: Second Chances

I can listen no longer in silence. I must speak to you by such
means as are within my reach.

JANE AUSTEN, *PERSUASION*

Tamar arrived in the Southern Highlands on the morning train
from Sydney. She was a striking sight, a woman with short jet-black
hair and a sculpted jawline. We embraced with warmth. I had not
forgotten how much I loved the company of my laughing Israeli
friend. While waiting for her on the station platform I had been
flooded by memories of our friendship, and in particular our long
conversations about life, love, relationships and books – always
books – during the years I had spent in Israel.

From the beginning of our friendship I was struck by the
connections in our life stories. We had been born in different
parts of the world but in the same year, 1932. The shadow of
the Second World War had hung over my early life in remote
Australia, while Tamar, born in Romania, was a true child of the
Holocaust. Her older sister, Marguerite, had tried to escape the
Nazi advance in 1942, sponsored by a Jewish youth movement;
she was one of a small group of children who joined seven

hundred paying passengers in an attempt to escape to Palestine. Tamar had not given me the details, but I read about the chain of inhumanities that flowed from greed and racism. Passengers and crew of the ill-fated MV *Struma* drowned when the already stricken and overcrowded ship was torpedoed.

When the family learned about the loss of Marguerite after the war, Tamar and her heartbroken mother grieved as one, but her father's grief was tinged with anger. He had implored his favourite daughter not to leave, to remain in Europe with her family. He mourned his daughter and he blamed her. Tamar found it hard to accept that his daughter's disobedience added to his pain, and she also felt guilt for being the one who survived.

Our parents were no doubt poles apart culturally. But when Tamar talked about the powerlessness of her mother and the vitality and intellectual curiosity of her extroverted father, I sensed another connection. She, too, had grown up with parents who were mismatched, and both our mothers failed to find their voices. Tamar, like me, had been born three decades before second-wave feminism discovered a new language to describe structural inequalities in the relationships between men and women. But when the time arrived at last she was stirred to follow the changing tide more boldly than I. She had responded enthusiastically to the call of Betty Friedan and Gloria Steinem in the early 1970s. My own self-confidence was then at such a low ebb that I failed to notice that these women were actually talking about me. As Tamar and I came to know each other, we both fretted about the ineluctable ways in which men prioritise their own needs. And as different as we were by nature and personal histories, we recognised immediately that we were of the sisterhood.

Another of those random connections that have blessed my life was responsible for what developed into a precious friendship. Tamar's aunt, her father's sister, had married a Greek diplomat and moved to Australia before the war. Her son and I were fellow graduates of The University of Sydney, although we were not close friends. However, by the time we were married and raising children in the 1960s, we moved in the same crowd, among whom the likes of the Crawfords abounded. The Saturday night dinner parties that were de rigueur for young suburban professionals meant that we often met socially. When we were living in Tel Aviv in the mid-1970s, I received a surprise phone call from Alec to say that he was in Israel on business. I mentioned that I was enrolled at Tel Aviv University and he told me that his cousin Tamar was chief librarian for the Faculty of Exact Sciences so I invited them both to lunch. I am glad I did, because it led to a lifelong association. My friendship with Tamar blossomed until the third and fourth generations, as they say in the biblical idiom. Two decades after my family returned to Australia, she acted in loco parentis whenever my granddaughter and her Israeli fiancé visited Tel Aviv from their home in Jerusalem. She became as close to them as a family member in the years before she died, and they named their first child Tamara in her memory.

We soon agreed that we were meant to be friends. From the beginning we talked about everything that we had in common as well as the differences in how our lives had unfolded. Mine had been sheltered, privileged and secure. Tamar had lived with less security and more danger, but she had a zest for life and had always taken risks. She left Romania as soon as the war came to an end, against the wishes of her parents, who followed her to Israel a few years later. She married a kibbutz member at seventeen and left behind a young son when the marriage failed to meet her expectations. She agonised over love all her adult life.

For my part, I had dared nothing at all. I was still clinging desperately to middle-class conventions, like Prufrock in the poem by T.S. Eliot. I realised that my life in Israel had failed to change the basic imbalance of the marriage relationship, and that still I had not dared to disturb the universe. Prufrock's absurdly trivial questions spelled out my own timidity. I, too, was besieged by anxiety over trivialities; perhaps not, like the man in the poem, about how to part my hair, or whether I dared to eat a peach, but similarly unimportant details of everyday existence. Tamar had always been undeterred by the sort of indecisions that beleaguered me. I envied her courage and her readiness to take risks, but how little we understand the paradoxes of the human condition. We discovered in time that as I was admiring Tamar's unfaltering engagement with life, she envied the patience and selflessness that she attributed to me as an ideal homemaker. I think the wry humour with which we eventually shared our initial views was partly responsible for the special quality of our friendship. We trusted each other with failures that had become our secrets. When our friendship took a firm shape, we discovered something even more precious: a shared moral compass that kept our relationship on course even across space and time.

Our warm embrace on the station platform wiped out the years that had passed since we both lived in Tel Aviv. As I drove her to my cottage, we talked about how long she might be able to spend with me. Her relatives in Sydney were reluctant to part with her for too long; she had had major surgery for cancer and the prognosis was concerning. But I told her about my reading project and suggested that at the very least she should stay until we had read Jane Austen's last novel together.

We were turning into the driveway by now, and she gasped at the breathtaking loveliness of a row of flowering pink and white crabapple trees on the verge. She gasped again as we approached the covered porch and she caught sight of the Frank Lloyd Wright-inspired stained-glass front door.

After depositing her capacious overnight bag in the guest room, we sat down in the reading room to drink coffee and catch up. I explained to Tamar that I was on a mission to overcome a malaise that I hadn't been able to shake off. I was now re-reading Jane Austen's six novels, which had helped shape my view of friendship, marriage and identity early in my life, in the hope of renewing my life force. I wanted nothing so much as to share with her the last of Austen's novels, *Persuasion*. 'Let's read it aloud,' I requested, hoping that the prospect of performing to an audience, if only an audience of one, might tempt my friend. Among the dreams we had shared in the past were our stage ambitions. While my natural inclination had always been for the dramatic, Tamar was born for comedy. She exhibited her gift for comic mimicry in her everyday conversation, one of the reasons we laughed so much when we spent time together.

Having Tamar as a friend on the Tel Aviv campus had transformed my university experience during the period that I lived abroad. We met at least once a week, and I was delighted to discover that she herself was a passionate reader. She was widely read, especially in European literature, and she had introduced me to novels that she was reading in French, Italian and Hebrew. She was as curious about my reading as I was about hers, the theory as well as the literary texts. It was my first taste of academic reading in the twenty years since I had graduated, and literary criticism and literary theory had moved on. I attended Professor Dorothea Krook's lectures on Henry James. She had been a lecturer at Cambridge, where she mentored the American poet Sylvia Plath. I often found myself in deeper intellectual water than I was accustomed to, and conversations with Tamar following lectures helped me to dive into these unplumbed depths.

I was intrigued and mesmerised by Krook's course on James, but I was too intimidated to contemplate writing my thesis under her supervision. I was more at ease with a historical course on Charles Dickens and decided to write my master's dissertation on the treatment of love in the mature novels, those that were written after he dealt with his autobiographical conflicts in *David Copperfield*. My dissertation was framed by an interpretation of love developed by the social psychologist Erich Fromm, who proposed that love is the only rational answer to the problems of existence – hard work but ultimately rewarding as we progress from one stage to the next. Fromm spoke of these progressions as 'being and becoming', and my analysis of Dickens's characters, especially the domestic angels so close to his heart, showed them evolving in this way, as distinct from the rounded characters described by E.M. Forster and epitomised in Austen's fiction. At that time little was known of Dickens's personal life, his alienation from his wife and his relationship with a girl much the same age as his daughters. If, as Fromm postulated, love is the only satisfactory answer to the problem of human existence, Dickens, we now know, failed in life in ways that cast a shadow over his fictional domestic angels as victims rather than, as I argued in the dissertation, highly evolved representations of his vision of love. Such is the importance of biographical context.

In her thirties, Tamar had travelled to New York with a lover who she thought was her soul mate. He had started to make a name for himself as an actor in Israel and Tamar became his protégée. In New York it became painfully clear that Tamar's partner expected her to defer her own ambitions and devote herself to furthering his career. She came close to an emotional collapse as she faced the loss of both love and ambition, but she found the strength to consider an alternative future. She qualified as a librarian and returned to Israel by herself. When we met, we were both in our early forties and she was established as a head librarian in one of the faculty libraries on campus. By the time she visited Australia in 2006 she had resigned from this position and become a consultant for library design. She had taken control of her own life and transformed it.

Tamar's love of reading was part of her professional life as a librarian. She urged me to read experimental fiction that was being published in the 1960s and 70s, the burgeoning nouveau roman, or 'new novel'. Out of curiosity, I read *La Jalousie* by Alain Robbe-Grillet, because I wanted to understand what it meant to write, and presumably to read, with the eye always focused on the object. I found it difficult to read in that way, but I related to the French novelist's ideas about the formation of a personal identity from the 'fragments' of memory and those fictional characters with whom he feels a connection as strong as a family tie.

Tamar was pleased to be reminded that her introduction to the nouveau roman had been instructive, and that I wholeheartedly agreed with Robbe-Grillet's view that memory, too, belongs to the imagination.

Later in the day we drove over the hill to browse in Berkelouw's Book Barn. I confessed that I had never warmed to Nathalie Sarraute, another of Tamar's favourite authors, because I found her too cerebral. Her preoccupation with the psychic life, with anxiety, frustration and rage, overpowered any pleasure that might be derived from the aesthetic dimensions of her work. I tried to convey to Tamar my reasons for preferring to read the realistic novel to which Jane Austen brought an inspired fidelity. Her novels belonged, as Walter Scott informed the public, to a class of fiction that rose in her own time. They introduced readers to lives not unlike their own and changed the rules of the novel.

For me, little had happened to subvert the rules of fiction since; neither the modernism of Virginia Woolf and James Joyce between the wars nor the nouveau roman of the mid-twentieth century had engaged my imagination in the same way. I promised Tamar that when we read *Persuasion* she would meet a character unlike any that Sarraute offered. I gave her a hint of what was to come: we were about to read a novel that dived deep into the consciousness of a heroine whose subdued passion sustains her independence of spirit and moral principle.

When we arrived at the Book Barn we browsed the shelves and made some purchases before ordering afternoon tea. Tamar presented me with a book by the cultural commentator Roger Scruton, *An Intelligent Person's Guide to Modern Culture*. I didn't tell her that I was sceptical about Scruton's conservative position, especially his blanket rejection of Marxist theory. I let her know that although I continue to value Matthew Arnold's belief in literature as the best that has been thought and said, I welcome opportunities to temper his enthusiasm with scepticism about past certainties and respect for new insights.

My gift to Tamar was a second-hand edition of Arthur Schnitzler's novella, *Fräulein Else*. I condensed the story as I offered the gift: a romantic teenage girl is preyed on by an older man in cahoots with her bourgeois parents. I had a story to go with the gift. As an undergraduate, I watched spellbound as the actor Elisabeth Bergner performed the role of Else in the Palace Theatre in Sydney. In another of life's coincidences, my mother had become friendly with a postwar refugee from Vienna; Mrs Wagner turned out to be a first cousin of the famous actor and offered to arrange a meeting. That was how I came to visit the star in her dressing room in an exquisite small theatre in the centre of the city of Sydney. The Palace Theatre no longer exists.

Ms Bergner, who had left Austria for London in 1933 and pursued her already successful stage and screen career, was gracious; perhaps she appreciated the friendship we had shown her cousin. I had prepared Katharine of Aragon's speech from Shakespeare's *Henry VIII* for an elocution examination, so I delivered the queen's dramatic address in the star's dressing room. Ms Bergner was encouraging, assuring me that if I ever came to Europe I could contact her and she would do what she could to help me, but, of course, that never happened, and I never saw her again. And much as I loved the novel *Fräulein Else* as Bergner had read it on stage, I confessed to Tamar that at the time I was influenced by the erroneous belief that such exploitation of women was personal and psychological rather than systemic.

The conversation flowed, as it always did when Tamar and I were together. Perhaps, my friend suggested, I should read Simone de Beauvoir. She might help me more than Jane Austen to explore the complexities that beset modern women and men when they try to live together. Did I know about the struggle of the celebrated and influential woman to maintain her equilibrium in her intimate relationship with Jean-Paul Sartre? But I was determined that it had to be Austen, and she agreed to stay with me until we reached the final chapter of *Persuasion*, though warning me that an English writer of a previous century might have nothing relevant to say to a cosmopolitan pragmatist, as she described herself. I shook my head; I had already re-read the opening chapters of the novel and imagined otherwise.

We reached a compromise to hurry the reading along. I would read the novel during the day, and in the evenings I'd read key passages and fill in the gaps with abbreviated accounts of the narrative. But first things first. Tamar wanted to buy gifts to take home, so the following day we drove over the hill, turned left towards Berrima, and parked outside the Magpie Cafe. Over lunch she brought me up to date on her health, her work and also on her son, whose birth name, Nimrod, taken from the Bible, denotes a hunter, the first on earth to be a mighty man. How like Tamar to have an adventurer's dream for her son. To her amazement, the spirit that matched her son's name in his youth and early manhood had changed. In recent years he had moved to Jerusalem to study religion. He adopted an ultra-Orthodox way of life and changed his name to Avraham. Now he was named for the first Jew rather than the first hunter. Once a month my atheist friend covered her head with a scarf and spent the Sabbath in his pious company. I was in awe of her capacity to give unconditional love.

As we waited for our coffee, Tamar and I compared the dreams we'd had for our children and their outcomes. My three daughters had developed strong relationships with Tamar while we were living in Israel. We talked about their distinctive personalities, the ways in which each of the three had struck out independently into areas that reflected individual interests and talents: the oldest committed to the empowerment of people on the margins of society; the middle daughter with psychotherapeutic techniques that combined body, mind and spirit; and the youngest, whose life was emotionally disrupted by our Israeli sojourn, pouring her energy into art and education as a spiritual journey. I shared with Tamar my astonishment at their maturity, the empathy with which they related to me and their father, and their ability to deal with gossip and conjectures about a family break-up when I established myself permanently in the Southern Highlands.

We were finishing our coffee when Tamar asked me to explain more clearly what had persuaded me to undertake this Austen reading marathon. I listed my reasons for deciding on a reading rehabilitation – the first time I had analysed them with someone outside my intimate family. I reminded her of conversations in Israel about a gnawing sense of failure in spite of outward successes, told her about the onset of vertigo when I had reached the age of sixty, and described the dawning idea that I needed to do something about my inner disquiet or live forever with a feeling that I had been cheated, or had cheated myself, of my share in life's pleasures.

I paused, wondering how I could be more explicit. 'To put it bluntly,' I said aloud, 'I short-changed myself when I decided to stay within the bounds of convention. I settled for life in a comfort zone, only to find myself spinning out of control. Instead of securing my place in the world, I found myself in danger of falling off the edge. The sense of disappointment in myself and in what I was getting out of life was overwhelmingly debilitating.'

She understood, Tamar said, nodding reassuringly. But how did I think that reading Jane Austen's novels would help?

Well, I confessed, I wasn't sure yet. But I could talk about the five novels I'd read so far.

I explained that I started with *Northanger Abbey* because I didn't have a clear memory of reading it before, and I was surprised to learn something significant from sixteen-year-old Catherine's life: that a mother who knows how to love is probably the most important blessing a girl can receive, and that friendship is about understanding your own values and standing by them even if it means abandoning friends. From *Pride and Prejudice* I learned how important it is to weigh up evidence before making judgements, and I was inspired by Elizabeth Bennet's commitment to the idea of a companionate marriage. Reading *Sense and Sensibility* I had discovered that the conflict between the two sisters – Marianne's tempestuous feelings and Elinor's controlled common sense – was raging within me, and I felt the need to reconcile my stormy feelings with my desire for rationality. *Mansfield Park* had a special place in my heart because I, like Fanny, moved into a strange home as a child and, like her, I had felt the need to make uncomfortable choices between people like the Crawfords and my moral precepts. *Emma*, the novel, and Emma, the heroine, had shown me that if a mother was not there to love her daughter, the daughter had best learn to love herself for the right and most intelligent reasons. As for *Persuasion* and the heroine Anne Elliot, I was looking forward to rediscovering the pleasure of previous readings; from these I remembered the autumnal mood cast by an older heroine as she noticed 'the tawny leaves and withered hedges' on one of her many walks, but the opportunity to read Anne's story again with a trusted friend would, I was sure, bring me new insights.

And so we began our reading of *Persuasion* that evening and continued until we came to the final page three evenings later. We joked that Jane Austen could be our Scheherazade if we finished each night by reading aloud a passage that would excite our curiosity about what was to happen next. Four nights instead of a thousand and one, we agreed, would be easy; time enough, I hoped, to persuade Tamar that Jane Austen had something to say to every woman, and to compare our opinions about what was at stake for her last fully drawn heroine.

We started at the beginning. I wasn't surprised when Tamar asked me to read the first chapter twice. As in the opening chapter of *Sense and Sensibility*, the introduction to a family history in *Persuasion* is dense with detail. We needed to understand the baronetage and the tradition that supported Sir Walter's aristocratic status before we could fully grasp the family dynamic. A vain, foolish and spendthrift widower who upholds two sets of values – class and property first and foremost, and then physical appearance – is revealed as a partial and prejudiced father who favours his oldest daughter because she resembles him, ignores the second because her beauty has faded, and despises the third because she has married beneath her.

We read on; it was clear that Austen has selected Anne, the middle daughter, as the person of chief interest in the narrative: 'Anne, with an elegance of style and sweetness of character, which must have placed her high with any people of real understanding, was nobody with either father or sister: her word had no weight; her convenience was always to give way; – she was only Anne.'

Tamar was clearly moved by this passage. The first part of the description of Anne reminded her of her exceptionally talented and popular older sister and how she had always felt guilty that she, not Marguerite, was the one who had survived the Holocaust. She was struck now by the thought that she herself had felt a little like nobody in her father's eyes, and that she needed to unburden herself of the weight of her father's grief over the death of his favourite daughter.

Tamar and I then discussed how our own families contrasted with the Elliots and considered the ways in which both our fathers had been caring but controlling figures. We were connecting our own lived experiences with Anne and Sir Walter. I pointed out to Tamar that Jane Austen, the English author from whom she had presumed she would feel alienated, was talking to her as much as to me. Tamar, I noticed with delight, was hooked on Austen's book.

The idea of being hooked on books has been around for a long time. When I was teaching English at the American International School in Israel I always tried to find the special interests or passions of reluctant readers. Sometimes I started with writing, believing that writing and reading form a continuum that encourages fluency in both. I noticed that one of my most recalcitrant students, with a marked lack of interest in every aspect of language in the classroom, was a spectacularly graceful skateboarder. Encountering him one morning in the car park, where he circled my car and came to a bravura halt alongside it, I asked him if he would talk to the class about his technique. He agreed. For the first time, he took the lead in a conversation with other students. Subsequently he drew pictures in his exercise book to illustrate his talk and went on to write a short piece that described how it felt to be in motion. It was not a masterpiece, but it was superior to anything he had previously produced and gave him greater confidence in his ability to express himself. It captured his mood in a writing process that Roslyn Arnold has referred to as 'magic in the brain.'

Reading, I have found, also performs magic in the brain. Certainly I have experienced it that way; I have rejoiced in the recent groundswell of voices that call for a new way of talking about reading. New, that is to say, in the sense of moving the goalposts of reading into new territory, from the field of texts and theory to the more accommodating land of relationships and enchantment. Rita Felski's book *Hooked: Art and attachment* is a pioneering work about the seduction of fiction – in fact, the enticement of all the arts. Felski sets out to explain how people become attached to particular works of art; to explain, for example, how I have come to care so deeply for Jane Austen's novels and her heroines. She does not offer a challenge to the idea of reading critically that has become familiar in schools and universities, but she regrets that attachment doesn't get much respect in academia, which is more interested in detachment.

If only Rita Felski had been present as Tamar and I entered a different kind of reality, she would have found a perfect example for her argument. Attachment is a fair description of what happened when we read the first chapters of *Persuasion*. Sir Walter captured our attention, and then Anne captivated us. And as we talked about the failures of the father and the damage to the daughter, we reflected on our lived experiences, conflicted memories of paternal authority. That, of course, brought us to the core dilemma of women of our generation. How do we counter the anxieties that stem from a combination of the unique relationships we have with our fathers and other male authority figures, and the invisible assumptions that constrain women's expectations of what they can achieve in their own right?

We compared Tamar's determination to make it in life, even if it meant going it alone, with my determination to preserve the smooth surface of a nuclear family despite doubts about the durability of what was underneath. We exchanged places temporarily as each of us cast the other's experience in a gentler light. We comforted each other; we agreed that we were enjoying our shared readings and were eager to continue the search for our own meanings in Anne's narrative.

Thus we proceeded, first to the narrative flashback that retrieves Anne's brief and youthful romance in Somersetshire. Persuaded by her godmother, Lady Russell, whom she has always relied upon, to break her engagement with her handsome, charming and impecunious naval suitor, Anne has faded into insignificance. Now, more than eight years later, she is persuaded, presumably in her own mind, that 'she should yet have been a happier woman in maintaining the engagement'. Tamar found it hard to accept Lady Russell and her powers of persuasion, but then we read the fourth chapter, where twice Anne is *persuaded* that engagement is the 'wrong thing'.

Tamar suggested that it would be interesting to count the number of times the words 'persuade' and 'persuasion' were used in the novel, to which I replied jokingly that time spent in the world of the exact sciences with which she was familiar might reduce reading to a laboratory experiment. Instead, I introduced my grammar fetish and pointed out Austen's use of the passive voice to emphasise the heroine's passivity and foreshadow her struggle to retrieve her own will.

We talked and read and talked again, parting each night like the sultan and the storyteller in *Arabian Nights*, curious about what will happen next. How will Anne's autumn visit to Uppercross affect her when she meets her beloved Captain Wentworth again? How will she endure his hostility towards her and his flirtations with the Musgrove sisters? Is Frederick changing his mind about Anne during the excursion to Lyme? Will Anne revert to 'only Anne' when she returns to her father's abode in Bath?

Our curiosity was satisfied each time. Anne endures the conduct of her previous suitor with dignity and grace; Captain Wentworth becomes increasingly gracious to an increasingly pretty and confident Anne; finally, to Bath, where Anne joins her father and older sister and quietly asserts herself with a new strength of character, and Captain Wentworth revises his views on Anne's surrender to Lady Russell and dares to avow his love once more. His declaration 'pierces the soul' in more than one way, with optimism and despair, 'I must speak to you by such means as are within my reach. You pierce my soul. I am half agony, half hope. Tell me not that I am too late, that such precious feelings are gone forever. I offer myself to you again with a heart even more your own, than when you almost broke it eight and a half years ago.'

Persuasion has been called an elegiac or autumnal novel, but that is only part of the story, as Tamar and I discovered over the final three nights. Transformed by her experiences, Anne has been accepted among a community of old friends at Uppercross and new friends at Lyme. 'Only Anne' is now valued, loved, admired and respected. Arriving in Bath to live again with her father and sister, she holds hard and with dignity to her second chance.

In environs that represent everything Anne Elliot rejects, she is blessed with a second spring as the emotional season defies those of the calendar. Now, at seven and twenty, Anne has every beauty except the bloom of youth. She proves herself to be wiser than her father and sister, capable of seeing through her cousin's insincerity, empathetic to a friend in distress, beyond the persuasive reach of Lady Russell and worthy of Captain Wentworth's love.

This, I suggested to Tamar, was what I might take from the novel: a second chance, for Anne, for Captain Wentworth, and maybe for me.

As we read, Tamar gradually became accustomed to Austen's language, and she started to take delight in it. We marked a paragraph for special notice and read it several times. Tamar was persuaded to read the passage aloud herself. We both savoured the elegance of the sentences, the grace with which thoughts and characters are blended, the subtle infusion of a moral perspective into her observations:

> The evening came, the drawing rooms were lighted up, the company assembled. It was but a card party, it was but a mixture of those who had never met before, and those who had met too often – a common-place business too numerous for intimacy, too small for variety; but Anne had never found an evening shorter. Glowing and lovely in sensibility and happiness, and more generally admired than she thought about or cared for, she had cheerful or forbearing feelings for every creature around her.

It was remarkable, Tamar observed with unreserved admiration, that Jane Austen brought about a character transformation without a hint of contrivance or sentimentality. 'I think that is how it happens in real life,' I suggested; 'Perhaps we don't change just because we try; we change when we learn from people who love us how to love ourselves.' That is what happened to Anne Elliot; from the moment she arrived in Uppercross after leaving Kellynch, she received first affection and then the love that she had not received in her father's home. The attributes of her character and disposition were affirmed by the regard in which she was held, and her confidence and assurance blossomed. The nobody Anne who leaves Kellynch Hall, her father's property, is not the Anne who arrives in Bath. Love has changed her. I am certain this is what Jane Austen believed; because Anne's will, like the will of each of the very different heroines, is forged by a transforming love.

Tamar and I were not of one mind about everything. I had read in one of the letters to Cassandra that the author thought this heroine might be 'almost too good for me', and Tamar was inclined to agree. I did not. She quoted a Hebrew aphorism: When it comes to smell and taste there is no point in arguing. So we agreed to disagree. That's what friendship allows you to do.

I said goodbye to Tamar at the station. Happily we met once again, two years later, in Tel Aviv. I was in Israel to visit my granddaughter, who had graduated from the Hebrew University. Tamar asked me for a progress report. I was doing well, I told her, reading the novels again and paying more serious attention to the historical and literary contexts of the fictions. I felt that my understanding of the novels was bringing new insights to my life. But nothing, I told her, was more significant than the reading experience we had shared. That was responsible for planting the idea of second chances in my consciousness. I was on my way now, in a happier place than I had been for years. The only persuasion I now acknowledged was my own.

When I asked Tamar how she remembered her time with Jane Austen and me, her answer was everything I could have hoped. She, like me, felt that even in such a short time we had learned new ways of seeing and being in the world. We compared our conclusions. Tamar now celebrated a mother who, although submissive, had been both loving and available. And she had come to terms with her father's vanity and authority, and remembered his better parts. Her determination never to be persuaded to act against her best interests was affirmed by the narrative and affirming to her sense of wellbeing. My conclusion was less an affirmation of my past life than the foreshadowing of a new beginning that, when we met in Tel Aviv, had already started. The idea of a second chance had sprung from our shared reading of *Persuasion*. The experience was like a fanfare, heralding the arrival of unimagined possibilities.

Finale

Where Angels Care to Tread

I must learn to brook being happier than I deserve.
JANE AUSTEN, *PERSUASION*

A book is sometimes given as a gift for a good if mysterious reason. Call it providence if you like. That's how I think of it, anyway, because providence has been an enduring presence in my consciousness. It may not be immediately obvious how such a gift should be received and it may take years for its place in the pattern of a life to be revealed. My late friend Deirdre, who died before her time in a car accident, gave me such a book. Her adult life, a series of romantic fantasies that failed to produce the spiritual union she craved, is a fragment that appears in the fabric from which this memoir has been woven.

In her short life Deirdre rose above a succession of abusive encounters. Abandoned by her father, she escaped from a mother who seemed to punish her daughter for her own loss. As a young girl, she fled to her grandfather's house, where she was harassed sexually, and fled again – this time into the arms of a bullying husband from whom she managed, as before, to break free. I am ever grateful for her example, and forever sad that her final chance was aborted by her death.

Deirdre's gift, a book of essays by Anne Morrow Lindbergh, was called *Gift from the Sea*. It has served me in different ways as I have tried, as indeed both Deirdre and I tried, to reconcile dreams with realities. Written twenty years after the notorious kidnapping and murder of Lindbergh's baby son, the slim volume consists of eight reveries on seashells. The author examines and reflects on them as she also examines and reflects on the shape of her life during a brief period of solitude at the beach. It is a wonderfully poetic book, and though it is slight it successfully weaves together, in a huge metaphorical arc, the writer's daunting experiences as a contemporary woman with her reflections on the natural structures of shells. When the book was reissued in the 1980s Lindbergh looked back with astonishment at her achievement, particularly that of finding common ground with so many other women. In working out *my* problems I hope that I, too, might write for other women, especially those who continue to speculate about the uneasy relations between men and women, who wonder why issues of power and control persist. I no longer feel like a Ms Prufrock; I have at last arrived at my own moment of daring, and that has given me the courage to share a precious gift, my reading remedy.

My generation believed that our daughters' generation of women would be able to rest easy, no longer stigmatised for wanting their autonomy and miraculously offered a means by which they could take control of their own reproductive system. Sex without babies! How well I remember the arrival of the contraceptive pill and the relief of redefining the word termination; no longer termination of pregnancy but termination of a flood of anxiety each month. And yet their experiences, revealed dramatically in the spectacular rise of the Me Too movement, give the lie to our belief that the battle is over, let alone won. By comparison, my obsession with personal happiness seems self-indulgent.

A woman I had known for years asked me, when I took leave from my marriage, why I thought I needed, or indeed deserved, a second chance in life. 'Don't you think you should make the best of the good life you have?'

She had been a good friend during some of my lowest moments, so I felt obliged to consider her question seriously, to untangle what she perceived as an ethical puzzle. I took her point. Like Jane Austen, like Anne Morrow Lindbergh, like Deirdre and most of the women I have known and loved, I have led a life of comparative privilege. Who are we, who am I, to seek a second chance in a life that has already dealt an abundance of good cards? I could have taken refuge in the idea that everything is relative, but that seemed too glib. So I told her about my sixtieth birthday party, the grim reality that it took my body to tell me about the needs of my soul. And, I told her, I claim the right to put my soul in order.

The polymath A.C. Grayling talks about twelve challenges to the methods of enquiry; one of them is the pinhole challenge, the need to look outside the tiny aperture of experience that constrains our perspectives. Looking outside the pinhole, I see women who are content and even fulfilled by the lives they are living. Lindbergh commented on the 'porcelain perfection' of lives that seem to be smooth and unproblmeatic. I try not to be distracted by the many women who appear to preside over perfect families; perhaps something there is a little mistaken or a little disguised; and if not, I have no reason to envy them. The disruption of my emotional life has become a condition of my past experience, part of my unique reality.

Then there are history's strongest women. They shake up the world. Jane Austen did it gently but incisively in her fiction. Mary Wollstonecraft shook the foundations of her society, in her life and in her writings. And there are those of us who are less brilliant than Austen and less daring than Wollstonecraft. We simply want to change the patterns of our lives. If we are honest, we acknowledge that we have already been blessed, but our blessings, for whatever reasons, personal and cultural, have been cast in the subjunctive mood; I think of Jane Austen's novel *Emma*. Everything 'seemed' to be in Emma's favour. But the rules of grammar and Jane Austen's imagination conspire to show us otherwise. Emma is not blessed, because she does not have the capacity to see what lies outside her pinhole view of the world. Her author gives her a second chance, and a perfect novel, if not a perfect heroine, is born.

I couldn't pinpoint exactly when my second chance had its beginning. Perhaps it was when Tamar and I read and discussed *Persuasion* over four magical nights. Perhaps it was when I became a regular member of the Bowral branch of the Jane Austen Society; or when our guest lecturer, Susannah Fullerton, long-time president of the national society, introduced her audience to the technique of free indirect discourse and Austen's representation of the inner consciousness of her characters. Or it might have been when I finally had the confidence to research and deliver my own evolving approaches to Jane Austen and her fiction: first to the Bowral branch, in a paper with the title 'Jane Austen Matters', and then the paper 'Re-reading Jane Austen' to a larger Sydney audience.

There are other wider possibilities. My conversation with a teacher about how she and her students enjoyed or didn't enjoy reading Jane Austen's fiction in the classroom triggered an interest in the relationship between reading and life that grew from miniscule to mighty. And the world seemed to be smiling at me again when, at the instigation of Nancy from the Brown Bookshop, I organised and moderated a series of conversations about books in a local vineyard. The highlight was a discussion about human rights and literature led by Nicholas Jose, the Australian president of PEN, the international organisation that defends writers under political duress; Nicholas was supported by the eminent poet David Malouf and the children's writer Libby Gleeson. I could feel myself coming alive on my own terms as I participated in conversations with purpose and gravitas. It was a return to something I thought lost only a decade before when my connection with the wider world seemed severed forever.

When I had made the decision to live independently in the Southern Highlands I knew that I also had to live by my own rule. I recognised a history of being persuaded to change my mind long before I read about Anne Elliot and her second spring. So, apart from practicalities, I maintained a distance from my former life in Sydney as one half of a couple, although sometimes I felt my heart breaking.

Separate lives led us both into new ways of life and different relationships. But as we grew accustomed to the change, we were able to resume occasional contact by phone. In time, we started to meet again as part of a family. We celebrated our oldest grandson's birthday combined with the announcement of the forthcoming birth of a child to him and his partner. When we met at Berrima for a birthday luncheon at the Magpie Cafe, the ice started to thaw. We parted not only amicably but affectionately. When our first great-grandchild was on the way we renewed our conversation as human beings with a shared destiny.

As time passed, I knew that the relationship was changing; we spoke on the phone more frequently and we occasionally met at weekends in companionable harmony. It occurred to me that as long as I lived independently, making daily decisions in my own right, the relationship might work for both of us. In the third year of our separation we had a family reunion in London. On a glorious English summer day we drove to a riverside restaurant with a literary history that touches on *Wind in the Willows*, *Three Men in a Boat* and *Mr Polly*. It was, as Ratty might have said, a jolly time, and when I look at the photograph of us farewelling the river scene, I see that, unlike the persona in Stevie Smith's startling poem, I'm no longer drowning; I'm waving – and I'm smiling as well.

The following year my husband phoned me in Bowral to tell me about an apartment for sale in the building where he lives. 'It's not in very good shape,' he said, 'but you can see the Harbour Bridge from the bedroom.' Now my heart leaped. The thought that I might one day catch sight of the bridge from my own window excited me. I was not thinking of leaving my Southern Highlands dream home, but I had an eye to my future old age. I rejoiced when the bid was successful.

And so it came to pass. Four years later I made my farewells to Lantern Hill. My husband and I were about to become, according to my younger granddaughter, who was studying social anthropology, 'LATs': people who live apart together. I would live with my morning glimpse of the Harbour Bridge and he would prepare the evening meal for us to share at the end of my writing day. It has proved to be a good and long-lasting solution. And it worked well with my planned project to understand better the power of Jane Austen's fiction. Somehow I wanted to repay the debt of gratitude I felt to an author who had formed and sustained beliefs and values with which I could live at peace. I wanted to provide evidence for the public discourse; to defend Jane Austen's novels for their relevance to young people today as they form relationships and navigate critical situations. It was starting to look like a serious research project, and I wondered if I were up to it. Everyone who knew about my passion for Jane Austen encouraged and offered to support me as an Austen project shaped itself in my mind.

That project was why I was sitting beneath the late summer foliage of a spreading plane tree in Woollahra in early 2015, waiting to have coffee with someone I had not seen for three decades. I was not sure that I would recognise her, but there was no mistaking her slender build as she walked toward me in a cornflower blue dress that matched her eyes. Roslyn was a connection from my past. When we returned from Israel to live again in Sydney, I had been inspired by her lectures on classroom methods for English teachers. I had now approached her in her professional capacity as an educational consultant; she had responded as a gracious friend. 'Let's have coffee,' she suggested, 'and you can explain to me why you want to write a PhD dissertation on Jane Austen and empathy.'

There is a truism that once you are in a field of interest, references to that field appear all around you. When you buy a blue car, for example, the roads seem to be filled with blue cars.

My project to position a study of Jane Austen in the field of empathy, although I had no idea how it might be done, connected immediately with Roslyn's expertise in the field of empathetic intelligence. It certainly could be done, she assured me – and, better still, it was worth doing. With her encouragement, I applied and was admitted to the PhD program in the School of Education at The University of Sydney.

It felt good, if slightly strange, to be walking down Science Road again and wandering through the quadrangle. I noticed changes everywhere: the digitised library, learning hubs, unisex toilets and no dining facilities that were accessible by male invitation only, as in my day; and faces no longer reflected an exclusively white Anglo-Saxon society. Everywhere I went I received encouragement and affirmation. My age attracted attention; I was eighty-four when my enrolment was confirmed. Christine, the librarian who delivered research tutorials to higher degree students, was helpful beyond the call of duty. And younger people in the tutorials I attended on research methods were fascinated by the idea of researching how and why Jane Austen's novels were read and studied at school.

I can't pretend that it was smooth sailing. It took a year longer than it should have, and it was painful to lose the empathetic thread that I thought I shared with my initial supervisor. But despite that disappointment, a flight of angels accompanied me to the completion of my task: a daughter whose filial loyalty and sceptical understanding of the politics of research degrees ensured that I was not left stranded; an auxiliary supervisor whose faith in what I had to say and and the skills and imagination to guide me in how to say it supported me through a crisis of confidence; and a replacement supervisor whose wisdom and expertise honoured four years of research and helped me channel it into a thesis that, according to both examiners, made a significant contribution to the way young people learn to read Jane Austen's fiction. When the morning newspaper announced a successful eighty-eight-year-old doctoral candidate as 'a Ruth Universally Acknowledged' I was filled with gratitude for the compliment and the abundance of good wishes. I wished that my father were still alive to drink with me; as in the psalm I read at his memorial service, my cup was running over.

My doctoral research was more than an academic enquiry. It brought a lifetime of reading to the final phase of a journey that started when I was sixty and reached its conclusion when I was close to ninety. If I had been told on the day I walked down the hill to replace my lost copy of *Northanger Abbey* that I would write a dissertation that would say something new and even significant about the experience of reading Jane Austen's fiction, I would have questioned that expectation. But nearly two decades later, I feel like a character caught up in the resolution of an Austen novel. Perhaps Fanny Price feels the same every time her novel is read. The narrator of *Mansfield Park*, who does not concern herself with sin and guilt, guides Fanny and Edmund to a better life. I have been guided, too.

There is no way that I could have predicted the happy ending to my Austen odyssey. I was deeply unsettled by the emotional turbulence that accompanied my decision to set out on a solitary life, but it gradually subsided. I willed myself to take control as the years rolled by, and I gradually returned to a more active life. Unlike Ulysses, I came home at last to a peaceful household.

Living now in our separate abodes and continuing to share our evening meals, my husband and I make the best of company, enjoying endless conversations about the prospects of our children, who are now in their sixties, our grandchildren, who are establishing themselves in life, and our eight great-grandchildren, whose reading tastes are lovingly nurtured. We talk about those aspects of the world we live in that are, in equal parts, exciting and frightening. And we have other topics of conversation as well; even, from time to time, the latest news from the world of Jane Austen.

Is my life now light, and bright and sparkling? Well, yes, often it is; although I know that clouds lurk behind blue skies, not only because of climate change. So it isn't idyllic, and it doesn't need to be. I have never been Elizabeth Bennet and the man I married was never Mr Darcy. Fiction shows us possibilities; in real life we make our own choices and learn to live with them, one way or another. So, in the life I live now, apart and together with the person whom I once mistook for my hero but who has, in the long run, turned out to be my best companion, there are friendships we value and people we love. Sometimes we share them, sometimes our affections diverge. But it is more important to me that I have been given a second chance to make a life that is 'really and truly' good enough. And I owe it most of all to Jane Austen, the guide who still sits on my reading table.

Jane Austen's
Reading Remedies

Mixtures prescribed to enhance wellbeing

PRODUCED UNDER LICENCE TO JANE AUSTEN,
LITERARY APOTHECARY

Side effects:

temporary discomfort caused by new insights; can be alleviated
by deep reflection

Dosage:

take by reading immersion; ideal age stated on label; repeat as
frequently as desired

NORTHANGER ABBEY

A REMEDY PRESCRIBED FOR ADOLESCENT AILMENTS

Symptoms: delusions; impulsive behaviour

Treatment: exposure to ideas about the imagination, and the pitfalls of friendship

Dosage: once a year, between ages of fifteen and eighteen; as desired thereafter

Side effects: discomfort caused by recognising insincerity

Benefits: enhanced ability to distinguish between authentic and false friendships

EMMA

A REMEDY PRESCRIBED FOR GROWING PAINS

Symptoms: exaggerated sense of entitlement; denial of vulnerability

Treatment: exposure to ideas about boundaries and generosity of spirit

Dosage: once a year between ages of eighteen and twenty-three; as desired thereafter

Side effects: discomfort caused by self-examination

Benefits: clearer sense of boundaries; development of intelligent love

PRIDE AND PREJUDICE

A REMEDY PRESCRIBED FOR HEARTACHE

Symptoms: erratic judgements; lack of perspective

Treatment: exposure to high spirits and ideas about evidence-based decisions

Dosage: once during teens; yearly for life

Side effects: discomfort caused by feeling shame for flawed judgements

Benefits: sense of humour restored; sense of judgement improved; resilience encouraged

SENSE AND SENSIBILITY

A REMEDY PRESCRIBED FOR VERTIGO

Symptoms: erratic mood swings

Treatment: exposure to ideas about reason and balance

Dosage: early twenties, repeated at five-yearly intervals; more frequently if desired/required

Side effects: discomfort caused by renouncing old habits

Benefits: enhanced emotional stability

MANSFIELD PARK

A REMEDY PRESCRIBED FOR ANXIETY

Symptoms: social reticence; emotional cramps

Treatment: exposure to ideas about moral behaviour and the ethics of social behaviour

Dosage: mid-twenties, repeated at five-yearly intervals; more frequently if desired/required

Side effects: discomfort caused by recollections of past unkindness

Benefits: renewal of trust; affirmation of ethical standards

PERSUASION

A REMEDY PRESCRIBED FOR DYSFUNCTION

Symptoms: languishing spirits; faded appearance

Treatment: exposure to affirmation and affection

Dosage: yearly, between ages of thirty and forty; as desired thereafter

Side effects: discomfort caused by regret for time lost

Benefits: daring to live the truth; enhanced sense of wellbeing

Acknowledgements

In my dedication I acknowledged my debt of gratitude to Jane Austen and her novels. I also owe a debt of gratitude to the many works of literature and reference included in this account of my reading life. Personal acknowledgements start with Professor Roslyn Arnold, who helped conceptualise the dissertation at the heart of this reading memoir. Associate Professor Rebecca Johinke and Dr Olivia Murphy were inspired supervisors. They, together with my daughter Dr Julia Wolfson, sustained me through the formidable challenges of higher degree research. My thesis examiners, Professor Katie Halsey of the University of Stirling and Professor Devoney Looser of Arizona State University, unwittingly but significantly contributed to the interest in my reading life that led directly to the writing of a reading memoir. I have received generous encouragement from Susannah Fullerton, President of the Jane Austen Society of Australia, and invaluable editorial assistance from Dr Joanna Penglase.

My debt to Tessa Feggans, Ali Lavau, Angela Handley and Dannielle Viera for expert editorial guidance provided by Allen & Unwin is beyond measure.

When it comes to family I have been blessed. My daughters, Olivia and Laura, stimulated and encouraged me as we talked our way through relevant contemporary cultural issues, while my granddaughters, Jessica and Kate, were generous with conversations about what matters to young people today. I acknowledge especially the support of my husband, David, who has been a kind and thoughtful travelling companion on my writing journey.

Reading Lists

'I have seen a great many lists of her drawing up at various times
... and very good lists they were, very well chosen,
and very neatly arranged ...'

JANE AUSTEN, *EMMA*

The following list of books about Jane Austen is suggested by the author in the spirit of Mr Knightley in Jane Austen's novel *Emma*.

Biographies of Jane Austen

Austen-Leigh, J.E. (2002). *A Memoir of Jane Austen: And Other Family Recollections*, edited with an introduction by Kathryn Sutherland. Oxford: Oxford University Press.

Byrne, Paula (2013). *The Real Jane Austen: A Life in Small Things*. London: Harper Press.

Clery, E.J. (2017). *Jane Austen: The Banker's Sister*. London: Biteback Publishing Ltd.

Collins, Irene (1998). *Jane Austen: The Parson's Daughter*. London: Hambledon Continuum.

Jenkins, Elizabeth (1938/1986). *Jane Austen: A Biography*. London: Victor Gollancz Ltd.

Shields, Carol (2001). *Jane Austen: A Life*. New York: Penguin.

Tomalin, Claire (1999). *Jane Austen: A Life*. London: Vintage.

Jane Austen and reading

Halsey, Katie (2013). *Jane Austen and Her Readers, 1786–1945*. London: Anthem Press.

Murphy, Olivia (2013). *Jane Austen the Reader: The Artist as Critic*. London: Palgrave Macmillan.

Wells, Juliette (2011). *Everybody's Jane: Austen in the Popular Imagination*. London and New York: Bloomsbury Academic.

Jane Austen's letters

Brabourne, Lord Edward (ed.) (1884). *Letters of Jane Austen*. London: Richard Bentley & Son.

Le Faye, Deirdre (ed.) (2011). *Jane Austen's Letters*. Fourth Edition. Oxford: Oxford University Press.

Books about Jane Austen and her novels

Barchas, Janine (2019). *The Lost Books of Jane Austen*. Baltimore: Johns Hopkins University Press.

Fullerton, Susannah (2012). *A Dance with Jane Austen: How a Novelist and Her Characters went to the Ball*. London: Francis Lincoln Limited.

Harman, Claire (2009). *Jane's Fame: How Jane Austen Conquered the World*. Edinburgh: Canongate.

Kelly, Helena (2016). *Jane Austen: The Secret Radical*. London: Icon Books Ltd.

Looser, Devoney (2017). *The Making of Jane Austen*. Baltimore:

Johns Hopkins University Press.

Tanner, Tony (1986). *Jane Austen*. London: Macmillan Press Ltd.

Todd, Janet (ed.) (2005). *Jane Austen in Context*. Cambridge: Cambridge University Press.

Jane Austen's fanfic

Fowler, Karen Joy (2005). *The Jane Austen Book Club*. London and New York: Penguin.

Goodman, Allegra (2010). *The Cookbook Collector*. New York: The Dial Press.

James, P.D. (2011). *Death Comes to Pemberley*. New York: Alfred A. Knopf.

McCullough, Colleen (2008). *The Independence of Miss Mary Bennet*. New York, London, Toronto and Sydney: Simon & Schuster.

Paynter, Jennifer (2014). *The Forgotten Sister: Mary Bennet's Pride and Prejudice*. Seattle: Amazon Publishing.

Russell, Roslyn (2014). *Maria Returns: Barbados to Mansfield Park*. Flynn: Bobby Graham Publishers.

Bibliography

A Daily Dose of Jane: The Austen Antidote for 2020. YouTube video. Devoney Looser and George Justice, 11/13/2020. Glendale Arizona.

Alcott, L. (1868/1989). *Little Women*. London: Penguin Classics.

Amis, K. (2009). What Became of Jane Austen? In S. Carson (ed), *A Truth Universally Acknowledged: 33 Great Writers on Why We Read Jean Austen*. New York: Random House Trade Paperbacks.

Arnold, Roslyn (2008), *Empathic Intelligence: Teaching, learning, relating*. Sydney: University of New South Wales Press.

Auden, W.H. (1937). She Shocks Me. In Southam, B.C. (2005/1987) *Jane Austen: The Critical Heritage, Vol II, 1870-1940 (1987/2005)*. New York: Routledge.

Austen, J. (1811/2006). *Sense and Sensibility*. Cambridge: Cambridge University Press.

Austen, J. (1813/2006). *Pride and Prejudice*. Cambridge: Cambridge University Press.

Austen, J. (1814/2005). *Mansfield Park*. Cambridge: Cambridge University Press.

Austen, J. (1816/2005). *Emma*. Cambridge: Cambridge University Press

Austen, J. (1817/2006). *Persuasion*. Cambridge: Cambridge University Press.

Austen, J. (1817/2006). *Northanger Abbey*. Cambridge: Cambridge University Press.

Austen, J. (2008). *Later Manuscripts*. Cambridge: Cambridge University Press.

Austen-Leigh, J. (1871/2008). *A Memoir of Jane Austen and Other Family Recollections*. Oxford: OUP.

Barrie, J. (1945). "The Admirable Crichton". In A.E. Wilson (ed). *The Plays of J.M. Barrie in One Volume*. London: Hodder and Stoughton Limited.

Bromwich, D. (1983). *Hazlitt: The Mind of a Critic*. New York and Oxford: OUP.

Bronte, Charlotte (1847/1997). *Jane Eyre*. London: Wordsworth Editions Ltd.

Bronte, E. (1847/?). *Wuthering Heights*. London: Gordon Classics Library.

Bruce, M. Grant. (1913/1997). *Norah of Billabong*. Sydney: Harper Collins.

Campbell, Sue (2003). *Relational Remembering: Rethinking the memory wars*. Lanham, Md.: Rowman and Littlefield.

Carroll, Lewis (1965/2015). *Alice's Adventures in Wonderland*. London: Puffin.

Carter, Angela (1979). *The Bloody Chamber and Other Stories*. London & New York: Penguin.

Chapman, R.W. (ed) (1955). *Jane Austen: Letters 1796-1817*. London: Oxford University Press.

Chevalier, Tracy. (1999) *Girl with a Pearl Earring*. London: HarperCollins Publishers.

Cochrane, H. (2nd July, 2021). "Quarries of Silence: The work and legacy of Geoffrey Hill, who died five years ago". In TLS, *Times Literary Supplement*, no. 6170, p. 20.

Cocteau, J. (1947/1979). *The Eagle Has Two heads*. London: Vision Press Ltd.

Cole, Toby (1947). *Acting: A Handbook of the Stanislavski Method*. New York: Lear.

Collins, W. (1868/1998). *The Moonstone*. London: Penguin Classics.

Cooper, J.F. (1826/1986) *The Last of the Mohicans*. London: Penguin Books.

Cunningham, M. (1999). *The Hours*. London: Fourth Estate.

Defoe, D. (1719/2001). *Robinson Crusoe*. London: Modern Library.

Deresiewicz, William (2011). *A Jane Austen Education: How six novels taught me about love, friendship, and the things that really matter*. New York: Penguin Books.

Dickens, C. (1838/2021). *Oliver Twist*. London: Puffin Modern Classics.

Dickens, C. (1849/2012). *David Copperfield*. London: Penguin Classics.

Didion, J. (1968/2017). *Slouching Toward Bethlehem: Essays*. New York: Open Road Media,

Drabble, M. (1965/1998). *The Millstone*. Boston: Mariner Books.

Eliot, G. (1871/1968). *Middlemarch*. Boston: Houghton Mifflin Company.

Eliot, T.S. (1954/2002). Selected Poems. London: Faber and Faber.

Engel, Marian (1981/1991). *Lunatic Villas*. Toronto: McClelland & Stewart Inc.

Ephron, Nora. (1983/1996). *Heartburn*. New York: Vintage.

Fadiman, Anne (1998) *Ex Libris: Confessions of a common reader*. London: Penguin.

Farrer, Reginald (1917/1987). Jane Austen, ob. July 18, 1817. In B.C. Southam (ed.), *Jane Austen Volume 2, 1870–1940*. New York: Routledge.

Felski, Rita (2020). *Hooked: Art and attachment*. Chicago: Chicago University Press.

Fitzgerald, Penelope (1878/2015). *The Bookshop*. London: Harper Paperbacks.

Fitzgerald, F. Scott. (1925/2008). *The Great Gatsby*. London & New York: Penguin Books.

Forster, E.M. (1910/1973). *Howards End*. London: Penguin English Library.

Forster, E.M. (1927/1949). *Aspects of the Novel*. London: Edward Arnold & Co.

Flanagan, R. (2008). *Wanting*. Sydney: Vintage.

Fraiman, Susan (1995). 'Jane Austen and Edward Said: Gender, culture and imperialism'. *Critical Inquiry*, pp. 805–21

Fromm, Erich (1956/1971). *The Art of Loving*. London: Unwin Books.

Fussell, P. (1975/2013). *The Great War and Modern Memory*, Oxford: Oxford University Press.

Goodman, A. (2005). 'Pemberley Previsited: *Pride and Prejudice.*' In A. Fadiman (ed.), Rereadings. New York: Farrar Straus and Giroux.

Gornick, V. (2010). *Unfinished Business: Notes of a chronic re-reader*. Carlton: Black Inc.

Grayling, Anthony C. (2021). *The Frontiers of Knowledge: What we know about science, history and the mind*. New York: Viking.

Greene, Maxine (2003). *Releasing the Imagination: Essays on education, the arts, and social change*. San Francisco: Jossey-Bass.

Greer, G. (1970). *The Female Eunuch*. London: MacGibbon & Kee.

Grenville, K. (2020). *A Room Made of Leaves*. Melbourne: The Text Publishing Company.

Griffin, Walter Burley, 'The City Plan of Griffith', *Irrigation Record*, vol. 3, no. 6, 1 June 1915; no. 7, 15 June 1915.

Grimm, W. &. J. (2015). *A Favourite Collection of Grimm's Fairy Tales.* .London: Floris Books.

Gunn, J. (2014). *We of the Never-Never and The Little Black Princess.* Sydney: Harper Collins.

Guppy, Shusha (interviewer) (1986). Alain Robbe-Grillet, The Art of Fiction No. 91. *Paris Review,* Issue 99.

Hall, Radclyffe (1928/2015). *The Well of Loneliness.* London and New York: Penguin.

Hampton. J. (2003). *Joyce Grenfell.* London: Hodder & Stoughton.

Hughes, L. (1995). Hold Fast to Dreams, In A. Rampersad & Roessel, D. (eds). *The Collected Poems of Langston Hughes.* New York: Vintage Classics.

Ibsen, H. (1949). *A Doll's House, Ghosts, An Enemy of the People, The Master Builder.* New York: The Modern Library.

Idriess, I. (1932/1973). *Flynn of the Inland.* Sydney: A&R Classics.

Ishiguro, Kazuo (1989). *The Remains of the Day.* London: Faber and Faber.

James, Henry (1881/2009). *Portrait of a Lady.* Oxford: OUP.

James, H. (1905). "The Lesson of Balzac". In Southam, B.C. (ed) (1987/2009). *Jane Austen Vol II 1870-1940: The Critical Heritage.* New York: Routledge.

Jespersen, Otto. (1933/1948). *Essentials of English Grammar.* London: George Allen & Unwin Ltd.

Kennedy, Margaret (1925/2014). *The Constant Nymph.* London: Vintage Books.

Lamb, Charles and Mary (1810/2022) *Tales from Shakespeare: Introduced by Dame Judi Dench.* London: Puffin Classics.

Lawrence, D.H. (1915/1995). *The Rainbow.* Ware: Wordsworth Editions Ltd.

Leavis, Q.D. (1957). Introduction. *Mansfield Park*. London: MacDonald.

Lee, Hermione (1996). *Virginia Woolf*. London: Vintage Books.

Le Faye, D. (ed) (2011). *Jane Austen's Letters, Fourth Edition*. Oxford: Oxford University Press.

Lewes, G (1859). 'The Great Appraisal'. In B.C. Southam (ed) (1968). *Jane Austen: The Critial Heritage*. London: Routledge & Kegan Paul.

Lindbergh, Anne Morrow (1955). *Gift from the Sea*. New York: Pantheon Books.

Looser, Devoney (ed.) (2019). *Jane Austen: A year of quotes*. Chicago: University of Chicago Press.

Macaulay, Lord T. B. (1800/1932). *Miscellaneous Essays: The Lays of Ancient Rome*. London: J.M. Dent & Sons Ltd.

Mantel, H. (2009). *Wolf Hall*. London: Fourth Estate.

Mantel, Hilary (2007). 'Jane Austen'. In Joseph Epstein (ed.), *Literary Genius: 25 classic writers who define English & American literature*. Philadelphia: Paul Dry Books.

Marcus Aurelius (2006). *Meditations*. New York and London: Penguin.

Mead, Rebecca (2014). *The Road to Middlemarch*. Melbourne: Text Publishing.

Milliken, Robert. (2002). *Mother of Rock: The Lillian Roxon Story*. New York: Avalon.

Montgomery, L.M. (1908/2013). *Anne of Green Gables*. Vintage Children's Classics.

Montgomery, L.M. ((1937/1980). *Lantern Hill*. Sydney: Angus & Robertson Publishers.

Morrison, T. (1987). *Beloved*. New York: Vintage.

Mortimer, P. (1962/2015). *The Pumpkin Eater*. London: Penguin Classics.

Murphy, A. (ed) (2015). *The Works of Samuel Johnson*, LlD. London: Arkosa Press.

Owen, D. (02/01/2017). "The Enduring Monologue of Ruth Draper". In *The New Yorker*

Packard, V. (1957/2007). *The Hidden Persuaders*. New York: If Publishing.

Robinson, M. (2012). *When I Was a Child, I Read Books*. New York: Farrer, Straus & Giroux.

Rosenblatt, L. (2005). *Making Meaning with Texts: selected essays*. Portsmouth: Heinemann.

Said, E. (1994). *Culture and Imperialism*. New York: Vintage Books.

Sartre, J-P. (1938/2000). *Nausea*. London: Penguin Classics.

Schnitzler, Arthur (1925). *Fräulein Else*. New York: Simon & Schuster.

Scott, Walter. (1816). 'Walter Scott, an unsigned review of *Emma*', In B. Southam (ed.), *Jane Austen: The critical heritage*. New York: Barnes & Noble, p. 63–4.

Scruton, Roger (19980. *An Intelligent Person's Guide to Modern Culture*. London: Duckworth.

Shakespeare, W. (1959/2000). As You Like It. In D. Dolan (ed) *The Pelican Shakespeare*. London: Pelican Books.

Shakespeare, W. (1958/2017). Much Ado About Nothing. In P. Holland (ed) *The Pelican Shakespeare*. London: Pelican Books.

Shakespeare, W, (2016). *King Lear*. London: Penguin Classics.

Shakespeare, W. (2016). *Romeo and Juliet*. London: Penguin Classics.

Shaw, G.B.S. (1898/1947). *Plays Pleasant and Unpleasant*, Vols 1 & 2. London: Constable and Company Limited.

Shelley, Mary (1818/2003). *Frankenstein*. London: Penguin Classics.

Silber, Joan (2021). *Secrets of Happiness*. London: Allen & Unwin.

Southam, B.C. (ed.) (1987/2001). *Jane Austen: The critical heritage Vol. 2, 1870– 1940.* New York: Routledge.

Stevenson, R.L. (1883/2001). *Treasure Island.* London: Kingfisher.

Swift, Graham (1997). *Mothering Sunday.* London: Simon & Schuster.

Symonds, J. (1952). *Thomas Carlyle, The Life and Ideas of a Prophet.* New York: OUP.

Trilling, L. (1951/1964). *The Liberal Imagination: Essays on Literature and Society.* London: Mercury Books.

Turner E, (1884/1994). *Seven Little Australians.* Glebe: Walter McVitty Books.

Warner, Marina (2014). *Once Upon a Time: A short history of fairy tales.* Oxford: Oxford University Press.

Wiesel, Elie (1958/1981). *Night.* New York: Penguin Books.

Wilder, Thornton (2008). *The Selected Letters of Thornton Wilder.* Robin G. Wilder and Jackson R. Bryer (eds). New York: Harper.

Williams, Niall (2019). *This Is Happiness.* London: Bloomsbury Publishing.

Wilson, Ruth (2000). *A Big Ask: Interviews with interviewers.* Sydney: New Holland.

Wilson Ruth (ed.) (1996). *Say NO to Prejudice.* Sydney: Kenigsberg/Wilson.

Wilson Ruth, (1998). Sabina, My Friend. In R. Brampton (ed.). *I Remember, I Remember.* Double Bay: Woollahra Municipal Council.

Winch, Tara June (2019). *The Yield.* Penguin Random House Australia.

Wolanski, S. (2008). *Destined to Live: One Woman's War, Life, Loves Remembered.* Sydney: Fourth Estate.

Woolf, V. (1925/2003). *Mrs Dalloway*. London: Collector's Library.

Woolf, V. (1927/1972). *To the Lighthouse*. Harmondsworth: Penguin Books Ltd.

Woolf, Virginia (1928/2013). *A Room of One's Own*. Melbourne: Penguin Books.

Woolf, Virginia (2009). 'Jane Austen at sixty'. In Susannah Carson (ed.), *A Truth Universally Acknowledged: 33 great writers on why we read Jane Austen*. New York: Random House.

Zangwill, I. (1898/2015). *Dreamers of the Ghetto*. Scotts Valley: Createspace Independent Publishing Platform.

Zweig, S. (1939/1961). *Beware of Pity*. London: Cassell & Company Ltd.

Ruth Wilson read her first Jane Austen novel in 1947 and in 2021 completed her PhD on reading and teaching Jane Austen. In-between she taught English and worked on oral history projects including one with Holocaust survivors. She encourages her four children, five grandchildren and eight great-grandchildren to read widely, wisely and well. She and her husband are a married couple who live apart together.